C000157329

VEILS, TURBANS, AND ISI
REFORM IN NORTHERN I

AFRICAN EXPRESSIVE CULTURES

Patrick McNaughton, *editor*

Associate editors
Catherine M. Cole
Barbara G. Hoffman
Eileen Julien
Kassim Koné
D. A. Masolo
Elisha Renne
Z. S. Strother

VEILS, TURBANS, AND ISLAMIC REFORM IN NORTHERN NIGERIA

Elisha P. Renne

Indiana University Press

Acknowledgments

THE IMPORTANCE OF textiles in social life is a diverse topic that leads in many directions. This study represents my following myriad paths over the past thirty years, with the kind assistance of many individuals along the way. I have had the privilege of speaking with cloth traders, thread dealers, textile factory workers, hand embroiderers, designers, Islamic scholars and teachers, *alhajis* and *hajiyas* (men and women who have performed the hajj), government officials associated with textile manufacturing, and textile mill owners as well as professors, archivists, and emirate officials. Their trust and consideration in taking time to speak with me reflect one of the great benefits of long-term fieldwork. For it was through connections in Ibadan, where I first worked as a graduate student and research affiliate at the University of Ibadan in 1987, that I was able to meet with Alfa Khalifa Bamidele and visit his school and subsequently attend the wedding of Nuratu Raimi's granddaughters in 2013. Postdoctoral research, which began in Itapa-Ekiti in 1991, led to my long-standing research relationship with Chief Kayode Owoeye, who facilitated interviews in Ikole-Ekiti with Jama'atu Tabligh members and traveled with me to Ilorin in 2014 where Professor Lateef Oladimeji, an expert on the history of Jama'atu Tabligh in Nigeria kindly spoke with me.

My work in northern Nigeria began in October 1994, when I took up residence in a family house in the old walled section of Zaria known as Zaria City, or Birnin Zazzau. I thank the Emir of Zazzau, His Royal Highness Dr. Shehu Idris, CFR, for granting me permission to stay and conduct research in Zaria City. I am indebted to many people in Zaria City, Kaduna, and Kano. While too numerous to mention all of them individually, here I thank Yusuf Abdullahi, Sani Ibrahim, Jimi Magajiya, Samaila Magaji, Mohammed Mohammed, Yahaya Muktar, Samaila Nabara, Rabi Wali, Abdulrahman Yahaya, and Umma Yahaya for their ongoing assistance. At Ahmadu Bello University, the kindness of six vice chancellors over the years has encouraged me in this project, and colleagues at Ahmadu Bello University and Nuhu Bamalli Polytechnic—both in Zaria— have, from the beginning, been most generous with their time and advice. They include Sheikh DanLadi, Rabi'u Isah, Salihu Maiwada, Mairo Mandara, Musa Muhammed, Mohammad Tahir, Dakyes Usman, and Mohammadu Waziri. Abdulkarim DanAsabe and Hannatu Hassan, faculty at the Federal College of Education, Kano, have also been extraordinarily helpful. At the University of Michigan, I have benefited from the comments and suggestions of faculty members and students, including Omolade Adunbi, Kelly Askew, Frieda Ekotto, Kelly Kirby (now at Moore College of Art and Design, Philadelphia), Jaclyn Kline, Stuart Kirsch, Anne Pitcher, and Ray Silverman. Julius Scott, as always, has provided astute editorial advice and answers to my incessant questions. Additionally, the exceptional help of librarians at the University of Michigan, the Herskovits Library-Northwestern University, Ahmadu Bello University, and the Bodleian Libraries-Oxford University; museum curators at the Museum of Science and Industry, Manchester; and in Kaduna, archivists at Arewa House, the Nigerian National Archives, and the Kaduna State Ministry of Information, have greatly facilitated this study. I also thank colleagues and friends on whom I imposed for advice, a second reading, and solace: Laura Arntson, Chris Bankole, Sue Bergh, Sarah Brett-Smith, LaRay Denzer, Gordon Hartley, Murray Last, and Ann O'Hear as well as the late Philip Shea. While hardly an exhaustive list of all those who deserve thanks, I acknowledge the special support of Ya'u Tanimu and Hassana Yusuf, who have helped me during my stay in Zaria from the beginning. Together, they helped me organize research assistance, provided excellent counsel and information, and patiently waited with me when I needed visa extensions. My visits to Hassana's parents' home in Kaduna were always a pleasant respite, and Hassana Yusuf continues to impress me with her willingness to pursue difficult leads as well as to accompany me on bus and taxi rides to and from Kano, Kaduna, and Yakasai. As always, I owe her great thanks.

This long-term research on textiles and Islamic reform in northern Nigeria would not have been possible without funding from various sources, which include the Department of Anthropology, the Department of Afroamerican and African Studies, the African Studies Center, the Advanced Study Center of the International Institute, and the Humanities Institute—all at the University of Michigan as well as the Fulbright US Scholar Program, the Pasold Research Fund, and the John Simon Guggenheim Memorial Foundation. I also thank the University of Michigan Office of the Vice President for Research for a subvention grant for photograph reproduction, which contributes immensely to readers' appreciation of the significance of textiles in the moral imaginings of Islamic reformers in northern Nigeria.

Three individuals have shaped my study of African textiles. Joanne Eicher shared her extensive knowledge of Nigerian textiles with me and, through her own research, encouraged me to look for internal and international textile trade connections. The late Annette Weiner enabled me to expand my understanding of the importance of textiles in social life—which included spiritual continuities fostered by cloth, cloth's embodiment of wealth and prestige, and cloth's use as essential objects of exchange at birth, marriage, and death. Thomas Beidelman taught me to think about cloth and moral imagination. I am indebted to him for helping me to understand the significance of the two sides of cloth and about the use of dress as deception. To these three teachers, I am truly grateful.

I am likewise grateful to the two anonymous manuscript reviewers; my copy editor; and Rebecca Logan, as well as Paige Rasmussen, Nancy Lightfoot, and design staff members at Indiana University Press, whose kind but firm organization facilitated the publication process. Dee Mortensen, editorial director at Indiana University Press, continues to provide outstanding support for African studies.

Finally, I acknowledge my contemporaries who lived and worked in Africa or who studied the role of textiles in social life who have gone before me: Mary Bivins, Charlotte Jirousek, Aisha Muhammed, Jeanne Raisler, Yedida Stillman, and Lillian Trager.

Inda ganyen doka daya ya fadi, a sa ganyen dorowa dare ba rufe wurin

(Where one *doka* leaf has fallen, it would require more than a hundred *dorowa* leaves to fill its place)

VEILS, TURBANS, AND ISLAMIC REFORM IN NORTHERN NIGERIA

1 Material Religion and Islamic Reform in Northern Nigeria

When 'Umar b. al-Khattāb sent out a governor, he would impose five conditions on him: not to ride mules, not to wear fine clothes, not to eat choice food, not to employ chamberlains and not to close the door against people's needs and welfare. . . . 'Attāb b. Usayd once said, "By God, the only thing I gained from the work the Messenger of God charged me with, was two garments which I gave to my client, Kaysan."

—'Uthmān dan Fodio, *Bayān Wujūb al-Hijra 'ala 'l-'Ibad*

The handsome girls in their gay cotton prints with their powdered faces set off by necklaces and earrings and headkerchiefs, and . . . the sober elegance of prosperous men in their flowing robes and shining dark-blue turbans.

—M. G. Smith, introduction to *Baba of Karo*

There probably exists no social unit in which convergent and divergent currents among its members are not inseparably interwoven.

—Georg Simmel, "Conflict"

In NORTHERN NIGERIA, Islam, politics, and textiles have historically been interconnected. Men, women, and children—working as cotton growers, spinners, weavers, dyers, cloth beaters, tailors, draughtsmen, embroiderers, and traders—were part of an elaborate system of textile production that flourished in the nineteenth century. This system was facilitated by the reformist Islamic jihād begun in 1804 that led to the establishment of the Sokoto Caliphate. Islamic scholars and students; royalty, commoners, and slaves; women and men distinguished themselves through dress, which marked their social status as well as religious affiliation in a Hausa-Fulani society framed by a political-economic hierarchy based on agriculture, crafts, and trade (Bello 1983; Bivins 2007; Bobboyi 2011; Kriger 1988, 1993, 2010; Last 1966, 1967, 1970, 1974, 2014; Lovejoy 1978, 1981; Shea 1975, 2006). While the advent of British indirect colonial rule in the early twentieth century undermined this system of politics and production, increased imports of European textiles expanded sartorial and production options rather than replacing handwork (Maiwada and Renne 2007). Even when industrial textile mills were

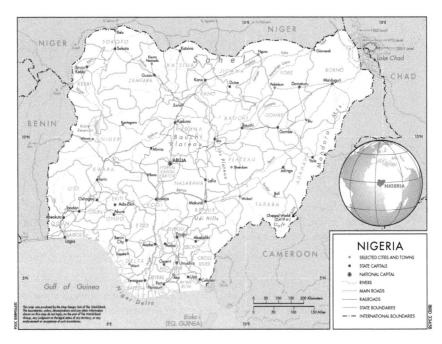

Map 1.1. Map of Nigeria, indicating the cities of Ilorin, Kaduna, Kano, and Zaria, September 2004. (Courtesy of the World Bank)

established in northern Nigeria after independence in 1960, textile-related work employed many in the cities of Ilorin, Kaduna, Kano, and Zaria (map 1.1) (Andrae and Beckman 1999; Maiwada and Renne 2013; Onyeiwu 1997). Yet by the twenty-first century, this constellation of textile production, consumption, and trade; political hierarchy; and religious authority had drastically changed. With most domestic mills closed and handweaving all but abandoned, the primary source of textiles for northern Nigerians is now China. I examine the consequences of this historical rupture in order to consider the emergence of Islamic reform movements in northern Nigeria over the past two hundred years. At a time when many are questioning the moral basis of a society in which many are unemployed and government services, such as the provision of electricity and pipe-borne water, are largely nonexistent, I reflect on how earlier examples of Islamic reform in northern Nigeria have shaped contemporary demands for religious, economic, and political revival (Mustapha and Bunza 2014). These demands include Shari'a law, women's education, and new forms of religious dress. The specific trajectory that this disenchantment with modernity has taken in northern Nigeria, expressed in terms of religious reform, reflects a particular past. Elsewhere, this questioning of the moral basis of the contemporary political economic order is couched in terms of the environment and energy resources, socioeconomic inequality, and political repression (Fischer 2014). While massive unemployment, growing inequality, and authoritarianism, as well as environmental degradation, fuel this discontent, the particular actions taken to redress these problems in northern Nigeria, India, and Egypt, for example, reflect local conceptions of the moral basis of society. By situating Islamic reform groups in northern Nigeria within their specific historical, social, political, and material contexts, I seek to complicate simplistic depictions of these groups as "radical Muslim sects."

Furthermore, because textile production, trade, and use have played such a critical role in underwriting Hausa-Fulani social life, I consider sequential political-economic transformations and Islamic reformist movements in relation to textiles and dress used by Muslim women and men. Specifically, this perspective enables me to examine how changing ideas about Muslim piety and their material expression through the use of things—veils and turbans, wrappers and robes—are shaped by the everyday actions of women and men (Meyer and Houtman 2012; Morgan 2010). Their actions, in turn, have contributed to the shaping of larger political-economic circumstances with the successive changes in the practice of Islam and political rule in northern Nigeria paralleled by changes in textile production, styles, and sources. Indeed, during the time of the Sokoto Caliphate, founded in 1808, one might speak of political rule, religious practice, and textiles—their production, trade, distribution, and use as dress—as "a total social phenomenon" in the sense described by Marcel Mauss (1967: 1).[1] Several Europeans noted the varieties of dress worn by Muslim political leaders. For example, Hugh Clapperton, who stopped in Kiama on his way to Kano in 1826, observed, "I had a visit from the governor, who came in state. . . . [H]e had on a turban over a European foraging cap, two or three tobes [robes] of Manchester cotton; the rest of his dress was of country-made cloth" (1829: 71). Others, such as Heinrich Barth, who traveled in northern Nigeria in the early 1850s, remarked on the pervasiveness of handweaving, hand dyeing, and textile trade in Kano and its environs as well as the trade in textiles between Kano and other parts of the caliphate:

> Besides the cloth produced and dyed in Kano and in the neighboring villages, there is a considerable commerce carried on here with the cloth manufactured in Nyffi, or Nupe, which, however, extends only to the . . . "riga," or shirt worn by men, and the "zenne" [*zane*] or plaid: for the Nyffawa are unable to produce either turkedi or rawani [shiny black indigo turbans, mentioned by M. G. Smith in the epigraph]—at least for export—while they seem with the exception of the wealthier classes, to supply their own wants themselves. The tobes brought from Nyffi are either large black ones or of mixed silk and cotton. (1857: 1:512)

Barth approvingly mentions the domestic basis of this extensive system of textile production and trade. "Commerce and manufacturing go hand in hand," he observes, favorably comparing this situation with that of Europe, with its "immense establishments, demeaning man to the meanest condition of life" (1:512).

This moral assessment of work forms, specifically processes of textile production and trade, relates to the ways that textiles themselves have been intimately linked with Islam—through Qur'ānic verses that prescribe covering the body (Lombard 1978; Stillman 2000), through Islamic conversion reinforced by the allure of textiles and clothing (Abba 1981), and though the conflation of textiles with particular Muslim identities (Baker 1995; Renne 2012). Indeed, some leaders of Islamic reform movements in Nigeria in the late twentieth and early twenty-first centuries have used textiles to represent their transcendence over earlier religious practices, prescribing new styles of dress, particularly veils and turbans, to distinguish reformers from those following earlier Islamic mores. Others make use of what they envision as dress "in the time of the Prophet Muhammad," as a way of emphasizing their return to fundamental Islamic texts.

The recent demise of handweaving in all but a few areas of northern Nigeria and the decline of textile manufacturing in the cities of Kano and Kaduna have led to widespread unemployment that is related to the rise of twenty-first century religious reform movements, whose leaders seek to address a sense of moral and economic disorder through a return to Islamic practices and Shari'a law (Lubeck 2011). While these leaders have not explicitly called for a return to local textile production—either of handwoven or industrially produced textiles (as in Mahatma Gandhi's advocacy of *khadi* cloth during the nationalist movement in India [see Bayly 1986]), their disapproval of the Nigerian government's failure to provide employment and sustenance for many northern Nigerians is reflected in a longing for the reintegration of religion and law, family and community, politics and work as the moral basis for social life. Precisely how this moral basis has been imagined, however, differs even within particular Islamic reform groups. In the context of this rapid social change—especially during the years of oil boom and bust of the 1970s and 1980s, the droughts of the 1970s, and a highly disruptive structural adjustment program (SAP) and economic policies of the 1980s—"many Muslims are confronted with awkward questions to which they have had to find individual answers: What does it mean to be a Muslim in these circumscribed circumstances? How does one reconcile the religion with modernity?" (Mustapha 2014: 6). What is the morally right way to be in the world—theologically, socially, materially, politically? These are questions that many seek to answer.

Material Religion: Islamic Reform and Textiles

Connections between cloth—material—and religion have long been made in practice, even while those who make distinctions between the mundane and the spiritual often situate them in different spheres (Morgan 2010). As Birgit Meyer and

Dick Houtman have noted, the study of religion has tended to focus on theological questions and conceptions of belief and to disregard material things: "The antagonism between religion and things, spirituality and materiality, is a legacy of the 'religious past'" (2012: 2). Furthermore, assumptions reflecting "a broader secularist idea of religion as interiorized and private" have tended to discount public expressions of religious belief as inappropriate or disingenuous (2). Yet it is precisely such public expressions and their material manifestations that enable an understanding of the succession of Islamic reform movements in northern Nigeria. Meyer and Houtman suggest that "we can 'know' religion only, though not completely, through its past and present manifestations," and they also note the importance of examining "the particular forms and elements through which religion ... materializes" (2012: 4)—both useful frames for understanding Islamic reform movements in northern Nigeria. For Islamic reformers there, from Shehu 'Uthmān dan Fodio and his son Muhammad Bello in the nineteenth century, to Abubakar Gumi and Mohammed Marwa in the twentieth century, and to Muhammad Auwal Albani and Mohammed Yusuf in the twenty-first, all were concerned with material things such as veils and turbans, which have been part of the public sphere of religious expression of belief. Even in the distinction between this world (*duniya*) and the afterlife in paradise (*Lahira da Aljannat*), a critically important matter in the writings of northern Nigerian Muslim scholars, this contrast was represented at times by material things, specifically textiles. The nineteenth-century Fulani writer Muhammadu Tukur, in his poem "Black Leg-Irons," describes both the transience of life in this world and the eternal life in paradise in terms of cloth. In the former, "the weaver of fine black and white cloth [*saki*] and the weaver of open-work cloth too,[2] are today no more, only the spider who weaves to give the monkey" (quoted in Hiskett 1975b: 33). In paradise, however, "fine clothes will be bought and will be laid out for the Believers, that we may mount, horses and camels, clothes of silk" (35). This poetic connection between moral states and textiles underscores the spiritual and material intersections with which Islamic reformers in northern Nigeria have historically conceptualized a proper Islamic path.

Islamic Reform, Education, and Gender

Islamic reform in northern Nigeria has in the past reinforced, and continues in the present to reinforce, new ways of thinking about religious practice, legitimate political authority (and associated legal systems), education, proper gender roles, and dress. As Nana Asma'u, the daughter of Shehu dan Fodio, writes in her work *A Warning, II*:

18. The love of the Qur'an is to love God: For the Prophet's sake, read it constantly.
19. This is the Path of the Almighty, He who follows will never turn.

20. Women, a warning. Leave not your homes without good reason
    You may go out to get food or to seek education.
21. In Islam, it is a religious duty to seek knowledge
    Women may leave their homes freely for this.
22. Repent and behave like respectable married women
    You must obey your husband's lawful demands.
23. You must dress modestly and be God-fearing,
    Do not imperil yourselves and risk Hellfire. (Quoted in Mack and Boyd 2000: 167)

In this passage, Asma'u stresses the importance of women's Islamic education as well as respectful behavior (showing *kunya*) and dressing modestly, as discussed in chapter 5. Nonetheless, the idea of dressing modestly, which has implications for both women and men (Lewis 2003), has been reinterpreted over the years, reflecting reformers' new ways of thinking about proper Islamic practice. For example, in the 1930s, Sheikh Salami Bamidele introduced his followers to the wearing of *burqa*-like *jellabiya* by women and large turbans (*lawani* in Yoruba) by men as a particular way of asserting a visibly Islamic identity (Tarlo 2010). Yet the complete covering of their bodies and faces by women followers of the Bamidele movement differed from earlier forms of women's veiling. Similarly, women associated with the Shi'a Islamic Movement of Nigeria (IMN) initially took up the wearing of black *niqab*, which distinguished them from followers of other Islamic reform groups.

The Importance of Appearance: Veiling and Turbaning

Thus, an important aspect of the material expression of religious reform and piety relates both to the gender identities and technologies of production, particularly to the types of material forms that are produced. What sorts of textiles are available for the expression of new beliefs and practice, and how are the meanings associated with new styles of textiles constituted? The dialectical process whereby material things are selected, seen, and made meaningful—and consequently, that these things with their associated meanings then shape the viewers' perception of a particular object, as described by Émile Durkheim (1915: 262)—frames the book's focus on two such objects, veils and turbans.

While there is a considerable art historical literature on Islamic dress and textiles in the Middle East (Baker 1995; Lombard 1978; Stillman 2000; Vogelsang-Eastwood and Vogelsang 2008), relatively little has been published on veiling, turbaning, and Islamic dress in sub-Saharan Africa (Akou 2011; LeBlanc 2000; Masquelier 2013; Renne 2013a, 2013b, 2013d; Schulz 2007; van Santen 2013). Furthermore, the historical and political context that has informed the choices of women and men regarding the particular textiles that are selected, given meaning, and subsequently worn as veils and turbans—in various styles covering the

Figure 1.1. Small girls wearing imported print head kerchiefs (*kallabi* or *dankwali*) and handwoven cotton wrappers (*zane*), northern Nigeria. (Courtesy of the Duckworth Collection, Melville J. Herskovits Library of African Studies, Northwestern University)

head, body, and/or face as well as the circumstances of wearing them—have been infrequently examined. While turbaning, like veiling, is closely associated with Islam in sub-Saharan Africa, there is even less discussion of turban types and turbaning practices. Yet the subject of veils and turbans has a particularly interesting gendered cast in northern Nigeria, where throughout the nineteenth and twentieth centuries, both women and men have worn veils and turbans, underscoring how turbaning and veiling have historically marked social and political rank as well as gender identities (fig. 1.1). Women may wear turbans, but they may only do so as emirate officials (Smith 1960), as *jaji* Islamic teachers (Boyd 1989: 51), or as brides (M. F. Smith [1954] 1981: 89), while emirs may cover their faces with *amawali* veils at their discretion, as discussed in chapter 5. Thus, a consideration of the types of materials used, including their specific qualities such as texture, opacity, patterning, and color; styles of tying; textile names; and sartorial restrictions associated with veils and turbans clarifies connections between changes in political authority, Islamic reform, and gender ideology. Indeed, by wearing *hijab* when attending *Islamiyya Matan Aure* classes for married women in Zaria, women followers of the Islamic reformist movement Jama'atu Izalat al-Bid'a wa Iqamat al-Sunna (Society for the Removal of Innovation and the Reinstatement of Tradition), also known as Izala (Kane 2002; Loimeier 1997), enabled its leaders to expand their efforts there in the 1980s. The introduction of new forms of head coverings as veils like the *hijab* suggests another dynamic of these interconnected processes—namely that religious reforms and textiles may structure attitudes about the gender roles in social life more generally—particularly on the attention paid to women's comportment and covering in public spaces (Mauss 1973). Indeed, it is through particular types of textiles and restrictions on their usage that ideas about gender are reinforced and reassessed. While Muslim women's participation in religious reform is less remarked upon than their use of veils, an approach that focuses on the material piety of women as well as of men clarifies their changing and respective roles in these processes.

Islam and the Moral/Material Bases of Social and Political Life

Throughout these chapters, various aspects of the fundamental conflict over the moral basis for political authority—between governance based on scholarly accomplishment and austere simplicity or on ascription and magnificent displays of wealth—may be seen. As the excerpt from Shehu dan Fodio's *Bayān Wujūb al-Hijra* in the epigraph that begins this chapter suggests, he believed that the regulation of wealth—by neither wearing fine clothes nor eating choice food—was part of one's moral obligation to attend to "people's needs and welfare" for the well-being of the entire community. Alternately, the rulers of Gobir, one of the seven Hausa kingdoms, supported a system of political hierarchy based on royal birth, with levies and tribute supporting the emirs and their courts, along with the emirs' distribution of gifts to their subjects. Even after the defeat of Gobir in 1808 and the administration of the former Hausa kingdoms through Fulani caliphate officials in conjunction with Hausa kings, the oscillation between ideals of austerity and scholarship and those of wealth and hereditary hierarchy as the basis of political authority continued. Dan Fodio's son Bello, who became caliph in 1817, realized that accommodation was necessary to maintain relative control over caliphate warriors and peaceful cooperation with emirate rulers (Last 1966). Yet the prosperity that the relative unity and security of the Sokoto Caliphate made possible provided the wherewithal for the very distinctions in court dress—reflected in silk-embroidered robes, turbans, and peacock-feather sandals—that reinforced the reemergence of former political hierarchies.[3] This alternating dynamic between ideals of austerity and of wealth as the moral basis of political life may also be seen in the establishment of the Ilorin Emirate (Danmole 1980), discussed in chapter 3. Following the death of Malam al-Sālih, the Fulani Islamic scholar known for his modest ways, the new emir, his son

'Abd al-Salāh, sought to gain official recognition for the emirate as part of the Sokoto Caliphate. The subsequent growth of Ilorin as a center of industry and trade contributed to a parallel expansion of ranks, distinguished by dress in the Ilorin court (O'Hear 1997). Nonetheless, this development coincided with the expanding community of Islamic scholars who traveled throughout southwestern Nigeria and established schools that were renowned in their time (Reichmuth 1997; see also Ware 2014). Several students who trained in these schools went on to lead Islamic reform movements in the years that followed (Oladimeji 2005).

This alternation between religious simplicity and distinctive display may also be seen in the wearing of *hijab* in Zaria City (Renne 2013a). Initially, plain dark *hijabs* were preferred, although they eventually were replaced by successive *hijab* fashions with different colors, styles, and decorations. Yet there are passages in the Qur'ān that celebrate beauty (e.g., Sura 18:31).[4] Thus, aesthetic tastes may also have an ethical aspect (Levinson 1998), suggesting the complications that surround dualisms such as austerity and wealth, simplicity and adornment. Indeed, such states do not stand in isolation but rather are interconnected, each one dialectically defining the boundaries of the other (Simmel 1950).

Some Recurring Themes

Such complicated conceptions regarding the moral basis of governance and meanings of dress—for example, as modest authenticity or as appealing opulence—are recurring themes throughout the following chapters. As discussed earlier, a succession of Islamic reformers has utilized textiles and dress as a way of representing and distinguishing their group's beliefs. Perhaps one of the most graphic examples of this connection between Islamic reform and proper Islamic clothing was the Maitatsine movement, led by Alhaji Mohammed Marwa, who was known as Maitatsine.[5] In 1980, Marwa led a group of disenfranchised rural poor in a revolt against the political and religious elite of Kano, whom he believed Allah cursed (*tsini*) for their corruption and extravagance associated with the oil boom years (1975–1981). He insisted that his followers neither wear garments made with zippers and buttons nor use bicycles, cars, or buses—all expensive Western imports—which related to his instructions that members should not "'believe generally in earthly possessions of luxuries' and to regard rich Muslims 'with extreme abhorrence and contempt'" (Isichei 1987: 195; see also Lubeck 1985). Some of Marwa's Islamic reforms were equally unorthodox, which included rejection of the hadith and avoidance of prayer facing toward Mecca.[6] Yet as Paul Lubeck observes, "As a social movement the 'Yan Tatsine [followers of Maitatsine] falls clearly into the Mahdist-millenarian tradition, one that is associated with violent social protest during periods of social crisis," (1985: 370) a dynamic that reemerged in the twenty-first-century Boko Haram and Ansaru movements examined in chapter 8.

Another theme relating to the complex meanings of dress in relation to Islamic governance and legitimacy pertains to the practice of gift giving, particularly the tradition of distributing robes by Muslim political leaders to members of their constituencies (Heathcote 1972; Kriger 1988; Renne 2004a). For example, in the seventeenth century, the king of Kano, Sarkin Mohamma Nazaki, was said to have distributed a thousand robes to the workers who extended the Kano City walls (Palmer 1908: 83). Similarly, Murray Last mentions the nineteenth-century Sokoto Caliphate practice of both receiving robes as revenue and distributing them as gifts during Ramadan and with administrative appointments: "Presents were the form that much of the revenue which Sokoto received from the emirates took. [For example], the Zaria payment referred to was 20 slaves, 70 gowns, of which 20 were fine Nupe gowns. . . . Another letter, just before his appointment [Emir Muhammad Sambo of Zaria], carries compliments and a present of four black tobes" (Last 1967: 105, 105n59, 169). Robes were also given to chiefs by Hausa caravan leaders traveling west as part of the kola trade: "These varied in price and quality, and the caravan leader was responsible before leaving the Hausa cities, for the purchase of enough gowns of the right kind to use as *gaisuwa* [literally, greetings, refers to a gift]" (Lovejoy 1980: 108–109).

This practice of gift giving continued well into the twentieth century. In the early 1950s, one colonial official described the distribution of over 150 robes by one emir during the observance of Eid-el-Fitr (the celebration that marks the end of Ramadan, also called Sallah) (Northern Region of Nigeria 1954: 5), while Ahmadu Bello distributed many robes during his conversion tours in 1964 and 1965 (Abba 1981). Such distributions of robes as gifts played an important role in maintaining the political authority of Hausa-Fulani political leaders, particularly emirs, and good social relations with their subjects. Following independence in 1960, when royal tribute in kind—which could be in the form of agricultural produce, livestock, and robes—essentially ceased, emirs commissioned hand embroiderers to produce robes, which were amassed by the court for future distribution of gifts. This practice provided employment not only for embroiderers but also for cloth and thread sellers, designers, tailors, washers, and beaters. Mauss, in the conclusion to his essay *The Gift*, argues for just this sort of beneficial gift giving, wealth redistribution, and meaningful work: "The mere pursuit of individual ends [the accumulation of wealth] is harmful to the ends and peace of the whole, to the rhythm of its work and its pleasures, and hence in the end to the individual" (1967: 75).

Despite the political and economic benefits that these exchanges and distributions contributed to community cohesion and well-being, the distribution of so-called customary gifts, such as robes, was nonetheless questioned as a form of bribery and corruption by British colonial officials during the postwar years. Prompted by provincial reports on "the customary exchange of presents between Chiefs, District or Village Heads, and their people" (Northern Region of Nigeria 1954: 1) amassed in late 1951, the chairman-legal secretary (a colonial official), two members of the Northern Nigerian Executive Council, and twelve members the Northern Regional legislature met in Kaduna in February 1952 to discuss the issue of gifts and corruption.[7] The majority of members followed the chairman's lead in condemning gift distributions as "purely secular and in far too many cases nowadays (whatever may have been the case in the past) [that] merely served the ends of *Neman Girma* [literally, looking for bigness], prestige, ostentation or avarice" (Northern Region of Nigeria 1954: 3). This document is an extraordinary example of colonial naïveté[8] and possibly of deception.[9] While almost all committee members reiterated what colonial officials wanted to hear, a few were more forthcoming. One member stated, "It would not be possible to forbid the customary exchanges of gifts in any form on the ground that these exchanges were an integral part of social behaviour, that the gifts from the richer to the poorer were alms the giving of which was a religious duty and that many poor and aged people who at present lived in reasonable comfort would find themselves destitute if the giving of presents, which often in their case were return presents, was forbidden" (Northern Region of Nigeria 1954: 3).[10]

The committee, however, supported the long list of customary gifts that were to be abolished. The ten emirs from the Northern Region who met on August 31, 1953, to consider the final report also backed this list—with one exception. They rejected the resolution that chiefs should not receive or distribute presents, which included robes, during Sallah: "We agree 'that Chiefs should not receive any presents at Salla time,' but we do not feel it justified that Chiefs should be prohibited from distributing presents as they wish at Salla time. After all it is the Chief's own property and he should be allowed to do whatever he likes with it" (Northern Region of Nigeria 1954: 14). While the report and its prescriptions may have affected some, in general the impact was inconsequential, and robe distributions continued long after Nigerian independence in 1960. For as Simmel observes, such gift giving and the "atmosphere of obligation" it supports "belongs among those 'microscopic,' but infinitely tough, threads which tie one element of a society to another, and thus eventually all of them together in a stable collective life" (1950: 395). The emirs who met in Kaduna in 1953 and refused to end the giving of gifts during Sallah knew that the advantages incurred by their fulfilment of this obligation were too beneficial to give up.

Perhaps one other aspect of this report should be noted. The colonial officials who sought to restrict the distribution of customary gifts made some exceptions: customary gifts were to be made with monetary payments that could, at least theoretically, be accounted for by Native Authority treasury officials. For example, "When a person has been selected for an important Native Authority appointment or traditional title he may be given a present of gowns or cloaks

Figure 1.2. Native Authority Police wearing uniforms with *Ajami* script that reads, 'Yan Doka Zaria" [Zaria N.A. Police] on the road leading to the emir's palace in the background, Zaria City, 1938. (Photograph by George Howard Gibbs, courtesy of the Bodleian Libraries, Oxford)

with the traditional 'kayan sarauta' [things of royalty], but this is to be paid for from the Native Authority funds" (Northern Region of Nigeria 1954: 13). Yet several provincial respondents to the government's survey "pointed out that bribery and corruption were more prevalent outside of the Native Administrations than within [it] [see fig. 1.2], and were common in Government services such as in the Nigerian Police, the Railway, the Medical Department (especially in hospitals) and in the cotton markets" (Northern Region of Nigeria 1954: 3; see also Smith 1964). Moreover, these bribes and corrupt transactions were mainly in the form of cash.[11] Ironically, during the early twenty-first century, even as robe distribution as gifts has declined—further alienating people from traditional rulers—the levels of corruption associated with local, state, and federal officials absconding with government funds have increased (Opoola 2016), thus alienating people from the Nigerian government as well.[12]

Regarding what they considered to be the immoral accumulation of wealth, both Mauss (1967: 75) and dan Fodio (1978: 152) cite the Qur'ān, specifically Sura 64:15: "Your wealth and your children are only a trial," although the specifics of their interpretations differ. For dan Fodio, the passage suggested the transience of this world and the need to prepare for the next; for Mauss, it suggested the folly of pursuing wealth for individual rather than societal ends. Yet both decry the harm done to communities by the excessive accumulation of wealth by the rich that is not redistributed.

Many Islamic reformers who followed dan Fodio have had goals that reflect distinctive social values and religious mores in northern Nigeria—"alternative constructions of the world" as Bray (1997: 11) puts it—and like dan Fodio and Mauss, they have questioned the moral bases of Western capitalist societies. Yet such forms of political economy based on "the spirit of capitalism" (Weber 1946: 302) in Nigeria and elsewhere are neither permanent nor the evolutionary pinnacle of human social life (Hocart [1936] 1970; Orwell [1946] 1984). The questions raised by Islamic reformers in northern Nigeria—where textile mills representing the optimism of an earlier set of Muslim political leaders are shut down and many former workers are unemployed—about the benefits of modernity and associated forms of large-scale industry represent a rethinking of the moral basis of work and economies of scale in manufacturing, trade, banking, and agriculture. These questions have implications for us all.

Order of Chapters

This chapter sets out the general themes concerning the historical interconnections of Islamic reform, political authority, gender, and textiles in northern Nigeria. In the remaining chapters, I specifically address different facets of a succession of Islamic reform movements and their material representations.

In chapter 2, I consider the establishment of the Sokoto Caliphate and associated Islamic reforms and administrative practices that contributed to an expansion of Islamic scholarship as well as of textile production and trade. In the nineteenth century, this situation led to the movement of people and things throughout the caliphate and beyond—between Kano and Tripoli via trans-Saharan trade routes in the south, east, and west—by caravans carrying indigo-dyed textiles and wild silk thread. Caliphate textile production and trade generated prosperity and fostered not only relative internal security but also the growth of political hierarchy within the emirates. Chapter 3 continues this theme of Islamic reform and governance in relation to textile production and trade connections by examining the extension of caliphate rule to the southernmost emirate of Ilorin. The city of Ilorin, geographically situated between the Hausa-Fulani region of northern Nigeria and the Yoruba areas of southwestern Nigeria, was well suited for the expansion of Islamic education, trade, and innovation in handwoven work. The two Islamic reform groups that grew out of Ilorin's religious milieu, the Bamidele movement and the Jama'atu Tabligh—each with its own distinctive theology and dress—are also considered. Chapter 4 examines a specific question—namely, why the Sardauna of Sokoto, Ahmadu Bello, wore a wide variety of turbans. Unlike his predecessor Shehu dan Fodio, who was said

Figure 1.3. Ahmadu Bello wearing a *babban riga* with a *harsa* turban tied in Sokoto fashion on a visit to India. (Courtesy of the Kaduna State Ministry of Information, Kaduna)

to have one turban, Ahmadu Bello wore turbans of many colors and styles and, in general, dressed attractively in a range of beautifully embroidered robes and cloaks. Yet despite his apparent appreciation of magnificent dress, Ahmadu Bello did not live extravagantly. Rather, he followed a middle road between abstemiousness and royal display as well as between advocacy of Western and Islamic education, which paralleled his positions as a government official as the premier of the Northern Protectorate and as a member of the Hausa-Fulani aristocracy as the Sardauna of Sokoto (fig. 1.3). The chapter also discusses the different forms of turbans used in marking the distinctive identities of Islamic reform groups.

The fact that in northern Nigeria some women and some men wear turbans while some women and some men wear veils is examined in chapter 5. Specifically, this chapter considers the historical connections of gender identity and material expressions of Islamic piety and political authority as expressed by the wearing of veils and turbans. The association of women's veils with Islamic education and reform movements has been complicated by the ways that "fashion always comes in," as one Zaria man put it, referring to new styles of veiling. The practice of veiling has been affected by the notoriety that *hijab* and *niqab* have also achieved in regard to certain counter-pious associations with deception and disguise.

Some of the new styles of veils, turbans, and clothing seen in northern Nigeria have been obtained through the performance of the hajj, the subject of chapter 6. Performing the long pilgrimage to Mecca by road enabled some pilgrims to study with Islamic scholars along the way as well as to learn new styles of hand embroidery. For example, one pilgrim introduced the embroidery style known as *mai rumi* (a type of North African *passementerie* embroidery) to his home community in Zaria upon his return. This itinerant form of Islamic education also facilitated the spread of the Tijāniyya movement in northern Nigeria, which was led by Sheikh Ibrahim Niass, who first met the Emir of Kano, Abdullahi Bayero, in Mecca in 1937 (Loimeier 1997: 34). With the advent of regular flights to Mecca, many more Muslims could perform the hajj, underscoring how modernity may enable both the fulfillment of an Islamic tradition and the spread of new forms of Islamic reform.

In chapter 7, I consider a specific example of the relationship between different styles of veils and turbans, Islamic reform, and politics during the three decades following Nigerian independence in 1960. Despite extreme political upheavals—such as the assassinations of Ahmadu Bello and Abubakar Tafawa Balewa and the Nigerian Civil War (1967–1970)—it was also a period of economic growth exemplified by the textile industry in Kaduna and Kano. In Kaduna and Jos, this situation was paralleled by the growth of the Islamic reform movement Izala, associated with the introduction of *hijab* and women's education, as well as with splinter groups in Kano, such as the Daawa movement, which encouraged women's education through its sponsorship of the Aminu Kano Hijab Factory. However, it was also a time of increasing socioeconomic inequality in northern Nigeria, which contributed to political uprisings such as the Maitatsine riots of the early 1980s, demands for Shari'a law, and to a splintering of Izala into smaller reform groups in the late 1990s with their prescribed forms of dress and textile use, both as a way of referring to their doctrine and as a means of distinguishing themselves from other Muslims.

By the early twenty-first century, many of the textile mills established at the beginning of the independence era were closed. In chapter 8, I discuss the associated decline in cotton production and textile manufacturing as well as the subsequent unemployment—both rural and urban—that have coincided with the expansion of the Islamic reform group *Jama'atu Ahlus-Sunnah Lidda'Awati Wal Jihad* (JASLAWJ), more commonly known as Boko Haram. Following the extrajudicial death of the group's founder, Mohammed Yusuf, in Maiduguri in 2009 (Amnesty International 2012: 7), aggressive attacks against government and military sites and associated personnel expanded from 2010 to 2015. During this period, simple Islamic dress, which included turbans and short pants for men and veils for women, was transformed into a combination of military-style uniforms and Palestinian-style *keffiyeh* turbans for men and all-encompassing *hijab* worn by women, which some used to hide explosives. The transformation of uniforms and *hijab* from their associations with legitimate authority and modest piety, respectively, to forms of disguise and concealment is considered in the context of government and civilian efforts to contain increasingly sophisticated means of Boko Haram terror. However, with the election of a new administration in 2015 and a reversal of the tremendous theft of government funds that weakened military efforts, this violence has been somewhat reduced. In December 2016, the Boko Haram headquarters in Sambisa Forest was overtaken by government troops, and its captured flag was presented to President Muhammadu Buhari on December 30 (*Daily Trust* 2016b). Yet as late as February 6, 2018, military officers announced the destruction of Boko Haram's bomb-making factory in Sambisa Forest (*Daily Trust* 2018b). The chapter ends with a brief discussion of the government's continuing efforts to assist displaced people and plans to rebuild the areas affected by this situation. One poignant example of efforts to reintegrate Boko Haram victims was reported from an internally displaced persons (IDP) camp in Maiduguri. There, two young women who had been "married" to their Boko Haram captors, sat silently as they embroidered a type of Borno cap (known as *zawa* or *zana*) for which the area is renowned (Dan-Ali 2016).

In the epilogue, I return to the moral connections made between successive Islamic reform movements and textile production and use in northern Nigeria, where people have continued to seek the path that is straight and an understanding of the proper Islamic way of being in the world. Textiles and dress have often been an integral part of this process as reform movement members express their religious beliefs, in part, through material means. These material things—*abin duniya* (things of this world)—may also be used for hateful harm, as Boko Haram fighters have shown. Taking into account the complexities of such moral imaginings, the book concludes with a consideration of the continuing struggles between those who envision society as best served by communal efforts and those who see individual accumulation of wealth as the best way forward—spiritually, politically, economically, and environmentally—for life in this world.

* * *

These chapters are based on a range of primary and secondary materials. Primary materials include archival documents, photographs, and films; private family photographs; field interviews carried out in Zaria, Kaduna, Kano, Ilorin, and Ibadan from 1995 to 2017; my own field photographs; doctoral dissertations; websites; industrial textile samples; and museum textile collections. Secondary materials include newspaper articles, published trade records, and books and articles in the large secondary literature on northern Nigeria. These materials have been clarified by innumerable conversations and correspondence with acquaintances, friends, and colleagues in Nigeria, Europe, and the United States, without which this book could not have been written.

Notes

1. Mauss is referring to the interconnected aspects of society—religious, legal, moral, and economic—noting that "each phenomenon contains all the threads of which the social fabric is composed" (1967: 1). Other sociologists and historians, such as Georg Simmel (1950) and Francesca Bray (1997), also frequently use textile metaphors when discussing social conditions.

2. During the nineteenth century, a type of open-work (leno weave) cloth was woven on Zagoshi Island, opposite Rabba. Two undyed pieces were collected during the Niger expedition of 1841 to Egga (Johnson 1973: 356).

3. According to M. G. Smith, "To secure the support of non-Fulani subjects, Dabo [the emir of Kano] wrote Mamman Bello [the caliph of Sokoto] asking permission to employ the old Habe [state] titles and offices of Kano as machinery for its administration, together with essential insignia and procedures of Habe rule" (1964: 175).

4. "30. But surely We do not let the reward of those who believe and do the right to go waste. 31. There will be gardens of Eden for them; with rivers flowing by, where they will be decked in bracelets of gold, with silken robes of green and of brocades to wear, reclining on couches" (Sura 18:30–31, The Cave [*Al-Qur'ān* 1993]).

5. Andrea Brigaglia (2012: 13n13) points out that the nickname Maitatsine, which translates literally as "the owner of the Allah's curse," is actually an example of Marwa's foreign background and faulty Hausa: *Allah ta tsine* would translate as "Allah may she (*ta*) curse you." His feminization of Allah was not intentional.

6. The sole focus on the Qur'ān and the rejection of the hadith characterize a later Islamic reform group, the 'Yan Kala Kato, which began in Zaria in the late 1990s and is currently based in Kaduna (Sa'idu 2009a, 2009c).

7. Dan Fodio had also questioned an aspect of the practice of *gaisuwa* in Hausa kingdoms, suggesting that it may be seen as a bribe to gain influence with the recipient (Hiskett 1960: 568, 576).

8. For example, the committee recommended several measures, including notices to be posted "in railway stations, markets, dispensaries, post offices, Native Authority Offices, District Council halls and District offices" as well as "announcements to be made to the people when they are all gathered together for the Salla [Eid-el-Fitr]" (Northern Region of Nigeria 1954: 8).

9. It is not clear from this document who, within the colonial service, instituted the surveys and organized the meetings on which the report was based. In some instances, colonial officers "made work" as a way of promoting their careers. It is also possible that the colonial officials involved, "upholding middle class values of morality" about monetary transactions, did not understand the larger context of gift giving (Beidelman 2012: 293).

10. Similarly, kola caravan leaders viewed gifts of robes to the rulers of towns through which they traveled as a voluntary "symbol of respect and appreciation to the ruler and an

offering which pledged their good faith in the market exchange with local people" (Lovejoy 1980: 109).

11. M. G. Smith (1964: 187–190) conducted research in the Zaria Emirate in 1949–1950 with follow-up research in 1950–1951, around the same time that the materials for the report on customary gifts were collected. Smith found that village heads collected considerable amounts of cash as gifts for appointments they made and also profited from large amounts of grain purchased for the Native Authority, some of which they resold for profit. Smith concluded, "It will be seen that almost every practice prohibited by Shehu [dan Fodio] was to be found in Zaria during 1949–50, together with many innovations by which modern administrative duties and opportunities were reinterpreted to fit traditional patterns" (1964: 190).

12. Latifat Opoola (2016) reports that, based on information provided by the minister of information and culture, Alhaji Lai Mohammed, "55 people stole a total of N1.34 trillion, in seven years—between 2006 and 2013 . . . [which] represented more than a quarter of last year's national budget."

2 Islamic Dress, Textile Production, and Trade in the Time of the Sokoto Caliphate

Reports of European travelers repeatedly referred to the thriving textile industry and trade, and by the early twentieth century, when the British compiled their census reports, the numbers of people occupied in textile work were surpassed only by those in the agricultural sector.

—C. K. Meek, *The Northern Tribes of Nigeria*

The development of trade in the past has of course been the normal result of political unification.

—Max Weber, "Structures of Power"

IN NORTHERN NIGERIA, textiles and particular forms of dress—turbans, robes, and veils—have long been associated with the founding of the Sokoto Caliphate. In this chapter, I consider the significance of Islamic dress in relation to the nineteenth-century religious reforms instituted by Shehu 'Uthmān dan Fodio and his son Muhammad Bello. Islamic dress, particularly robes, turbans, and veils, provide insights into the historical processes—both religious and material—involved in the legitimization of political power and authority to rule. The anthropologist A. M. Hocart (1970) has referred to the tension between government based on the knowledge of sacred councilors, as he puts it, and government based on the political authority of kings. This tension was evidenced in the relations between Shehu dan Fodio and the kings of the seven Hausa city-states (Hausawa Bakwai), the former claiming authority based on Qur'ānic learning and religious instruction from Islamic scholars, the latter claiming authority based on royal birth and ideas about the divine right of kings. This mutual mistrust is suggested by the belief in the pre-jihād period "that a scholar compromised himself if he associated with kings. Indeed, for scholars to be seen entering the gates of palaces was a sign of the approaching end of the world" (Last 1966: 57). In *Kitab al-farq*, dan Fodio expresses this moral distinction regarding "the difference between the governments of the Muslims and the governments of the unbelievers" in terms of political authority and dress: "One of the ways of their government is succession to the emirate by hereditary right and by force. . . . One of the ways of their governments is their . . . wearing whatever clothes they wish, whether religiously permitted or forbidden" (quoted in Hiskett 1960: 566, 567).

Beginning with the period immediately preceding the 1804 jihād that led to the establishment of the Sokoto Caliphate in 1808, this chapter examines the changing contours of this intersection between Islamic governance, textile production, trade, and dress. Shehu dan Fodio wrote extensively on the reforms he prescribed for the proper observance of Islam—which reflected his extensive knowledge of the Qur'ān, hadith, and the opinions of distinguished Islamic scholars—and on what he considered to be appropriate Islamic dress and inappropriate royal dress. Indeed, the connection between the production of glossy blue-black turbans and large embroidered robes, *babban riga* or *rigar giwa*, which were made in several parts of the caliphate, reflected the combined efforts of enslaved and free men and women—as farmers, hand spinners, handweavers, dyers, designers, embroiderers, tailors, beaters, and traders. The results of their efforts functioned not only to visibly unify the caliphate but also to delineate the particular ranking of officials within it (Candotti 2010; Kriger 1988, 2006; Last 1967; Shea 1975). Furthermore, the materiality of cloth—its color, texture, appearance, hand, and odor contributed to its association with particular moral or aesthetic states (Bayly 1986; Schneider and Weiner 1986). For example, regarding color, within the Sokoto Caliphate, dan Fodio, citing Islamic jurist Ahmad al-Zarrūqin's commentary on *al-Waghlisiyya*, wrote: "It is desirable for a scholar, as well as a pupil, to adorn himself particularly with white clothes" (dan Fodio 1978: 92), while the blue-black dan Kura turbans and *kore* robes associated with kings and courtiers were distinguished by "the smell of the dyed cloth but more particularly from the beauty of its metallic sheen" (Flegel [1885] 1985: 7).

This connection between Islamic reform and textiles was made possible, paradoxically, through two aspects of caliphate rule—namely, the relative security that enabled production and trade connections between various parts of the caliphate and the insecurity of slave raiding, which provided agricultural labor for cotton and indigo production (Lovejoy 1978), as discussed in chapter 3. Here, the focus is on production and trade connections between different areas of the caliphate with its system of walled outposts (or garrison towns; *ribats*) and caravan fees instituted to maintain a certain amount of protection for travelers, both internally within the caliphate, and externally via trans-Saharan trade. This situation was made possible through administrative measures established by the shehu's son, Muhammad Bello.

Finally, the importance of economies of scale and of technological improvements in indigo dyeing of both thread and whole garments is considered. This industry—along with cotton growing, hand spinning of cotton and wild silk, handweaving of narrow cotton strips, tailoring, embroidery, and beating—contributed to the growth of the great urban textile production centers, most notably in Kano but also in Zaria, Bida, and Ilorin and in many smaller towns such as Kura and Zarewa. Young men migrated from villages throughout the caliphate to urban areas to obtain seasonal work in dyeing centers while also pursuing Islamic education (Shea 2006: 7), which was another aspect of this connection between Islam and textiles.

Just as Shehu dan Fodio viewed the corruption within the Gobir kingdom and its residents' extravagant dress and gifts as evidence of its disregard for the well-being of its subjects and as un-Islamic practice (Last 1967: lxx), so his son Bello understood the importance of both Islamic education and agricultural and commercial prosperity for maintaining the unity and security of the caliphate (Bello 1983; Last 1966; Lovejoy 1978). Caliphate efforts to institute Islamic reforms, the growth of Islamic education—for men and for women (Bivins 2007)—as well as increased textile production, trade, and consumption contributed to a sense of moral order in nineteenth-century northern Nigeria.[1] This is not to say that slavery and the insecurities associated with slave raiding did not exist or that a continued chafing at caliphate boundaries as well as discord between caliphate officials and emirate leaders did not occur. Rather, through the combination of agriculture and commerce, Islamic governance and scholarship—what Ahmadu Bello (1986) would refer to as "work and worship" in the following century—"the ideals, and to a large extent the practice, of Sokoto did not change . . . [as] the Caliph and his court upheld the traditions of the Shaikh" (Last 1967: 235). These traditions continued until 1903 when British colonial rule was imposed.

Islamic Reform, Textiles, and the Sokoto Caliphate

Much has been written about the background for the jihād led by Shehu dan Fodio and the founding of what came to be known as the Sokoto Caliphate. One aspect of the justification for jihād that relates to later Islamic reform movements in northern Nigeria concerns corruption and the accumulation of excessive wealth for one's own personal benefit.[2] The shehu wrote and spoke on several occasions about the evils of such excesses in his work *Bayān Wujūb al-Hijra 'ala 'l-'Ibad* (dan Fodio 1978). For example, in chapter 58, "On the way the Prophet acted (*Sira*) with people when he was sent to them," dan Fodio cites the story of Qarun from the *Al-Qur'ān*, Sura 28:76–81):

> 76. Verily Qarun was of Moses' people, but he began to oppress them. We had given him treasures, so many that a team of wrestlers could hardly lift their keys. His people said to him: "Do not be exultant. God does not like those who exult.
>
> 77. So seek the abode of the Hereafter through what God has given you, and do not forget your part in this world. Do good to others as God has done good to you, and do not try to spread corruption in the land. Surely God does not like corrupters."

78. He said, "This has come to me through my own acumen." Did he not know that God had destroyed many generations before him who possessed far more acumen than he, and more wealth? The sinners will not be asked about their sins.

79. Then he came before his people in all pomp; and those enamoured of this world, said: "Ah would that we had what Qarun had been given! He indeed possesses great good fortune."

80. But those who knew better, said: "Alack-a-day! God's guerdon is better for those who believe and do the right. Only those who persevere will receive it."

81. So We opened up the earth and sunk him and his mansion.

Dan Fodio continues in his chapter to describe the humility of the Prophet, who ate "as a slave" and who "sat among his Companions . . . with nothing to distinguish him from them." He also notes the writings of *Salih*: "The Messenger of God did not leave, on his death, a dirham, or a dinar, or a slave-girl" (1978: 152).

This theme was taken up by caliphate writers such as Muhammadu Tukur, a much-revered contemporary of Shehu dan Fodio, in his work known as "Sharafiyya" (The Noble). Tukur considers the theme of ostentatious wealth and distinctly refers to the Hausa kings and their courts:

You should know that death will take us all under the ground;
Leave off causing us to strut proudly about the earth, . . .
No longer will horns be blown for you, nor will you hear the drums,
He will no longer put on his gowns of silk
Whether he is a king of the Muslims or of the unbelievers.
(Quoted in Hiskett 1975b: 95)

This extravagance, condemned by Muhammadu Tukur and 'Uthmān dan Fodio alike, contrasts with the ascetic practices of dan Fodio, who was said to have one robe, one set of trousers, and one turban (Hiskett 1973: 31).

It is also interesting that in Tukur's work, textiles and dress serve as metaphors for immoral, un-Islamic behavior, specifically the "gowns of silk" but also the handwoven *saki* cloth used in expensive gowns worn by royal members of the court. In a verse from his poem "Black Leg-Irons," Tukur writes of those who have had children by adultery, "let them be warned, their adornment is a gown of fire" (quoted in Hiskett 1975b: 34). Yet there are also positive associations with dress as Muslims were often referred to as the "people of the gown" (Last 1979: 239). Indeed, an important aspect of Islamic identity was being properly covered with cloth.

The Importance of Turbans, Robes, and Veils

Turbans played a critical role in legitimating what dan Fodio considered to be a moral form of governance as an Islamic state. Indeed, Muhammad was said to be "'the wearer of the turban' (*ṣāḥib al-'imāma*), and like many of the accoutrements associated with a hero of epic proportions, his turban had a name—*al-ṣiḥāb* or the 'cloud'" (Stillman 2000: 17). This association of turbans with Muslim piety and leadership is evidenced in a vision recounted by dan Fodio, in which 'Abd al-Qādir al-Jīlānī, the founder of the Qādiriyya order, appears to him and presents him with a robe and turban. Mervyn Hiskett attributes the description of this vision to dan Fodio's *Wird*:

> When I reached forty years, five months and some days, God drew me to him, and I found the Lord of djinns and men, our Lord Muhammad—may God bless him and given him peace. With him were the Companions, and the prophets, and the saints. Then they welcomed me, and sat me down in their midst. The Saviour of djinns and men, our Lord 'Abd al-Qadir al-Jilani, brought a green robe embroidered with the words, "There is no god but God [Allah]; Muhammad is the Messenger of God"—May God bless him and give him peace—and a turban embroidered with the words, "He is God, the One." (Quoted in Hiskett 1973: 66)[3]

That the robe was green was significant as this color is associated with Muslim identity (Lombard 1978; Weir 1989: 64), while the phrases embroidered on both the robe and turban reflect the connection between Islamic texts and embroidered patterning of other forms of dress, particularly robes. Shehu dan Fodio first studied with his father, Muhammad Fodio, and then with a relative, 'Uthmān Bindari, both in Degel in what is now northern Sokoto State. From there, he later traveled to Agades (in present-day northern Niger) to study with Shaykh bin Umar, a renowned Berber Islamic scholar in the late eighteenth century. Thus, Shehu dan Fodio would have been influenced by the turbaning practices of Muslim teachers from the north and east, who were, in turn, influenced by Middle Eastern turbaning styles.[4] Similarly, Middle Eastern turbans reflected influences from the Ottoman Empire; the English word "turban" "derives from Persian *dulband* via vulgar Turkish *tulbant* or *tolibant*," as Yedida Stillman (2000: 16) suggests.[5]

While wearing a turban in the early nineteenth century was a widely accepted sign of being a Muslim, it could also be seen as a visual challenge to the political authority of a reigning emir. When Shehu dan Fodio, wearing a turban, visited Bawa, the king of Gobir, it was perceived as a potential threat to the king. However, Bawa, having been impressed by his sermons, acceded to Shehu dan Fodio's five demands for himself and his followers in Degel (Last 1974: 5). Two of the concessions granted to the shehu included the "freedom of preaching and conversion to Islam" and "freedom to wear a turban (or a veil) and not to pay tax" (Last 1974: 5n6).[6] Dan Fodio remained at Degel, on the western border of Gobir, during the pre-jihād period of 1792 to 1804. Yet when the new king of Gobir, Sarkin Nafata, came to power in 1794, he saw the Degel community as a threat to his moral authority and "therefore rescinded the rights of teaching and conversion and tried to disrupt the cohesion of the Muslims by banning their distinctive turbans and veils" (Last 1974: 7).[7] This event, along with the order by the subsequent king of Gobir, Sarkin Yunfa, that the shehu and his followers leave Degel, marked the second phase of the Sokoto jihād.

In 1804, the shehu and his followers moved to Gudu, just outside of Sokoto, where the armies of the shehu and Gobir fought for four years and the shehu's followers suffered from famine and sickness. The final battle of the jihād took place in Alkalawa, the capital of Gobir, which fell to jihād forces on October 3, 1808. "Resistance to the Muslims was broken everywhere," according to the shehu's son Bello (Last 1967: 39). Following this defeat, the administration of the Sokoto Caliphate under Islamic law began in earnest and the wearing of turbans was once more encouraged, if not required, for Muslim men.[8] Yet even as turbans came to be more routinely worn in the Sokoto Caliphate, previous distinctions—that some turbans were associated with religious scholars and some with royal political leaders—reemerged (see chapter 4). This dynamic was exemplified by the emir of Kano, Ibrahim Dabo (1819–1846) (Palmer 1908: 95), who devised a particular style of turban tying using white cloth that distinguished royal Muslim men of his lineage from commoners, with "two short ears of material, a way of visibly reckoning and honoring those from the ruling family" (Nast 2006: 96; see also Perani and Wolff 1992). More recently, a twenty-first-century expert in turban tying in Zaria City, Samaila Magaji, the Sarkin Kwal-Kwali Zazzau (the chief of decoration of the Zaria Emirate), explains this historical development:

> That turban [was devised by Ibrahim Dabo]; the other emirs learned from him. Zaria changed their own *kunne*, at the side, in order to differentiate their own turbans from that of Kano. And turbaning from Kano, they start tying it from the top of the head down, while in Zaria they tie it from down to up. . . . Zaria, Kano, Katsina, Daura, Bornu, Sokoto, and Gombe—there are similarities and differences. In Kano and Daura they have the same turbaning, they are doing the *kunne* at the middle; in Sokoto they are doing it at the back. Katsina [does it] at the back or in the middle, but small. In Gombe, they are doing theirs with a very large turban, sometimes with *kunne* at the side, but it's very large. (Samaila Magaji, interview by the author, September 1, 2012, Zaria)[9]

Such visual contests over styles and sizes of turbans and the techniques of tying them underscore Shea's point that, along with religion, "politics [has] . . . played a role in determining what kind of apparel people wear" (1975: 57).

What, precisely, did early eighteenth-century *rawuna Sunnah*—turbans associated with the practices of the Prophet—look like? We know something about how dan Fodio viewed turban wearing from his comment in chapter 56 of *Bayān wujūb al-Hijra*, "On a quality that makes it easy for the commander of the faithful and others to be friendly with all people":[10] "When you meet a man who

Figure 2.1. *Reception of the Mission by the Sultan of Bornu,* based on a sketch by Dixon Denham, engraved by E. Finder. (From Denham, Clapperton, and Oudney 1831: vol. 1, between pages 264 and 265)

Figure 2.2. *Veiled Woman on Horseback,* based on a sketch by Dixon Denham, engraved by E. Finder. (From Denham, Clapperton, and Oudney 1831: vol. 2, between pages 118 and 119)

persistently adorns himself as a bride, bleaching his clothes all the time, adjusting his turban, taking care that nothing should touch him, looking at his shoulders and having no interest besides preening himself, then class him with the peacock and keep away from him" (dan Fodio 1978: 149).

One might assume from this commentary on the excesses of a Hausa-Fulani dandy that simple white turbans would have been worn as *rawuna Sunnah.* While white was preferred, other colors were acceptable as dan Fodio noted in chapter 22, "On the law concerning the wearing of silk in a jihād": "Ahmad al-Zarrūqin in his commentary on *al-Waghlisiyya* said: 'It is desirable for a scholar, as well as a pupil, to adorn himself particularly with white clothes, [though] without prejudice to the wearing of other colours. The Prophet used to wear green, red, black and yellow, although not blue and nothing has been transmitted to approve or disapprove it'" (dan Fodio 1978: 92; see also Lombard 1978; Stillman 2000). However, his ideas about the specifics of turban styles and size are unclear (fig. 2.1), other than that he advised that Muslim men wear them and that Muslim women wear veils (fig. 2.2) (Ogunbiyi 1969; see also Mack and Boyd 2000).

Europeans' Accounts of Islamic Dress

Hugh Clapperton noted these nineteenth-century variations in Muslim men's turban styles when he was staying in Sokoto in November 1826, shortly after the death of dan Fodio:

> The dress of the men is a red cap, with a blue tassel of silk, a white turban, part of which, or a fold, shades the brow and eyes; another fold is taken over the nose, which covers mouth and chin, hanging down on the breast; a white shirt, close at the breast and short in the skirts, a large white tobe, and white trousers, trimmed with red or green silk, and a pair of sandals or boots: this is the dress of the greater part of the wealthy inhabitants. When travelling, they wear, over the turban, a broad-brimmed straw hat, with a round low crown. Some who do not affect great sanctity or learning wear check tobes and blue turbans over the forehead, with the end hanging down behind; the poorer, a white check tobe, white cap and trousers, and sandals. Some are content with the straw hat only, but all wear a sword, which is carried over the left shoulder [fig. 2.3]. (1829: 211–212)

Twenty-five years later, in January 1851, Heinrich Barth described a member of the *serki-n-turawa* (counsel of the Arabs) in Katsina wearing a "green and white striped tobe, wide trowsers . . . ," with an embroider[y] of green silk in front of the legs . . . round his red cap a red and white turban was wound crosswise in a very neat and careful manner" (1857: 1:446). On arriving in Kano, Barth noted the importance of cloth production and trade there (fig. 2.4), which included the making of blue-black turbans: "The principle commerce of Kano consists of native produce, namely, the cotton cloth woven and dyed here or in the neighboring towns, in the form of tobes or rigona (*sing. riga*); turkedi, or the oblong piece of dress of dark-blue color worn by the women; the zenne [*zane*] or plaid, of various colors; and the rawani baki or black *litham* [a black turban, also known as dan Kura]" (1857: 1:510). While in Kano, Barth also observed "some Arabs leading their camels, . . . heavily laden with the luxuries of the north and east (*kayan-ghabbes*) to the quarter of the Ghadansizen" (1857: 1:293), which provided another source of turbans for wealthy Muslims.

Figure 2.3. Young man wearing embroidered robe and *malafa* straw hat with the requisite sword—similar to the dress described by Hugh Clapperton in 1826. (Courtesy of the Duckworth Collection, Melville J. Herskovits Library of African Studies, Northwestern University)

Figure 2.4. Emirs, chiefs, and supporters wearing turbans—some with veils—and *babban riga*, waiting for an audience with His Excellency Frederick Lugard, Kano [1914?]. (Photograph by C. J. Chaytor, courtesy of the Bodleian Libraries, Oxford)

Paul Staudinger, who visited Zaria in September 1885, described an audience with Sarkin Muhammad Sambo, who reigned from 1881 to 1890: "After a few minutes' delay we were called to the king. . . . On a kind of clay platform in oriental fashion sat a venerable man, dressed simply but in garments of fine quality. His face was obscured by the dark blue face veil. . . . Later we saw the sultan's face unveiled; he had dignified, kindly features; a thin grey beard bore witness to his age. The ruler of Zaria's name was Zambo [Sambo]" ([1889] 1990: 1:173).

Staudinger, like Barth, also described trade cloths from two sources— European cloth brought from the south by traders associated with what he referred to as the English National African Company and North African and Middle Eastern cloth and clothing brought from the north by North African traders to Kano. In Zaria, Staudinger also described clothing that was locally made:

> Cloth and ready-made garments are of course much in demand . . . here the materials are predominantly local ones. The most popular and most eagerly sought are those deep blue black garments which are dyed so excellently here and in the Kano area. The gowns which are made of a blue and white material woven in a lattice-like pattern (according to [German explorer] Nachtigal and Barth "guinea fowl coloured") are more expensive, but the most expensive are those made of the finest white material edged with an attractive red [silk] band,

and the best of these come from Nupe and Ilorin. The narrow strips of cotton cloth woven in this country are still much bought and sold. ([1889] 1990: 1:181)

All these sources provided cloth from which turbans could be made. During his travels in northern Nigeria, Staudinger himself lamented, "Unfortunately, we had no fine linens or muslin, so popular here for turbans" ([1889] 1990: 1:103). Charles Robinson, who visited Zaria in 1895, was also disappointed: "[While] our supply of English cloth was practically exhausted . . . we could find no ready sale for the silks we had brought with us" (1897: 85). The wearing of plain white cotton *turkudi*[12] turbans or shiny blue-black ɗan Kura turbans, made by caliphate craftsmen, continued to prevail.

Administrating Islamic Reform and Textile Production in the Sokoto Caliphate

The production of handwoven textiles used for turbans, robes, veils, and wrappers within the caliphate was made possible through the administrative efforts of dan Fodio's son Muhammad Bello (Bello 1983; Last 1966). Bello, in his *al-Ghayth al-Wabl fi Sirat al-Imam al-'Adl* (The Comprehensive [Work] on the Conduct of a Just Leader), writes of his administrative objectives as the new leader of the caliphate, which included unity, defense, justice, and communal worship as well as socioeconomic development and Islamic education (Bello 1983). His attempts to achieve these goals contributed to the tremendous growth of the nineteenth-century textile industry in northern Nigeria. One of the primary measures that made their achievement possible was through the establishment of *ribats*—garrison towns situated in fertile areas where new Fulani-Hausa communities could prosper (Bello 1983; Last 1966). Consequently, mosques and schools were built, and "with scholars appointed to those towns as Imams, judges, *muhtasibs* (legal inspectors), and teachers, Bello hoped to maintain both the practice of Islam and the military control of the area" (Last 1967: 79–80; see also Lovejoy 1978: 351). Indeed, Bello sought to foster unity among people with different backgrounds and occupations. Yet as Last observes, "To establish a Muslim state in Hausaland Bello must have been aware . . . of his need for Hausa cooperation. . . . One way of achieving co-operation was to leave the communities under rulers loyal to Sokoto and to improve conditions so that trade and agriculture could prosper" (1966: 57–58). Thus, Bello emphasized the importance of emirs' responsibility for distributing land to those who sought to farm and by providing "public amenities for the people of his state for their temporal and religious benefits. For this purpose, he shall foster the artisans, and be concerned with tradesmen who are indispensable to the people, such as farmers and smiths, tailors and dyers, physicians and grocers, butchers and carpenters and all sort of trades which contribute to the proper order of the world" (Bello 1983: 102).

For example, textile production was particularly important for Bello's founding of a *ribat* in Sokoto: "Textile industries were located in separate quarters of the city; one produced white cotton cloth (*fari*) and the other, manned by Nupe, produced blue checked cloth (*saki*)" (Bello 1983: 102). Furthermore, the establishment of plantations for growing the cotton and indigo necessary for textile production expansion were made possible through the security that the *ribats* provided (Lovejoy 1978). For Bello, this security was enhanced further through the social cohesion fostered by community worship: "The benefit of residing in towns lay in living together and performing prayers in congregation. The idea of congregational prayer is to promote social cohesion as people living in one quarter, mahallah, meet one another five times a day; and on Friday all people living in various mahallahs of the city meet one another once a week for Jum'at prayer; and people living in the suburbs meet the people living in the city twice a year for 'id prayers; while people from different parts of the globe meet one another on the 'Arafat day" (Bello 1983: 99). By providing for community well-being, both materially and spiritually, Bello hoped to promote caliphate unity and avoid the destructive violence of the past.

Islamic dress supported this cohesion, not only by visibly marking their wearers as Muslim but also by promoting the demand for a range of textiles and garments throughout West Africa (Kriger 2006: 86), which was addressed by the economic expansion of their supply. Distinctive sizes and styles of robes—made with diverse materials, simply or elaborately embroidered and finished—were produced in different parts of the caliphate, although mainly in urban areas. Thus, "the quality and prices of garments varied," Colleen Kriger (1993: 389) notes. This range of possibilities contributed to distinctions among robes wearers based on wealth and political position. Much as turban-tying styles associated their wearers with particular emirates within the Sokoto Caliphate, so the most elaborately embroidered and/or indigo-dyed robes made with the finest handwoven cotton strips, perfectly tailored and finished through hand beating, reflected a wearer's status as well as the robe recipient's standing within emirate court hierarchies: "Skillfully tailored and embroidered garments were the most expensive textile products made in the caliphate, and they were worn and distributed as gifts by the Muslim elite.[13] . . . Very elaborately tailored garments worn by the Muslim elite were made from specialized cloth designed particularly for the tailoring process" (389).

Thus, although an ideal of simplicity in dress and disparagement of ostentatious garments was expressed by Shehu dan Fodio and reiterated by his son Muhammad Bello, the countervailing tendency among the emirs and members of their court to distinguish themselves through very finely discernable grades of robes contributed to the demand for these garments. The expansion of production in many areas of the caliphate—of plain white (*fari*) handwoven cotton strips as well as of blue-black and white (*saki*) cotton strips and handwoven strips made with imported magenta silk (*alharini*) or local wild silk (*tsamiya*)—made the expression of these different religious and political sentiments possible. The expansion of trade networks did so as well.

Internal and Trans-Saharan Textile Trade

While much as been written about the trans-Saharan trade, nineteenth-century trade networks within the Sokoto Caliphate were also extensive. Traders traveled in caravans, often by foot, with donkeys laden with goods and sometimes with porters, bringing commodities for sale to one area where demand was great and supply limited (fig. 2.5). Thus, most traders adapted themselves to what was available and what was in demand rather than specializing in a particular commodity. Some men, particularly Islamic students, traded more informally, buying and selling when necessary as they sought out particular Islamic scholars with whom to study (Mohammed 1978). This connection between trade, travel, textiles, and Islam may clearly be seen in pilgrimage (Yamba 1995) not only to Mecca but also in journeys to religious shrines elsewhere in Africa (see chapter 6). However, long-distance trading practices within the Sokoto Caliphate of the nineteenth century (and at times beyond its borders) are exemplified by the biography of one caravan leader, Madugu Mohamman Mai Gashin Baki, who related his trading experiences in Nigeria and Cameroon to German explorer Eduard Flegel in the 1880s (1885, [1885] 1985).

Internal Long-Distance Trade

Madugu (literally, caravan leader) Mohamman Mai Gashin Baki was born in Kano in the late 1820s (fig. 2.6). When he was around sixteen years old, he traveled with one long-distance trader (*fatake*) to Ledde, in the Nupe kingdom, where they "sold horses to the king in exchange for Nupe cloth" (Flegel [1885] 1985: 6). They then returned to Kano after about six months. Following a short stay, they traveled together to the Adamawa region, where they purchased elephant tusks before returning to Kano (Johnson 1978). On his third expedition, Madugu Mohamman went to the Bauchi area and then on to Kuka (the capital of Adamawa at that time), where he bought galena (a mineral used for eye makeup), which he took back to Kuka. He then returned to Bauchi with five large oxen that he had purchased and had loaded with natron (see Barth 1857, 1:515), which he subsequently sold. The success of these early trips reflected his business acumen and flexibility, buying local commodities when they were available at low prices and selling them in places where prices were dear. Thus he, like many long-distance traders, did not focus on a single commodity but bought and sold according to circumstance. On his next trip, he planned, along with "a friend from Nupe, Agole by name," to take tiny cowries and "Bukin tuffa" (*Bakin tufafi*;

Figure 2.5. Donkey caravan near Miya, in Bauchi State. (Photograph by Eric Lardley Mort, courtesy of the Bodleian Libraries, Oxford)

literally, black clothing)—the pride of Kano city—to sell in Ngaundere, in what is now Cameroon: "'Bukin tuffa,' the indigo dyed cloth with the metallic sheen, is prized throughout the whole of the Western Sudan" (Flegel [1885] 1985: 7). In the following years, Madugu Mohamman continued to trade in elephant tusks, kola, beads, and cloth, depending on market conditions.

One aspect of this arduous and sometimes dangerous life[14] that impressed Flegel was the importance of the evening prayer after the business of the day had been completed: "The call of the Mallam has a special character . . . [and] the company are turned to the east in recollection of him whose words they use. The call to prayer is beautiful and deeply moving to the traveller. . . . On the participant in this beautiful and emotionally rewarding experience a peace of mind descends, contributing to happiness at work, the pleasure of companionship at the camp fire, and sustaining him until the following morning when, as the sun first touches the horizon, sounds out the call once more" ([1885] 1985: 11). While Flegel surely did not know the writings of Muhammad Bello, the sentiment expressed in this passage mirrors Bello's description of the sense of security and well-being that communal prayer could convey.

Nonetheless, Magudu Mohamman faced adversity during his career as a caravan leader, with false promises of safe passage by one village head as well as agreements for payments that were never received. As an independent caravan leader, he had the support of a network of Muslim contacts in some of the areas where he traveled, but as a stranger, he was also in a socially vulnerable position. Another

Figure 2.6. Madugu Mohamman Mai Gashin Baƙi and Madugu ɗan Tambari shown with Eduard Robert Flegel. Madugu Mohamman (*bottom left*) has a black beard (*gashin baƙin*), while Madugu ɗan Tambari's face is covered with an *amawali* face veil. Both are wearing embroidered *babban riga*. (From Flegel 1885)

group of men, based in several Katsinawa-Ungogo District villages just outside of Kano, who were involved in the long-distance trade in wild silk (*tsamiya*) had more social support in their travels, mainly because the wild silk trade in northern Nigeria was "in the hands of a fairly closed community" (Shea 1980: 108).

It is unclear precisely when the concentrated efforts in collecting, processing, and trading wild silk by a small group of villagers living outside of Kano began. Shea suggests that since this trade was well established in the Kano area when it was investigated by the British in 1907, it had probably "developed together with the general expansion of Kano trade in the first half of the nineteenth century, sometime after the Jihad" (1980: 99). As has been discussed, the security provided by the growth of the Sokoto Caliphate in areas both south (toward Bida and Ilorin) and eastward (toward Bauchi and Adamawa) enabled traders to broaden their collection areas of wild silk cocoons as well as to sell their product—degummed wild silk lint and silk thread. Indeed, presuming these silk traders were traveling in the nineteenth century as Shea suggests, they would have been traveling on some of the same routes as Madugu Mohamman.

During the dry season, traders would travel in small caravans using donkeys to bring goods from Kano that they could trade "along the way, then gather silk (both by collecting and by purchasing small lots) and [return] after several months to Kano" (Shea 1980: 102). One older trader described the route from "Wudil, Takai, Kafin Gana, Birnin Kudu . . . and then Yola" (102). Once an area was identified as having wild silk cocoons, the traders would proceed in a group and then fan out to gather as many of the large, loose cocoons as possible. In some places, villagers would collect and keep cocoons in anticipation of Kano traders' arrival. As one German businessman observed in 1913, "The number of people engaged in the collecting is very great and most of the material changed hands several times even before it was treated" (quoted in Shea 1980: 98). After collecting a sufficient number of cocoons, which could take several days, they would take them in sacks to be processed in their home villages at the Mile Nine Area outside of Kano City. While the degumming of *tsamiya* cocoons was not a difficult process, it was time-consuming and best done in large quantities when possible. Degummed *tsamiya* silk or silk thread could then be sold in the Kano market or taken to markets in Bida and Ilorin or beyond, where it was used in handweaving and embroidery.[15] By "do[ing] most of the work themselves (from collecting the silk, to degumming it and spinning the thread), and even do[ing] embroidery" and working cooperatively, the people of the Mile Nine Area largely monopolized the silk trade (1980: 107). As Shea has observed, "Primarily rurally based, they seem to have been unaffected by the ostentatious way of life of many city people, and their thrifty habits have doubtless also contributed considerably to their impressive success in the silk trade" (107).

Trans-Saharan Trade in the Nineteenth Century

While wild silk thread was not widely used in handweaving in Kano and Zaria, it was frequently used in hand embroidery of robes and trousers (Shea 1980: 103). Rather, the silk that was used in handweaving along with a range of woven silk, woolen, and cotton textiles (and thread) that came to Kano in the nineteenth century was imported mainly via trans-Saharan trade routes: "The desert caravans to Kano . . . continued to function with few interruptions well into . . . [the twentieth] century, and English cotton goods, including unbleached and bleached calico in considerable quantities, formed half to two thirds of their cargoes. . . . It can be shown that Kano was importing considerable quantities of yarn for weaving, in addition to the traditional import of dyed waste silk for spinning from the Mediterranean countries; it was also importing made-up clothing from North Africa, and some made in Europe to North African patterns" (Johnson 1976: 97).

Barth noted that aside from cotton plain-weave and printed textiles, a large part of trans-Saharan trade from Tripoli to Kano consisted of the magenta waste silk known as *alharini* (Arabic, silk):

> The very coarse silk, or rather refuse, which is dyed in Tripoli, is imported to a very considerable amount, this forming the principal merchandise of most of the caravans of the Ghadamsiye merchants, and about one third of their whole commerce, amounting to not less than three to four hundred camel-loads annually, worth in Kano each about 200,000 kurdi. . . . But according to some well-informed sources thousands of loads of this article pass annually through Ghadames. . . . A good deal of this silk, I have no doubt by far the greatest part, remains in the country, being used for ornamenting the tobes, sandals, shoes, and other things. (1857: 1:518)

Evidence from his description of handwoven clothing sold in Kano as well as from cloth collected during the 1841 Niger Expedition would seem to confirm Barth's statement. For example, of the twenty cloths in the British Museum's 1841 collection, four cloths include red silk stripes made with *alharini* silk imported through Kano (Johnson 1973: 358).

Barth, who in visited the Kano market in 1851, lists several different types of *zénne* (*zane*, women's wrappers), which include silk: "'Fessagida,' with a broad line of silk; 'hammakuku,' with less silk; . . . 'zellumwami,' a peculiar zenne with a silk border; jumada, another similar kind; 'da-n-katanga,' once a very favorite article of female dress, . . . with red and black silk in small quantity, and a little white. . . . Besides, there are ten kinds of zennwa entirely of silk, but these are made better in Nupe than in Kano" (1857, 1:510).

The variety of cloths available when Barth made this assessment underscores both the enormous textile production and trade that was centered in Kano as well as textile specialization associated with particular areas of the caliphate. There was also great demand for imported unbleached and bleached calico, as indicated by trade records. This type of plain-weave cotton fabric could be used in the construction of lightweight white garments that might or might not be embroidered as well as for use as turbans. Indeed, Staudinger noted that North African traders brought "cloths for turbans . . . ; they also [brought] carpets made in their own country, burnouses, *haïks* [sic],[16] red caps (fez), saddles, and so forth" ([1889] 1990: 2:114). These imports along with textiles and garments produced in various parts of the caliphate were sold in Kano and traded through caravan networks to towns elsewhere in the caliphate (Shea 1975: 22; see also Johnson 1973: 354).

Staudinger, who visited Kano in late October and early November 1885, was surprised by low prices of European articles: "But the amazing fact is that they can sell European goods in Kano much cheaper than the English, indeed sometimes for half the price which the English charge for their goods in Loko [Lokoja] and this in spite of there being transport costs and customs duty already added on to them in Tripoli. What is more, the cheapest cottons, for instance, brought in by the Arabs are mostly of better quality than those sold by the Europeans" ([1889] 1990: 2:114). Marion Johnson (1976: 115) suggests that, as was the case for Kano silk traders, the family and religious connections of Muslim North African merchants involved in trans-Saharan trade (see Lydon 2009: 280) enabled them to travel with relatively few expenses, which allowed them to charge low prices for their goods (fig. 2.7).

North African traders had a further advantage in that they knew the market for Islamic dress in Kano, as described by Barth: "An important branch of import is formed by articles of Arab dress, chiefly bernúses, caftans, sedríyas, trowsers, red sashes, shawls. . . . The sort of dress most in request comes from Tunis, but a good deal also from Egypt; and from the latter country come all the white shawls with red borders, called 'subéta' in Arabic, 'aliyáfu' in Hausa. . . . The common articles of dress, of coarser workmanship, are made in Tripoli" (1857: 1:517). Notwithstanding the tremendous amounts of textiles and clothing shipped south from Tripoli, known in Kano as *kayan gabas*—things from the east—cloths such as indigo-dyed calicoes were sent from Kano back north to Tripoli, as Shea (1975) has observed.

Bigger Is Better: Economies of Scale in Textile Production

Indeed, in the nineteenth century, Kano was famous for indigo dyeing throughout West Africa. Barth wrote, for example, that "it was formerly supposed that Timbuktu was distinguished on account of its weaving, and that the export of dyed shirts from hence was considerable; but I have already had an opportunity of showing that this was entirely a mistake, almost the whole clothing of the natives themselves especially that of the wealthier classes, being imported either from Kano or from Sansandi, besides the calico imported from England" (1857: 3:357–358).

Figure 2.7. "Deposition of Tripolitan Arabs from Kano Town," exhibiting a range of men's Islamic dress styles. (Photograph by C. J. Chaytor, courtesy of the Bodleian Libraries, Oxford)

Two particular types of indigo-dyed textile garments produced in Kano and its environs were widely admired and purchased; they included *d*an Kura turbans (see fig. 4.7 and fig. 5.2) and *kore* robes, the latter purchased for trade by Madugu Mohamman (Flegel [1885] 1985). Shea (1975) discusses the production processes involved in narrow-strip handweaving and indigo dyeing in the Kano area. While initially, large clay pots (*kwatanniya*) were used for dyeing, they were later buried in beds of dyebath residue (*katsi*, removed from the bottom of dye pots); somewhat later these buried pots were lined with *laso* cement (Shea 2006: 7). This innovation in the indigo-dyeing process allowed Kano area dyers to produce quantities of the dark blue-black cloths at lower prices. One particular innovation involved the making of *katsi* balls, or bricks, from dyebath residue, which were dried, burned, ground, and mixed with other materials to produce the cement-like *laso*, which was used to make large dye pits at numerous dyeing centers, further enabling indigo dyers to process large quantities of textiles, garments, and thread (fig. 2.8) (Shea 1975: 153–155). This innovation also contributed to the diversity of indigo-dyed cloth available to customers, from indigo-blue textiles and garments that were dipped several times until the dyer obtained a deep blue color, to the blue-black cloths that were dipped many times, after which they were sometimes treated with a concentrated indigo paste known as *shuni* to produce a shiny black effect: "A distinction is commonly made between centers which specialized in ordinary, or 'blue,' dyeing and centers which specialized in 'black' dyeing. 'Black' cloths and gowns require not only longer and more careful dyeing, but also longer and more careful beating. The production of this 'black' cloth consumes more indigo in the dyeing process, as well as a great deal of expensive *shuni* (cooked or refined indigo) in the beating process. In addition, finer cloth is used for 'black' than for 'blue' cloth most of the time" (111).[17]

This specialization flourished in different parts of the Kano Emirate and led to another, less obvious innovation. To properly finish handwoven, indigo-dyed, and/or embroidered textiles, the cloth had to be beaten with wood mallets on a wooden log, a process that continues, at least in Kano and Zaria, to this day.[18] Shea (1975: 169) suggests that this practice preceded indigo dyeing. However, blue-black indigo dyeing presented certain problems, as any excess dye could stain mallets, logs, and subsequent white cloth that might need to be beaten; hence the need for separate beating establishments. This situation was further complicated by the introduction of indigo *shuni* paste, made from boiling down indigo leaves then whipping the concentrated indigo solution and drying it in lumps (171). While initially the paste was applied to a cloth and then carefully rubbed with stones,[19] the demand for shiny black turbans, robes, and wrappers led to the use of logs and special large mallets to beat the *shuni* into the dyed cloth. This shift to heavy Kano mallets, which required special training for their use and was forbidden to slaves (211), led to a range of different types of *shuni*-treated cloth:

> With the development of specialized beating centers, there was greater and greater differentiation between areas as to the kind of beating done. The ability to impart color to cloth after it was dyed meant that greater and greater varieties of cloth could be produced. Some cloths were given a much greater sheen than others. The cloths given the highest sheen were extremely expensive, and thus tended to be smaller than some of the garments given a lesser sheen. Thus, turbans and cloths for women's wrappers were often given a very great sheen, and large gowns were frequently given a somewhat less sheen. (Shea 1975: 173)

The different amounts of *shuni* used and types of beating contributed to very fine evaluations of handwoven textiles, turbans, and garments produced in dyeing and beating workshops in the emirate. These practices also contributed to very fine gradations in the evaluation of people who wore them and their worth.

The textile industry in Kano expanded during the nineteenth century, in part because of the administrative reforms associated with the Sokoto Caliphate, which enabled greater security and internal trade within an enormous geographical region. The transfer of raw materials, occupational mobility, and the cross-fertilization of knowledge about different forms of textile production through the relative ease of movement within the caliphate also contributed to innovations, particularly in large-scale indigo-dyeing processes. In this economic sense,

Figure 2.8. Indigo dyebath center (*marina*), Kano, 1930s. (Photograph by E. H. Duckworth, courtesy of the Duckworth Collection, Melville J. Herskovits Library of African Studies, Northwestern University)

bigger is better. However, the growth of Kano as a center of trade and wealth also contributed to another dynamic that in some ways resembled the religious challenges that Shehu dan Fodio sought to correct.

In the early years of the caliphate, the emir of Kano, Sarkin Kano Suleiman, was a pious ruler who did little to promote the economic development of Kano. Indeed, there are stories, perhaps apocryphal, that he sewed his own cloths (Shea 1975: 38). His successor, Sarkin Kano Ibrahim Dabo, took military action to consolidate the emirate, which further enhanced security and subsequent textile production and trade. However, in the last years of his reign, this emir "is reputed to have moved away from the austerity of his predecessor and to have instituted the custom of wearing sandals with ostrich feathers [fig. 2.9] and other items of apparel which were ostentatious and called attention to his wealth" (38). He is also believed to have instituted the distinctive tying of turbans that associated their wearers with particular emirates, as described by Samaila Magaji. This dynamic of distinction was continued by subsequent rulers so that by 1885, when Staudinger visited Kano, he was told about the emir's treatment of members of a

Figure 2.9. Emir of Kano Alhaji Abdullahi Bayero, wearing ostrich feather sandals. (Courtesy of the Duckworth Collection, Melville J. Herskovits Library of African Studies, Northwestern University)

delegation from Futa Toro who were sentenced to be beaten for showing a lack of respect. According to Staudinger: "At the court of the lord of Kano great pomp prevails. The original simplicity of the reigning Fulbe has disappeared and a strict code of protocol makes it difficult for subjects to approach their ruler, whereas they can penetrate unhindered to the mighty lord of Sokoto in order to present their pleas and grievances" ([1889] 1990: 1:230–231). The growth of the textile industry in Kano and the trade in robes and textiles between different parts of the caliphate were certainly beneficial in terms of employment and artistry, but they had their drawbacks as well.

Conclusion

Madugu Mohamman Mai Gashin Baƙi's career as a caravan leader for long-distance trade throughout the Sokoto Caliphate exemplifies the connection between increased security and trade within the caliphate. As Muhammad Bello had hoped, this situation contributed to a sense of Muslim unity and encouraged an expansion of agricultural production, the growth of textile-related industries, and an extension of trading networks. Madugu Mohamman's trade in Nupe cloth and black cloth from Kano as well as his travels with traders from various parts of the caliphate suggest the diversity of backgrounds of those involved in various aspects of textile production and trade. Furthermore, the administration of a system of governance based on Islamic principles was visually reinforced through Muslim dress—turbans, robes, and veils. Yet the Islamic reforms that Shehu dan Fodio sought to implement through his leadership of the Sokoto jihād were undermined by the economic success that the administrative policies introduced by his son, Muhammad Bello, supported. The tension between Islamic principles of simplicity and humility described by the shehu in his writings and the growing wealth associated with emirate rule was reflected through dress, with elaborate garments associated with the political authority of the emirs and modest, unassuming garments associated with the religious authority of Islamic scholars. This opposition was also visually represented in the continuing preference for and disapproval of silk garments. The tremendous quantity of waste silk imported to Kano from Tripoli during the nineteenth century, which was woven into narrow-strip textiles used in the making of magnificent *babban riga*, as well as the collection and processing of wild *tsamiya* silk used in hand embroidery and handweaving, contradict Shehu dan Fodio's initial injunction against the wearing of silk by men (dan Fodio 1978; Kriger 2010). Nonetheless, simple white garments continued to be preferred by some. As Georg Simmel has noted, the relationship between rights and obligations—between those who have great wealth and those who do not (either by ascetic choice, misfortune, or social consequences), contributes to a particular system of moral values:

Any social class that is not too low sees that its members spend a minimum on their clothing; establishes a standard of decent dress; and the one who does not attain this standard will no longer belong to that class. But it also establishes a limit at the other extreme, although not with the same determination nor in such a conscious manner; a certain measure of luxury and elegance and even modernity is not proper, indeed for this or that group; and he who overreaches this upper limit is treated on occasion as not belonging fully to the group. (1971c: 168)

In the early years of the Sokoto Caliphate, the "standard of decent dress" for Muslim men consisted of wearing a turban and some form of cotton gown and trousers, while for Muslim women, it consisted of a veil and large wrapper—of cotton and/or silk. Those who failed to cover themselves in such a manner might not be regarded as proper Muslims. Yet the tendency for those with great wealth and political power to distinguish themselves through "a certain measure of luxury and elegance and even modernity" may also be seen as overreaching an upper limit, placing such people outside of the group of proper Muslims. The tension between this tendency toward political hierarchy expressed in evermore luxurious dress and the countervailing movements against it expressed in simplicity of dress persists, just as the rights and obligations of those within the Islamic community continue to be contested. The spread of Islamic practice, education, and scholarship has affected how these relationships—and their associated rights and obligations—are understood as well. By both delineating and extending the impact of Islamic reforms in a wider area through expanded trade and Islamic scholarship, the nineteenth-century emirate of Ilorin was formed and integrated within the Sokoto Caliphate. The establishment of this southernmost emirate and its later development as the twentieth-century Kwara State are the subjects of chapter 3.

Notes

1. This sense of moral order was not held by all: the most common complaint in letters sent to caliphate viziers—high-ranking court officials—were concerned with "slaves who had either run away or claimed they were free men" (Last 1967: 199).

2. In a more recent example of such an offense, jewelry worth over £2 million (N593 million) was recovered from the former minister of petroleum, Diezani Alison-Madueke, and the wife of Jide Omokore, a political ally of former president Goodluck Jonathan, by the Economic and Financial Crimes Commission in April 2016 (Abdallah 2016a).

3. Hiskett (1973: 66n6) notes that the phrase embroidered on the turban, "He is God, the One," may refer to *Surat al-ikhlas* (Sura 112), which may have been embroidered in its entirety on this turban.

4. Nehemia Levtzion (1987) discusses the extent of interaction among Islamic scholars in West Africa prior to the jihād associated with the Sokoto Caliphate. Materials made available

by eighteenth-century trans-Saharan trade routes would also have influenced turbaning practices (Lydon 2009).

5. "The 'imāma or turban has been worn by the Arabs since pre-Islamic times.... The 'imama of Jahill and early Islamic times was probably not the composite headgear of the medieval and modern periods consisting of one or two caps (taqiyya or araqiyya and/or qalansuwa, kulak, or tarbush) and a winding cloth, but merely any strip of fabric wound around the head.... In the early umma, the 'imāma certainly did not have any of the significance it was later to have as a 'badge of Islam' (sima al-Islam) and a 'divider between unbelief and belief' (hajiza bayn al-kufr wa 'l-imari)" (Stillman 2000: 16).

6. F. H. El Masri describes one of the five demands made to Sarkin Bawa: "To treat with respect any man with a turban" (1978: 23).

7. According to Murray Last, "Though the wearing of a turban is not a duty (fard), it is sunna and recommended, this prohibition was a contributory factor in the decision to commence the jihad" (1967: lxix, n30).

8. Philip Shea notes that while "the wearing of turbans became a symbol of loyalty to the new regime in Sokoto . . . in Borno, never subjected to Fulbe [Fulani] rule, the turban even today is not worn by the Shehu or by any of his followers" (1975: 57). However, in a sketch by Dixon Denham based on his visit to the Sultan of Borno in the 1820s, the sultan and members of his court all wore turbans (see fig. 2.1).

9. According to Magaji, turbans may be tied to make visual reference to the spelling of Allah in Arabic (see fig. 5.5).

10. In El Masri's introduction to Bayān wujūb al-Hijra, he notes that dan Fodio sought to explain "the obligation of the faithful to enforce the law, hence hijra, jihad, and the establishment of Islamic rule" based on the writing of earlier Islamic scholars (1978: 14).

11. Barth describes the trousers as made "of speckled pattern and color, like the plumage of the Guinea-Fowl" (1857: 1:446). In Hausa, this patterned weave is known as saki and in Yoruba as etu, terms that mean "guinea fowl" (see chapter 3; see also Kriger 2006).

12. Turkudi refers to very narrow handwoven cloth strips approximately half an inch wide that are sewn together to the required size cloth (Lamb and Holmes 1980: 90).

13. Robes were also used as gifts to encourage consideration of a request made to a caliphate official. Last notes that when the vizier at Sokoto received "an in-coming letter [it] was often accompanied by some gowns or cloths, occasionally a slave or a horse or a parcel of kola-nuts" (1967: 196).

14. According to Mark Duffill, who translated Flegel's The Biography of Madugu Mohamman Mai Gashin Baki ([1885] 1985: 43) and who conducted interviews in Bakindi, where Madugu Mohamman had retired, the leader took special measures to ensure the safety of his caravans: "Like other Hausa caravan leaders, Madugu Mohamman would consult with a Malam in order to obtain a favorable day for setting out on a journey. In Bakundi he consulted one Malam Burba. He also took elaborate precautions to surround himself with mystical protection. He would wear a gown that had many charms sewn into it, special belts, and a special hat, when leading a caravan" (43; see also Goody and Mustapha 1967; Heathcote 1974).

15. Laurence Douny (2011: 406) mentions a Kano man, whose family had long been involved in the silk trade, collecting wild silk in the Bauchi area and selling it to Marka-Dafing people in Burkina Faso.

16. A *haïk* is a large piece of cotton, silk, or wool cloth worn as an outer garment in Morocco [Moroccan Arabic *ḥā'ik*; from Arabic, weaver; active participle of *ḥāka*, to weave].

17. Shea (1975: 111) observes that beating *shuni* into dyed cloth added considerable value to these cloths, which were comparable in weight and volume with less costly indigo-dyed cloth, hence justifying the expense of selling them through long-distance trade.

18. In Anguwar Limanci in Zaria City, several *gidan buga* establishments have beaters who specialize in three types of beating for embroidered robes—*buga lema, buga lallashe,* and *buga fashi uku.* The first is the most extensive form of beating and is expensive, while for the last, "we only beat the place where the embroidery is" (Renne 2004b: 106).

19. Shea notes that in the 1970s in Bida (Niger State), Nupe craftsmen "placed dyed cloth on a wooden slate . . . , wipe[d] the *shuni* (indigo paste) on the cloth, and finally rub[bed] the cloth with a fine polished stone" (1975: 172).

3 Muslim Identity, Islamic Scholarship, and Cloth Connections in Ilorin

[The emir of Ilorin] was richly dressed, habited in a fine, black cloth cloak; with his head covered by a turban, mounted on a beautiful bay charger.

—W. H. Clarke, *Travels and Explorations in Yorubaland (1854–1858)*

To consolidate his pride in his Fulani ancestors, the Emir Abdul Kadiri [of Ilorin] made a tour, in his own car, of the northern emirates in 1935 and was received by the Sultan of Sokoto and the Emir of Gwandu.

—S. J. Hogben and Anthony Kirk-Greene, *The Emirates of Northern Nigeria*

IN THE EARLY nineteenth century, the emergence of the emirate of Ilorin both as the southernmost emirate in the Sokoto Caliphate (under the Gwandu Emirate) and as a major center of Islamic learning and textile production in what is now southwestern Nigeria has had important consequences for Islamic practice there.[1] While Hausa, Fulani, and Yoruba Muslims have distinguished themselves by language and ethnicity, their historical interconnections in Ilorin, both politically and as Muslims in relation to the Sokoto Caliphate, continued throughout the colonial period—essentially the first half of the twentieth century—in Nigeria. The continuing influence of Islamic teachers, descendants of nineteenth-century scholars from northern Nigeria, on Yoruba Muslim scholars in Ilorin may be seen in the work of Sheikh Ahmad bin Abi Bakr. Abu Ikororo, as he was popularly known, subsequently taught Yoruba Muslim students in Ilorin and Lagos (Danmole 1980: 220). Other Muslim scholars from Ilorin established important Islamic schools elsewhere in southwestern Nigeria during the colonial era (Danmole 1980; Reichmuth 1997). These connections may also be seen in the system of nineteenth-century handwoven textile production in Ilorin in which many Islamic scholars and their students participated (O'Hear 1983). Furthermore, just as Muslim scholars from the north traveled to Ilorin to teach, there was an active trade in handwoven cloth from Ilorin, which was used in the making of *babban riga* robes elsewhere in the Sokoto Caliphate. These interconnections between Islam, handweaving, and official dress, which reflected a particular form of political economy, were nonetheless later affected by the imposition of British colonial rule.

This northerly infusion of Islam into southwestern Nigeria differed from Yoruba Muslim movements that began in Lagos in the 1840s, associated with the repatriation of freed Yoruba and Hausa slaves who established Islamic societies and mosques there (Gbadamosi 1978b). With the collapse of Old Oyo and the Oyo Empire at the end of the eighteenth century and the establishment of emirate rule in Ilorin around 1829 (Danmole 1980: 37; see also Hiskett 1984: 186), Yoruba Muslims living in nearby towns and villages, some of whom were handweavers, flocked to Ilorin (Gbadamosi 1978b: 11) as did Muslim Hausa and Fulani slaves (Danmole 1980: 44).[2] "Henceforth," as Tajudeen Gbadamosi describes it, "Ilorin remained to Yorubaland a sort of Islamic lighthouse, a local Mecca to which the Yoruba Muslim turned for study and guidance" (1978b: 10). O'Hear has noted that, "[while] some weavers declare that their families came to Ilorin 'because of Islam' . . . , many of the ancestors of present-day weaving families are said to have been Muslims even before they came to Ilorin" (1983: 126–128). She thus concludes that "there is a clear connection between Islam and the weavers in Ilorin" as a consequence of these early nineteenth-century migrations.

The emirate of Ilorin was ruled during the nineteenth century by a succession of Fulani rulers who were approved by leaders of the Sokoto Caliphate (Danmole 1980). As part of the caliphate's extensive textile industry (Shea 1975, 2006), Ilorin officials also provided support for middlemen who facilitated trade in textiles and agricultural commodities between the northern and southern regions of the caliphate (O'Hear 1983). The town's location south of Raba, a major crossing of the Niger River (map 3.1), also contributed to Ilorin's position as a major cosmopolitan center of trade, a position it held well into the twentieth century. While the position of middlemen traders was eroded following Ilorin's defeat by British Royal Niger Company forces in 1897 (O'Hear 1983) and the completion of the Lagos–Kano railroad in 1911, Ilorin retained its intermediary status during the colonial period to some extent (fig 3.1). It continued to serve as a link between northern and southern Nigeria; between Yoruba, Hausa, Fulani, and Nupe people; and between British colonial and Middle Eastern connections— through trans-Saharan trade and pilgrimage to Mecca. Handweaving and trade in narrow-strip cloth, as well as forms of Islamic dress—*babban riga* robes, imported turban materials, and handspun cotton thread from the north—supported these interconnected, yet distinctive identities.

During the period of British colonial rule (1903–1960), Ilorin was a political administrative center as well as the religious center of the Ilorin Emirate. As the provincial and divisional capital, Ilorin continued its role as an economic center, particularly in the production of handwoven cloth and trade in European textile imports coming from Lagos through the auspices of expatriate firms such as United Africa Company, John Holt, and Paterson Zochonis (Pedler 1974).[3] While northern Nigerian and trans-Saharan trade with North Africa continued

Map 3.1. Map of Yoruba, indicating location of Raba (present-day Rabba), the important Niger River crossing for traders traveling from the north to Ilorin. This map, which appeared in Thomas Bowen's *Adventures and Missionary Labours*, published in 1857, is also of interest for what is not shown. Neither Jebba nor Lokoja, which became major Niger River crossings in the twentieth century, are indicated.

during this period (Johnson 1976), cloth trade with southern Nigeria and Ghana expanded considerably (O'Hear 1983: 140). This combination of Islam and politics as well as textile production and commerce that had attracted teachers and students, politicians and administrators, weavers and traders to Ilorin led to the spread of particular forms of Islamic belief, practice, and dress through the travels of scholars, weavers, and traders.

This chapter considers three aspects of these interrelated processes. First, the intermediary position of Ilorin—as part of both the north and south—and the Islamic scholars and the handwoven textiles associated with this urban center makes it particularly useful for thinking about historical and contemporary connections between Yoruba, Hausa, and Fulani Muslims. I begin with a discussion of the position of the emirate of Ilorin within the religious, political, and economic system of the nineteenth-century Sokoto Caliphate. During this period, the production of textiles relied to some extent on the labor of slaves, who grew and harvested cotton as well as the indigo used to dye thread for the narrow-strip, handwoven cloths for which Ilorin was famous (Kriger 2006). Handweavers,

LIST OF GIFTS PRESENTED BY HER MAJESTY'S GOVERNMENT TO THE
KING, IMAM, AND CHIEFS OF ILORIN.

	£	s.	d.
1 Ivory-handled sword, gold-plated scabbard, with gold knot	11	10	o
1 Ivory-handled sword, gold-plated scabbard, with gold knot	9	o	o
2 Embroidered saddle-cloths, at £3	6	o	o
2 Embroidered saddle-cloths, at £2, 15s.	5	10	o
2 Musical boxes, at £6, 2s.	12	4	o
3 Broussa prayer carpets, at £4, 16s. . . .	14	8	o
3 Broussa prayer carpets, at £2	6	o	o
2 Broussa portiers, at £4, 15s.	9	10	o
2 Embroidered cloths (Koran inscriptions), at £2 10s. .	5	o	o
1 Bagdad embroidered turban cloth	1	13	o
1 Bagdad embroidered turban cloth	o	16	6
1 Indian tent-cover, 30 by 10 feet	2	o	o
2 Gongs and beaters, at £1, 10s.	3	o	o
2 Hand-mirrors, with oxydised silver backs, at 18s. 6d. .	1	17	o
2 Daghestan rugs, at £2, 2s.	4	4	o
Carry forward . .	£92	12	6

Figure 3.1. Good relations with the emir of Ilorin was deemed to be of considerable importance in the establishment of British control of the emirate, as evidenced by the gifts presented to the emir, imam, and chiefs of Ilorin by Major Claude MacDonald, who visited Ilorin in 1897 (figure from Mockler-Ferryman 1892: 299). According to A. F. Mockler-Ferryman regarding recommended gifts, "to some it is sufficient to give a packet of needles or a few yards of cheap cotton stuff, while to others (such as the Mahommedan emirs) handsome presents of English and Oriental goods are necessary" (1892: 299). Broussa prayer carpets are considered to be some of the finest of Turkish handwoven rugs.

however, were generally freeborn Muslims whose work arrangements reflected specific forms of Islamic practice and emirate rule, which included the wearing and distribution of robes.

Second, I consider the spread of Islamic reform and its influence on dress during the colonial period, focusing on a group of Muslim scholars associated with what Patrick Ryan refers to as "conservative reformers" (1978: 126) in the cities of Ilorin and Ibadan, which were historically connected with or influenced by developments in the Sokoto Caliphate (Danmole 1980). As Muhammad Umar (2006) has noted, during the colonial period, Islamic reform and resistance to British colonial rule were muted. Yet the continued importance of Islamic scholarship and dress, reinforced through the expansion of Islamic schools and new styles of clothing throughout the southwest, were one way that some could implicitly criticize British—Christian (Nasarawa in Hausa)—colonial rule and reject Western education.[4] This particular reformist position—the valorization of Arabic and knowledge of the Qur'ān, hadith, and *tafsir* as well as specific forms of Islamic dress—reflected an explicit dismissal of Western (and Christian) cultural practice and represented an indirect form of resistance to British colonial rule. This dynamic is exemplified by one group of Yoruba Islamic reformers associated with Ilorin through the teachings of Sheikh Yusuf Agbaji (Danmole 1980: 231; Doi 1969) and his many students, including Sheikh Abdul Salami Bamidele, who began what is referred to as the Bamidele movement, a small reformist group founded in Ibadan in the early 1930s (Doi 1969; Ryan 1978). For Bamidele, Muslims should appear distinctly as Muslims and should study Arabic Islamic texts; he rejected both Western dress and education.[5] Through their specific styles of dress, members of these groups stressed their Muslim identity as "visibly Muslim" (Tarlo 2010) and their affiliation with particular Islamic practice.

Finally, the chapter concludes with a discussion of the role of the Bamidele movement and its related movement, Jama'atu Tabligh, and their prescribed forms of dress in situating Nigerian Muslims within a global Islamic community with expanded ties to the Middle East (and, for the latter group, with southeast Asia). Bamidele insisted that women in the movement wear *burqa*-like gowns, which he associated with the Arab world. He also encouraged his followers to perform the hajj. Pilgrims from Nigeria initially journeyed by foot to Mecca, accomplishing the pilgrimage over a period of months and even years (Yamba 1995); this overland pilgrimage on foot continued through the colonial period. However, by the mid-1950s, Ahmadu Bello, premier of the Northern Region from 1954 to 1966, helped to organize pilgrim welfare boards (see chapter 6). In July 1955, Ahmadu Bello performed the hajj for the first time (Niven 1982), accompanied by several ministers and emirs, including Yahaya Madawakin of Ilorin, who was serving as the regional health minister (Paden 1986: 283). Indeed, with his frequent visits to Ilorin, Bello sought to maintain connections with this southernmost emirate of the former Sokoto Caliphate, which remained part of the Northern Region until 1967 when Kwara State was formed.[6]

Islam and the Emergence of the Emirate of Ilorin

At the beginning of the nineteenth century, Ilorin was a small town headed by Afonja, who served as the Are Ona Kakanfo (commander in chief) of the Old Oyo army. Yet the town's position significantly changed after Afonja revolted against Oyo and called a Fulani Muslim, Malam al-Sālih, to assist him both politically and spiritually due to his "considerable influence with his co-religionists and a great reputation for piety" (Hogben and Kirk-Greene 1966: 286).[7] Thereafter, Ilorin's freedom from the authority of Old Oyo under the protection of Afonja attracted Yoruba, Hausa, and Fulani Muslims, some of whom had been

enslaved under Oyo (Danmole 1980: 12).[8] While Afonja was successful in making Ilorin "into a large city" (Johnson 1921: 200), the presence of al-Sālih with
his large Muslim following had consequences for the basis of political authority
there. Although Afonja himself was not a Muslim,[9] he sought to establish his
own kingdom through an alliance with al-Sālih and the many Muslims who had
come to Ilorin. According to Danmole, Afonja and al-Sālih maintained "a common front" and Afonja subsequently agreed to al-Sālih's request that he bring his
sons to settle in the city (1980: 45). However, following al-Sālih's death in 1823, his
son ʿAbd al-Salāh led the Muslim population, who preferred to have a Muslim
political leader, against Afonja, who was killed in 1824. Thereafter, Emir ʿAbd
al-Salāh sought to establish official recognition of the emirate of Ilorin, which
was achieved around 1829. As part of the Sokoto Caliphate under the emirate of
Gwandu, this change in political organization had social and economic as well as
political implications for Ilorin.[10]

Islam, Textiles, and Trade in Nineteenth-Century Ilorin

The diversity of Ilorin's population, which was composed of a range of ethnicities
with varied knowledge and skills, contributed to its success as "one of the great-
est entrepots of central Africa and the commercial emporium of all southern
Sudan" (Clarke 1972: 185). Ilorin's geographical position also facilitated this trade,
as it was located just south of the Niger River where the town of Raba served
as a crossing point to large towns in the caliphate, while trade routes, however
insecure, led to urban centers such as Lagos to the south (O'Hear 1983: 64). Villages with large farms surrounded the city, where cotton and indigo as well as
foodstuffs were grown. As chapter 2 discusses, Shehu ʿUthmān dan Fodio's son
Muhammad Bello, who became caliph in 1817, emphasized the importance of
supporting Islamic scholarship through economic achievements in agriculture,
craft production, and trade (Last 1966). In this regard, the labor policies of the
Sokoto Caliphate, particularly a system of slavery that provided cheap labor for
agricultural production as well as for the processing of raw materials for spinning and weaving (Lovejoy 1981: 201–207), also contributed to Ilorin's economic
growth as a trade entrepôt. William Clarke, who visited Ilorin in 1855, described
the vitality of the large markets held in the different quarters of Ilorin (map 3.2):
"I entered Ilorin at night at the north-west gate and on the night following rode
three miles into the city to the stranger's home [where he was to stay] and every
four hundred yards passed a market beautifully lighted with lamps. This is the
case over the whole city; the din and confusion of which are like the roaring of
many waters and may be heard for several miles. From six until eight o'clock at
night during the time most of the marketing is done the city is . . . alive with human beings" (1972: 186).[11]

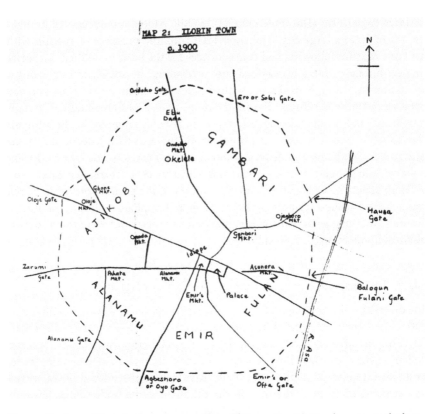

Map 3.2. Sections of Ilorin in the early 1900s (from O'Hear 1983: 367). Handweaving took place mainly within Agbaje and Okekere Quarters, which were also renowned for Islamic scholarship (O'Hear 1983: 127–128), and within the Yoruba-speaking wards of Ajikobi and Alanamu.

Ilorin played an important role in the production and trade of narrow-strip handwoven textiles, as observed by nineteenth-century travelers such as Robert Campbell and A. F. Mockler-Ferryman:

> An example of the extent to which cotton fabrics are manufactured [in Ilorin], we encountered one day in a ride of less than an hour more than one hundred and fifty weavers, busily employed at their looms. (Campbell 1861: 106)

> Just within the gates, I passed a weaver's house, where a number of men were seated at work by the side of the street; they ceased weaving as I went by, and clinked their shuttles together as in salutation, at the same time singing a kind of hymn of praise. (Mockler-Ferryman 1892: 207)

While a range of different types of named cloths were produced by Ilorin hand-weavers,[12] one particular type of narrow-strip cloth produced in Ilorin was in great demand by Muslim men during the nineteenth and early twentieth centuries. Called *etu* (Yoruba) or *saki* (Hausa), the name "guinea fowl" cloth refers to the alternating black and white warp and weft threads that give the cloth a slightly speckled appearance. *Saki* cloth, produced within the Sokoto Caliphate and widely distributed throughout West Africa (Kriger 2006: 85), was used to make the large *babban riga* worn by royalty, district heads, and scholars: "*Saki* was one of the most important and prominent types of cloth produced in the Sokoto Caliphate. . . . Over time, *saki* cloth became associated with caliphate officials and title-holders, lending a very special aura of power, position, and prestige" (85).

As Colleen Kriger (1988: 54) observes, the production of hand-embroidered robes from locally handwoven textiles was an urban occupation associated with courts of the emirs. Chapter 1 describes how the distribution of these large embroidered robes, *babban riga* (or *rigar giwa*), was part of a system of emirate gift giving (Heathcote 1972: 14; Last 1967), which was particularly important during Muslim holidays such as Eid-el-Fitr. These robes were in demand, in part, because of their connection with Islam. Thus, former slaves who were already Muslims or who later converted and became wealthy traders sought to wear these costly robes that associated them with their free status as Muslims (Reichmuth 1997: 241). Ilorin handweavers, tailors, and embroiderers played an important role in this process: "In the 1880s 'tobes' from Ilorin were said to be among the best [sold] in Zaria. In 1889, Ilorin cloth and gowns were much in demand in Kano, to which market they were being carried by Hausa traders who obtained them as a result of their ivory sales on the Niger. Ilorin traders also carried cloths to Kano and Bida, for example, for sale" (O'Hear 1983: 139).

This long-distance trade of finished embroidered robes between Kano, Zaria, and Bida during the nineteenth century also reflected the movement of expert weavers and embroiderers who could travel to Ilorin or Kano as the situation warranted.[13] Indeed, some Muslim men used their work as weavers, tailors, or embroiderers to finance their travels to study with renowned scholars throughout west and north Africa as well as their journey to Mecca and back (Yamba 1995; see also chapter 6).

Connections between Islam and Handweaving in Ilorin

Aside from the importance of wearing handwoven robes and of the migration of handweaver-teachers to study under revered Islamic scholars, there are other connections between handweaving and Islam within Ilorin as well. For example, in the early nineteenth century, many of the Yoruba weavers, some of whom may have also been Islamic teachers, moved to Ilorin, settling in two districts, Agbaje and Okekere, which "are noted as centres of Islamic scholarship" (O'Hear 1983: 123; see also Hermon-Hodge 1929: 274–275). More specifically, the compound of the celebrated weaver Alhaji Yahaya Kalu (fig. 3.2), who himself traveled to Mecca, is located near the compound of the Kamal-ud-Deen family, whose members are noted for Islamic learning (Danmole 1980: 221–225) and whose presence surely influenced the Islamic practices of his neighbors. As Reichmuth has observed, "The local weaving and textile industry, which still persists on a very large scale in the Yoruba quarters, has in many families remained closely connected with Islamic studies and Qur'ānic teaching" (1997: 235).

Modes of textile production and Islamic practice also intersected in more everyday ways. For example, the age of a child entering Qur'ānic school would have been around the same age as a child beginning a weaving apprenticeship, and "Qur'ānic and *'Ilm* [other Islamic texts] studies can be seen as part of an 'educational package' which the town had to offer and which contained religious instruction and professional training in different crafts" (Reichmuth 1997: 235). Clarke's description of "the warping by small boys who seem to be as expert in their department as those who throw the shuttle" suggests this sort of teacher-student relationship (1972: 273). Furthermore, the habitus of worship—the requisite five daily prayers—could be practiced by weavers without undue interruption to their work. Similarly, attendance at Friday mosque could be followed by trade in a range of commodities, which include selling textiles in the area surrounding the mosque.[14] These quotidian connections between handweaving and Islamic education are further exemplified by the *oniwala* pattern depicting a wooden board (known as *allo* in Hausa and *wala* in Yoruba). This rectangular board with a handle is used by children for memorizing portions of the Qur'ān, and its image has been incorporated into the supplementary weft designs of narrow-strip handwoven cloths for which Ilorin is renowned (fig. 3.3) (O'Hear 1983, 1988).

Islamic Scholarship in Nineteenth- and Twentieth-Century Ilorin

As part of the establishment of the new emirate, Emir 'Abd al-Salāh followed administrative practices set forth by the caliphate. Yet as Reichmuth notes, Ilorin was unique in that its governance effectively combined the aspects of prior Yoruba political rule with Fulani leadership, partly through the integration of Islamic scholars: "Fulani, Hausa, Nupe, Dendi and Kanuri, and even Arabo-Berbers are attested among the scholars who came to Ilorin before and after the foundation of the emirate. The Yoruba who formed the majority of the population were gradually absorbed into that group of Islamic scholars and imams" (1995: 36).

These different ethnic constituencies were reflected in Ilorin proper, which was divided into different quarters, with the head imams representing the religious-political hierarchy that was associated with the emirate; the Fulani imam headed the hierarchy, followed by the Yoruba imam and the imam for northerners (Hausa, Nupe and Kanuri) (Reichmuth 1995: 36). Yet while Fulani

Figure 3.2. Chief of weavers, Olorin Aso, Alhaji Yahaya Kalu, from Okekere District in Balogun Ajikobi Ward in Ilorin, was renowned for his early use of supplementary weft float patterning (O'Hear 1983, 1988). (Courtesy of Ann O'Hear)

Figure 3.3. Narrow-strip handwoven cloth with leno weave and rayon supplementary weft float *oniwala* patterning, which depicts the wooden board (*wala* in Yoruba; *allo* in Hausa) on which students write verses from the Qur'ān. Purchased in Ojé Market, Ibadan, January 2017, the fineness of the leno weave and the use of shiny lurex thread suggests that the cloth was woven in the early 1980s. (Photograph by the author.) An older example of this cloth, collected in 1901, is part of the Coker Adams Collection, in the Department of Africa, Oceania and the Americas, British Museum.

leadership was associated with the particular political hierarchy that prevailed within the emirate, the city's earlier history as well as the prevalence of the Yoruba population meant that it "belonged at least as much to Yorubaland as to the cluster of emirates established after 'Uthmān dan Fodio's jihad" (Danmole 1980: 68). The exchange of ideas and practices associated with the teachings of different Muslim scholars led to the flourishing of a "sacred community of scholars, saints, and emirs" described by Reichmuth (1995).

In the early caliphate period, the majority of Muslim scholars were Fulani, Hausa, and Nupe. However, by the end of the century, over 20 percent of Islamic scholars in Ilorin came from the Yoruba quarters, reflecting the increasing numbers of Yoruba students in the nineteenth century. Indeed, several Yoruba Muslim scholars began to attract large numbers of students not only from Ilorin but from other parts of Yorubaland as well. Malam 'Abd al-Qadir Afunso, for example, attracted students from Lagos (Reichmuth 1997: 238). Two religious teacher-scholars in Ilorin, Sheikh al-Labib Muhammad ibn Abd al-Qadir al-Iluri (known as Taj al-Adab) and Abu Ikororo, were renowned for their poetry and grammar and history texts as well as for their teaching methods (Danmole 1980: 221). With respect to teaching, two other Ilorin-trained scholars continued this concern with methods of Islamic education. Sheikh Kamalu 'd-deen and his followers started the Ansar ul-Islam Society, which established primary (and later secondary) schools in Ilorin that combined Islamic and Western education.[15] Another Ilorin scholar, Sheikh Adam al-Iluri, was renowned for his establishment of a system of Arabic *Markaz* schools, first in Abeokuta, then in Agege (near Lagos); since then nine Arabic and Islamic Training Centers (part of al-Iluri's *Markaz* network) have been created in Ilorin. These scholars and their students have had an enormous influence in Islamic education in southwestern Nigeria. Nonetheless, other Ilorin scholars have had varying views of Western education, which are reflected in their educational focus and in their forms of dress as Muslims.

Islamic Reform and Colonial Rule

Aside from more renowned Islamic scholars such as Abu Ikororo, Taj al-Adab, Kamalu 'd-deen, and Adam al-Iluri, less well-known scholars such as Sheikh Yusuf Agbaji also taught in Ilorin.[16] Agbaji had over one hundred students (Doi 1969: 104) who went on to teach elsewhere in Nigeria, as Sheikh Korede, an Islamic scholar from Ilorin and now living in Ikole-Ekiti, explains: "The Alhaji at Amunigun in Ibadan was taught by Alhaji Lagbaji [Agbaji] from Ilorin, Alhaji Lagbaji came from Saraki descent in Ilorin.[17] So every person in Ibadan, particularly in Amunigun and Agbeni learned under the elder Alhaji at Amunigun— and those who learned under him have begun to teach other people. The older Alhaji Bamidele was taught in Ilorin under Alhaji Lagbaji and it was this Lagbaji in Ilorin who also taught us. I received my own education at Ilorin and my teachers are from Ilorin" (Sheikh Korede, interview by the author, April 5, 2013, Ikole-Ekiti).

Despite his influence on many Yoruba Muslim scholars, not much has been written about Agbaji. It was Agbaji who taught Abdul Salami Bamidele, who studied hadith, *fiqh* (Islamic jurisprudence), and *tafsir*. According to A. R. Doi, Bamidele "travelled with his teacher to different parts of the country, including Ilorin, Lagos, Abeokuta and Ijebu-Ode. This afforded him the opportunity of meeting Muslim scholars from different parts of the world" (1969: 104). While Agbaji was associated with Ilorin, it was common for students to establish schools outside of the city where their teachers resided (Danmole 1980: 224). Bamidele subsequently established his own school in his house in Amunigun, Ibadan, in 1935.

Bamidele was referred to as *mujadded*—reformer—when he began his preaching. In Ibadan, he initially met with considerable resistance: "The rejection of people was very hostile. They used to bombard him with questions when he preached. On two occasions while preaching at Amunigun near his house, he was stoned by the angry crowd and his garments were torn" (Doi 1969: 105). Several aspects of Bamidele's doctrine would have been offensive to some Yoruba—Muslims or otherwise—in Ibadan. In his preaching there in the mid-1930s, Bamidele's exclusive focus on Islamic texts and his denunciation of certain Yoruba cultural practices such as masquerade performance and face marks or body tattooing would have been unpopular with other Muslims in Ibadan. In this sense, Bamidele was part of a group of Islamic scholars in the southwest, particularly Muslim scholars from Ilorin—such as Agbaji—who continued to be influenced by the writings of dan Fodio on the need to reform what were considered un-Islamic local practices.

The Bamidele Movement and the Importance of Appearing Muslim

As was the case for dan Fodio, one of the most distinctive features of the Bamidele movement was Bamidele's insistence that his followers wear turbans (*lawani*):[18] "What does it profit, if a man says he is Muslim but he does not look like one; he has no beard, he wears no turban, his dress is un-Islamic, his women go about shamelessly without purdah. Is his claim that he is Muslim justifiable? Is he a true Muslim? The answer is No" (quoted in Doi 1969: 110).

A photograph of Bamidele taken in the late 1960s (fig. 3.4) shows him wearing a hand-embroidered *babban riga* made with *saki* handwoven cloth strips and a large white turban. Similarly, in the school that he founded at Agbeni, Ibadan, his son Khalifa Bamidele teaches young students who all wear turbans (fig. 3.5). While Bamidele also prescribed "dress that covers them (*aso iwoleke*)" for women when they went out, the *jilbab*, an all-encompassing *burqa*-like garment, had not yet been seen in Ibadan (Badmos n.d.: 39). Instead, women wore *iborun* (stole) and *iboju* (face

Figure 3.4. In this family photograph, Sheikh Salami Bamidele wears a hand-embroidered *babban riga* made from handwoven *saki* cloth strips, possibly woven in Ilorin and embroidered by Nupe or Hausa men. He also wears the turban that characterized his movement. (Courtesy of Khalifa Bamidele)

veil), as did women of the Zumuratu Muminu (Zumratul Mumeenun), another small Islamic reform group that began in Ilorin in the 1940s (Danmole 1980: 234).[19]

However, on December 1, 1959, a member of the Bamidele group, Alfa Yusuf Okunola Ayegbami, was walking to Bamidele's house at Amunigun when "he saw one Arab woman [a Larubawa] who was begging. . . . The woman was wearing a jilbab" (Badmos, n.d.: 40) Ayegbami took the woman with him to see Bamidele, who on hearing what the woman said, gave her money to travel home. Bamidele "asked the woman the name of the dress that she was wearing and she said 'Jilbab'" (40). He believed that God sent the woman to him with this *jilbab*. He subsequently asked if someone could sew such a dress; Alhaji Musitafa Adedeji Oriare agreed to make such a garment. The following Saturday, Adedeij's wife appeared, together with the Arab woman, wearing a white *jilbab* made of guinea brocade cloth. "Now it was Taibatu Adedeji who was the first Nigerian *eleeha* to wear the *jilbab* in Africa" (40), although the color, white, was eventually replaced with black (fig. 3.6). When, as a pilgrim to Mecca and Medina, Bamidele later saw Middle Eastern women wearing the *jilbab*, it confirmed his belief that God wanted women to dress in this way (41). According to his son, Khalifa Ahmadu Bamidele, it was "*eleeha* dress—it is the House of God" (interview by the author, March 27, 2013, Ibadan).

Figure 3.5. Khalifa Bamidele and students at his school in Agbeni, Ibadan, March 27, 2013. (Photograph by the author)

Figure 3.6. *Eleeha* women at the Bamidele compound at Agbeni, Ibadan, March 27, 2013. (Photograph by the author)

In advocating that his followers wear turbans and *jilbab*, Bamidele made reference to precedents in Muslim dress set by others. For example, the use of turbans was introduced by nineteenth-century Fulani religious reformers who followed and preached the teachings of Shehu dan Fodio. In the case of the *jilbab*, Bamidele sought to link his group's connections with what he saw as proper Islam as it was practiced the Middle East. In both cases, he wanted to expand the scope of his movement and to attract followers to it. Yet there continued to be considerable resistance to his teaching. For example, many Muslims in Ibadan not only rejected his denial of all traditional Yoruba practice, they also wanted their children to receive both Western and Islamic education. Peter Clarke has suggested that the particular attraction of the Bamidele movement reflects the situation of those "who were left hanging between two worlds, in particular the semi-literate, whose standard of education tended to take them a step away from the old pattern of living but was not sufficient to enable them to succeed in the 'new order'" (1982: 228). Yet this assessment does not take into account the deep dissatisfaction with things Western, particularly education. As one person in Ibadan in 1929 expressed it in a letter to the *Yoruba News*: "Western education . . . has come to naught . . . it has been an increasing source of prolific affliction and poverty. Many formerly employed are now unemployed. A man who formerly ate from a table now eats from a leaf. . . . Our fathers were not Europeanised and could carry out their responsibilities" (Clarke 1982: 228).

Through his emphasis on Muslim identity, Islamic learning, and rejection of Western dress and education, Bamidele was making a virtue of a vulnerability. However, he was also maintaining connections with a reformist past, associated with the teachings of dan Fodio and, while he could not have realized it at the time, shaping Islamic reformist movements that would emerge in northern Nigeria in the twenty-first century.

The Legacy of the Bamidele Movement and Connections Elsewhere in Nigeria

Bamidele died in 1969 and was buried in an unadorned grave at his house in Agbeni; his extensive library is also preserved there. His firstborn son, Khalifa Ahmadu Bamidele, continues to hold classes in the school that his father founded (see fig. 3.5), while members of the sect in Ibadan continue their connections with those in other parts of southwestern Nigeria, including Ilorin and Ijebu-Ode. Like the other Yoruba reform groups that began during the colonial period, his followers maintain styles of dress that distinguish them from other Yoruba Muslims. Perhaps the continued wearing of the black *burqa*-like garment that they call the *jilbab* is one of the most distinctive aspect of their dress.

Yoruba Muslim women who wear such dress are referred to as *eleeha*, literally the owners of seclusion (*eha* means "seclusion" in Yoruba). By wearing the *burqa*-like *jilbab* with a mesh face covering, women can leave the confines of their family houses while simultaneously maintaining seclusion in public. This particular form of veiling, however, is not seen elsewhere in Nigeria and was particularly shocking to people in cities and towns in southwestern Nigeria such as Ibadan and Ikole-Ekiti when women first began wearing them. This reaction is suggested by Abdul Ganiyu Badmos's description of people's response to Taibatu Adedeji when she first wore a *jilbab* in 1959: "Many people were surprised, they had never seen such a dress anywhere and they were shouting, 'The dead have arisen!'" (n.d.: 41). They were making reference to the similarity in appearance to masquerade costumes worn at funerals and other traditional Yoruba ritual functions.

Four years later, in 1963, a similar response to a young woman wearing *eleeha* dress in Ibadan led to violence and arrests. A young unmarried girl named Nuratu, dressed in a *jilbab* and face veil, was walking to her father's house when she was accosted by a man who was a member of one of the Ibadan masquerade cults. He accused her of wearing their masquerade dress and as he tried to remove her *jilbab*, she grabbed his clothing as well. Alhaja Nuratu, who is now sixty years old, with many grandchildren (fig. 3.7), recalls the event:

> As I was coming from Aminugun where our father [Bamidele] was preaching, I ran into some masquerades. They challenged me and said, "What you are wearing, it is our masquerade!" They began to call me, saying, "Will you stop there, you masquerade?" I did not answer them. When we got to Sapata Street, at the corner, they just drew me back and challenged me: "Were you not the one we were calling and you decided not to respond to our calls?"
>
> Then they pulled off my *jilbab* and I resisted. From there we went to the Kabiyesi [king's palace] where the police came to arrest us. The masquerade people wanted to run away with my *jilbab*, but I refused to let them—so the police arrested all of us. It was settled that Muslims should find ways of identifying themselves and the masquerades should also differentiate themselves, instead of mistaking each for the other. The name of the traditionalist leader was Fajobi. I didn't know him nor had I seen him before. My *jilbab* that was torn remained in the police station ever since, it was never given back to me. I was very young then, I was still an *omoge*, an unmarried girl. (Nuratu Busari Ayodele, interview by the author, April 1, 2013, Ibadan)

In his biography of Bamidele, Badmos similarly describes this incident. He refers to it as a war, "*Awon Aborisa Gbe Ogun ti Jilbab* (The Orisa Worshippers Wage War Against the Jilbab)," and includes additional remarks about the actions of Bamidele. After Fajobi and his fellow traditionalists were arrested and jailed, they were taken to be sentenced in court:

> Before they took them to local court at Mokola, Alfa Bamidele went to see them. And he gave them a lecture, that they should stop their idol worship and become Muslims. They said that at the end [of the court hearing] that the

Figure 3.7. Veiled brides, the granddaughters of Nuratu Busari Ayodele, at their wedding in Ibadan on April 3, 2013. The young women seated behind them are wearing fashion *hijab*. (Photograph by the author)

government fined them £20; Bamidele helped them pay £10. After that, most of the idol worshippers converted to Islam. That Fajobi is now reading Qur'ān and now his name is Tijjani. Among those idol worshippers, they brought the masquerade cloth [*aso Eleeko*] to the mosque house and burnt it. And most people removed the mirrors [*jigi*] from the masquerade cloths before they burnt them. (Badmos, n.d.: 64)

This incident underscores the importance of religious dress in asserting a particular and new religious identity, in this case, the *jilbab* and veil, as well as rejecting an old one—exemplified here by the burning of the masquerade cloth by former *oriṣa* worshippers who had converted to Islam. Yet when Fajobi converted to Islam, he took the name Tijjani, indicating that he did not become a member of the Bamidele group but rather became an adherent of the Tijāniyya brotherhood, which by the 1950s had a small membership in Ibadan.[20] Thus, he indirectly continued to reject the wearing of the *jilbab* by his wives, who would have worn *iborun* and *gele* as did Yoruba Muslim women associated with other Islamic groups in Ibadan.

There were similar responses to *eleeha* dress elsewhere in southwestern Nigeria. For example, Sheikh Korede, who is now a member of Jama'at Tabligh, describes his experience, probably sometime in the 1990s, when he first moved to Ikole-Ekiti from Ilorin:

> My wives were the first *eleeha* since I came to Ikole-Ekiti. It was very strange for both old and young people here to see *eleeha* here. There was even a time I took a doctor to the palace for attacking my wife in the street. This man said my wife/*eleeha* should remove her *aso eleeha* dress that she was wearing. He accused her of being one of the thieves in Ikole, that she was using the *eleeha* dress to steal goats and other things in the town—so that she should go outside without wearing it [as if she were naked]. There came a time when my *eleehas* were afraid of going out of the house. Because whenever they went out, people would be watching them as if they were masquerades. (Sheikh Korede, interview by the author, January 2013, Ikole-Ekiti)

People were initially hostile toward this form of female Muslim dress in part because it challenged prevailing ideas about religious dress and in part because of the reformist Islamic doctrine associated with it. Yet by the early twenty-first century, in large Yoruba urban centers such as Ibadan and in smaller towns such as Ikole-Ekiti, women wearing *eleeha* dress, while not common, are not exceptional. "*Eleeha* is no longer new to everyone as it was when I got here. There are Muslims of Ikole origins who are now keeping their wives as *eleeha*," Sheikh Korede explained to me.

Other Yoruba Reformist Groups Associated with Ilorin

Eleeha dress distinguished Nuratu Ayodele and other Yoruba women followers of Bamidele from Yoruba women who belonged to other Islamic reformist groups in Ibadan, such as Ansar ud-Deen, which supported Western education and had ruled against the seclusion of women (Gbadamosi 1978a: 5). Yet the particular tailored details of dress distinguished the followers of other "conservative Islamist" reformer-teachers (Ryan 1978: 126), some of whom had studied with Agbaji in Ilorin. For example, when we were looking for the house where Nuratu was staying in the Eyelele area of Ibadan, Alhaji Ajeigbe, a Bamidele leader, asked directions from a woman dressed in a black *jilbab* with a *niqab*-style face veil, addressing her as "Eleeha." Later, I asked if she was a member of the Bamidele group and was told, "No, she's Tabligh." Thus, although both styles of black dress are referred to as *eleeha* dress, the small details of tailoring—the style worn by Bamidele women has tiny pleats at the top that form a sort of cap, much like Afghan *burqas*, whereas the Tabligh style consists of a *jilbab* worn with a *niqab*—distinguish these groups from one another.

Jama'atu Tabligh

Some members of the Tabligh group were trained by Islamic scholars in Ilorin and share some of the reformist ideas of Bamidele and his followers. While there are many similarities between the Bamidele movement and the Tabligh group, their origins differ. The Jama'atu Tabligh was founded in India by Muhammad Il-yas al-Kandhlawi in 1926. He focused less on conversion of unbelievers and more on the proselytization and teaching of those who were already Muslims, directing them to become better Muslims by concentrating on the Qur'ān and hadith. Ilyas himself taught in the context of political decline of the ruling Muslim aristocracy in northern India and the consolidation of British colonial rule throughout India. A central concern of Jama'atu Tabligh is the renewal of Muslim belief and practice by emulating the lifestyle of Muhammad. This aspect with its focus on the Qur'ān and hadith and stress on working with Muslims at the community (grassroots) level characterize the reformist Bamidele and Zumratul Mumeenun movements as well. Through *da'wah* (literally, invitation in Arabic), the proselytization prac-tice of inviting non-Muslims, as well as Muslims, to practice the faith, followers of Ilyas expanded membership in Tabligh, at first in India and subsequently globally.

The first Jama'atu Tabligh group that came to Nigeria was led by Mawlana Hassan Badawi, who traveled to Kano, Nigeria, in 1956. The group was taken to the chief imam of Kano, who did not attend to them. They subsequently returned to Pakistan to reassess the situation. They came back to Nigeria the same year but went instead to Lagos, where they settled at the Ali Balogun Mosque, having re-ceived strong support from the chief imam of Lagos, Alhaji Ligali Ibrahim (Olad-imeji 2012: 77). Tabligh proselytization in Nigeria continued with members sent from Pakistan and India through the 1950s. The first Nigerian Tabligh leader was Alhaji Sambo, who was born in Ilorin and began his leadership in the early 1970s, after which Tabligh groups were established outside Lagos in other southwestern Nigerian towns, including Ibadan.[21] By the early 1990s, the membership of the Movement in Lagos had expanded to extent that the leadership decided to move the national headquarters to Araromi Village, near Ilorin, on land that had been donated to the group. In 1995, the first annual religious celebration, known as the *Ijtima*, was held at Masjid Noor, which has continued to serve as the headquarters for Jama'atu Tabligh in Nigeria.

Despite organizational differences, leaders of these conservative reform groups stress the importance of the seclusion of women and of their being cov-ered when in public. Yet historical and theological distinctions are also evident in their dress—Tabligh wives of Sheikh Korede and another man we interviewed, Alfa Aminu, wear *eleeha* dress that completely covers them, although, as men-tioned, in a style distinct from that worn by women followers of the Bamidele group. Aminu—like Khalifa Bamidele in Ibadan—attributes the dress of *eleeha* to verses in the Qur'ān that were revealed to the Prophet:

> Tell the believing women to lower their eyes,
> guard their private parts, and not display their charms

except what is apparently outwardly,
and cover their bosoms with their veils
and not show their finery. . . . (Sura 24:31)

O Prophet, tell your wives and daughters, and the women of the faithful,
to draw their wraps a little over them,
They will thus be recognised and no harm will come to them,
God is forgiving and kind. (Sura 33:59)

Tabligh members also stress wearing dress that clearly identifies them as Muslim—particularly, for men, turbans and shortened pants—based on descriptions in the Qur'ān. As Alfa Aminu (2013) notes, "We are wearing short pants because it's one of the traditions of the Prophet, in one of his writings, it says that the follower is a good man. . . . [But] if the pant leg covers the ankle, he has no Sallah. The pant leg should not cover the ankle, it will block prayer. [For example], when you put on trousers and the pant leg goes down beyond the ankle, the remaining material will be in the hellfire. To avoid the fire, men should not allow trousers to come down over the ankle."

Another member of Jama'atu Tabligh also commented on the use of shortened pants (see also Janson 2005: 457):

We believe it is against the will of God to wear long trousers. It is a pride for anyone to wear such a long kaftan or trousers. God is against this. If you have much, try to share with others instead of wasting. This is one of the principles of this group. *We have so many poor people around us, why do you have to waste, you just have to share with others.* This is the reason why they are bearing that name, Tabligh, the moment this group found out that the name is not bad, they accepted being called that. (Sheikh Korede, interview by the author, April 5, 2013, Ikole-Ekiti; emphasis added)

This way of thinking reflects Tabligh members' sense that the Muslim community must support one another, implicitly suggesting that the present government no longer cares for its citizens.

Some Ilorin-based Islamic scholars, such as Mallam Musa, who was interviewed by Ryan in 1973, take this position. When asked about practices associated with Muslim adult conversion and about what a convert might give in appreciation, Ryan notes that "it is the ideal of Musa A. that the poorer convert, especially, should rather be the recipient of gifts from the mallam. Musa particularly singled out the gift of new clothing" (1978: 252).[22] Furthermore, that members of the Bamidele and Tabligh groups make reference to the Qur'ān in their decisions about dress and grooming is consistent with their reformist insistence that Islamic practice should be based solely on the Qur'ān and hadith, which reflect back on the "time of the Prophet." As in the teachings of dan Fodio, religious innovations (*bid'a*) such as praying at the tombs of saints and participating in certain forms of spirit possession are not acceptable. By wearing dress as described in the Qur'ān, they demonstrate their rejection of recent fashions and Western dress. Yet there is some leeway in how the Qur'ān may be interpreted. That women should "cover their bosoms" or "draw their wraps a little over them" presents the ideal of covered heads and bodies but not necessarily the covering of their faces. Similarly, Qur'ānic prescriptions about giving to the poor may be broadly interpreted (e.g., Sura 2:271), even as Bamidele and Tabligh men wear shortened trousers as a sign of their careful thrift, which enables their generosity to the poor. As discussed in Chapter 5, reformist Islamic groups in northern Nigeria have interpreted the practice of covering and shortening in somewhat different ways. Nonetheless, a common interest with appearing visually and distinctively Muslim may be seen in the religious, political, and trade connections between the area associated with the former emirate of Ilorin and the emirates of northern Nigeria—the Northern Region—during the colonial and early independence eras.

Early Twentieth-Century Islamic Dress and the Colonial Textile Trade

The robes and turbans, *jilbab, burqas*, and veils worn by members of the Bamidele movement came from a range of sources—Nigerian, European, Middle Eastern, and North African. Imports of European textiles (and also industrially spun thread, which became increasingly popular with Ilorin handweavers; see O'Hear 1987: 515) fluctuated during the 1930s and 1940s, affected by the Great Depression as well as trade blockades and embargoes associated with World War II. However, by the time Bamidele first saw the Arabic woman wearing a *jilbab*—who became the model for *eleeha* women followers—in December 1959, a range of imported textiles would have been available in Ibadan and Ilorin. When Adedeji volunteered to make a copy of the woman's *jilbab*, he purchased a type of white cloth referred to as *aso Ateginni*, or guinea cloth (cotton damask, known locally as guinea brocade or *shadda* in northern Nigeria). Such lighter weight materials would be more appropriate than handwoven strip cloth, which would not provide the requisite drape. While black was later adopted as the preferred color for *jilbab* used by Bamidele *eleeha*, deeply dyed black cotton damask was not as easily available. A photograph of Bamidele's wives taken sometime in the early 1960s (Doi 1969: 110) show them wearing a range of differently colored *jilbab*—from white to black. For some, the *iboju* appears to be made with the same material as the *jilbab* itself. For others, the face veil is made with a contrasting cloth. This range of options was made possible through the increased importation of manufactured cloth distributed by European mercantile firms.

Alternately, Bamidele continued to wear *babban riga*, which were made of handwoven cloth strips possibly woven, tailored, and embroidered in Ilorin. In a photograph taken during Id-el-Fitr prayers in 1968, he wears a robe made with handwoven material and embroidered with a large checkered pattern known as *malum malum*; he also wears a full white turban. However, in a photograph taken in his library, probably around the same time, he wears a light-colored robe with hand embroidery at the neck on material that appears to be damask. He is also wearing a patterned turban and a patterned shoulder cloth, both possibly made of silk. He may have received these garments as gifts or purchased them during his trip to Mecca. In either case, they exemplify the expansion of Islamic dress options made available through increasing textile trade and, after 1955, through Nigerians' ability to travel to Mecca by air. Indeed for Bamidele, his pilgrimage to Mecca in 1961 and his subsequent stay in Egypt may have reinforced his thinking about the importance of appearing Muslim.

Continuing Connections between the Ilorin Emirate and Descendants of the Sokoto Caliphate

In April 2013, we conducted an interview at a generator shop in Ikole-Ekiti, where Sheikh Korede was visiting some men. After the interview, I gave the sheikh some naira for his time, which he handed to the two men—alfas (Islamic scholars)—who were sitting with us, one of whom was the owner of the house. When I later asked about this, I was told that the sheikh gave it to them for fuel so they could attend a religious meeting over three hours away in Ilorin.

Travel by car to attend a religious meeting in Ilorin is just one of many road trips taken by Muslim scholars and political leaders that maintain connections between those living in southwestern and northern Nigeria. When in 1935, the emir of Ilorin, Abdul Kadiri (fig. 3.8), traveled north to Sokoto and Birnin Kebbi in his private car to visit the sultan of Sokoto and emir of Gwandu, he did so to reinforce his emirate connections with his Fulani antecedents and caliphate past (Hogben and Kirk-Greene 1966: 304). Later, in the 1950s and 1960s, the Sardauna of Sokoto and premier of the Northern Region, Ahmadu Bello, frequently traveled south on official business as well as privately to maintain connections with Ilorin as part of the Northern Region. He believed that emphasizing the common religious and cultural practices of the region was critical for the political unity of the north. After the death of Kadiri in June 1959, Bello attended the funeral for the old emir and the installation of the new emir, Sukarnaini Gambari, later that year (fig. 3.9). He subsequently returned to Ilorin to visit the emir in 1964 to provide political support (Paden 1986: 445) and to participate in the commemorative display held at the emir of Ilorin's palace in May of that year.

In addition to these geographical connections, the continuing engagement of Islamic scholars in Ilorin—both of Hausa-Fulani and Yoruba backgrounds—with the work of their religious predecessors suggests the "importance of maintaining

Figure 3.8. Emir of Ilorin Abdul Kadiri dan Shuaybu Bawa, in the 1930s, wearing a turban with multiple layers of robes. (Photograph by E. H. Duckworth, courtesy of the Duckworth Collection, Melville J. Herskovits Library of African Studies, Northwestern University)

Figure 3.9. On February 25, 1960, Ahmadu Bello (*standing*) spoke before the emir of Ilorin, Malam Sukarnaini Gambari, and his court. (Photograph by Mr. Alabi, courtesy of the Kaduna State Ministry of Information, Kaduna)

connections with the Sokoto Caliphate past and with the writings of Shehu dan Fodio," connections reflected in their teachings throughout southwestern Nigeria (Danmole 1980: 248). Indeed, with the expansion of new Arabic schools in Ilorin with students from Kwara and other southwestern Nigerian states, "Ilorin seems to have regained at least part of its former role as an Islamic centre for Yorubaland. From this it has also renewed its position as an intermediary between north and south within the cultural and political framework of modern Nigeria" (Reichmuth 1997: 245).

Conclusion

From the early nineteenth century, when the Islamic scholar from Sokoto Malam al-Salih settled in Ilorin, connections with the religious and political philosophy of dan Fodio continued to be seen during the colonial and independence periods. As Danmole has observed, "The consolidation of Islam during the second half of the nineteenth century and in the course of the present century has largely been the work of the mallam class. Partly through the encouragement given by the Emirs to Muslim scholars from Hausa and Yorubaland to settle in Ilorin, Islamic learning . . . was greatly stimulated" (1980: 249). Thus, many Islamic scholars trained in Ilorin who went on to establish schools elsewhere in the southwest—in Ibadan, Ijebu-Ode, and Lagos—were influenced by the writings of dan Fodio as well as by the works of other Islamic scholars. Their teachings thus reflected a range of interpretations of Islamic texts and methods. Some, such as Adam al-Iluri, stressed the importance of reading texts exclusively in the original Arabic. Others, such as Kamalu 'd-deen, established a school in Ilorin that incorporated study of the Qur'ān, Arabic, and Islamic law and theology using Western pedagogical methods (Danmole 1980: 224). Sheikh Bamidele and Sheikh Korede, among others, stressed the importance of Islamic dress and textiles as well as Islamic knowledge and texts. Indeed, the particular forms of Islamic dress advocated by these two scholars and worn by their disciples distinguished their educational styles and theological orientations. These garments also marked the continuing concern with Muslim distinctiveness and the importance of textiles in marking this difference among various Islamic reformist groups.

While Ilorin's particular role as a commercial entrepôt for all of West Africa and its extensive trade connections with northern Nigeria diminished during the colonial period, it remains a center of Islamic scholarship and handwoven cloth production. Even with the expanding diversity of textiles made possible through increasing mercantile house presence and overseas trade during the colonial period, certain styles of dress associated with particular forms of Islamic learning and political economic history—such as the handwoven *saki* cotton robe worn by

Bamidele—continued to be promoted by some. The opportunities for using new, simpler materials in slightly different ways enabled groups such as the Jama'atu Tabligh to set themselves apart from other Yoruba Muslim reformist groups, making reference to the simplicity of dress that they associated with "the time of the Prophet."

Bamidele had earlier expressed this association of proper Muslim comportment with the *jilbab* worn by the Arabic woman he had met in Ibadan in 1959. However, the ability of increasing numbers of Muslims from southwestern and northern Nigeria to fly to Mecca contributed to a sense of being part of a global Islamic community and provided the opportunity to acquire a range of new styles of garments associated with Islamic textiles, even as Ilorin handweavers continued their production of narrow-strip handwoven cloth (see fig. 3.3). While pilgrims from different countries were visually distinguished by dress, certain sartorial similarities—women's veils, men's turbans and caps—underscored and expanded a visibly Muslim commonality. The connections between textile production and Islamic scholarship, between dress and Islamic reform, exemplified in the distinctive turbans and veils worn by Muslim men and women in northern Nigeria, are examined in chapters 4 and 5.

Notes

1. This discussion of the interconnections between the histories of Islam, craft production and trade, and Islamic education in Ilorin is based on the excellent work of Hakeem Olumide Danmole (1980, 1984), Ann O'Hear (1983, 1987, 1988), and Stefan Reichmuth (1993, 1995, 1997).

2. Danmole notes that Islamic scholar "Malam al-Salih's encouragement to Muslim slaves in Yorubaland to desert their masters may have been prompted by the fear that Muslim slaves held by non-Muslim masters were unlikely to be treated according to Muslim law" (1980: 44).

3. Frederick Pedler (1974: 134–135) describes the Royal Niger Company's takeover of Ilorin in 1897.

4. Muhammad Umar cites a similar response to British colonial rule: "Qadi Abd Allah b. Ali added a familiar Islamic moral discourse on the treacherous attraction of *dunya* [the world]; he agreed with signing [a] truce with [the] British but saw it as a means of biding their time to regain Muslim ascendency. . . . [Yet he warned that] weak-hearted people will become accustomed to their [Europeans'] corrupt manners, children will grow up in their religion, and women and youth will be tempted to dress in their garments and adornments" (Umar 2006: 70–71).

5. In this regard, Bamidele preceded more recent Islamic reformers in northeastern Nigeria such as Boko Haram, which literally means "Western education is forbidden." As chapter 8 discusses, men belonging to this group also wear turbans.

6. See Paden 1986 for Bello's denunciation of "the agitation for a merger between Ilorin and the [southwest], [which] as I have repeatedly stressed, largely owes its origin to places outside the Region" (328).

7. Malam al-Sālih is also referred to as Malam Alimi. *Alimi* means "the scholar" or "the believer" (Reichmuth 1997: 232; see also Hogben and Kirk-Greene 1966: 286; Johnson 1921: 193).

8. According to Danmole: "By the late eighteenth and early nineteenth centuries communities of Muslims were well established in Oyo Ile and a number of provincial towns within the Alafinate. Trade was an important, but not exclusive, activity of such communities" (1980: 14). This trade included horses, slaves, and textiles.

9. He was, nonetheless, a great patron of Islamic scholars who specialized in making protective amulets (Danmole 1980: 34).

10. For a more detailed discussion of the historical reconstruction of the founding of the Ilorin Emirate, see Danmole 1980: 31–58. While the precise date of its recognition is unclear, Danmole (1980: 56) notes that it was well established by the time of Emir ʻAbd al-Salāh's death in 1836.

11. William Henry Clarke was born in Georgia and became actively involved in missionary work in Africa. In 1853, the Foreign Mission Board of the Southern Baptist Convention sent him as a missionary to southwestern Nigeria. Clarke's manuscript, which covered the four-year period from 1854 to 1858, was subsequently edited by J. A. Atanda and published by Ibadan University Press in 1972.

12. Red *alaari* cloth (see fig. 3.3) as well as white cloths and a range of blue-black and white warp-striped cloth were among the cloths woven (O'Hear 1983: 123).

13. See O'Hear's (1983) discussion of the role of textile-trading middlemen and handweavers in Ilorin.

14. This connection is given special emphasis in Kura, in Kano State: "On Fridays, there is a special market which meets just outside the mosque (some distance away from the regular market), and after midday prayers only white strips of the fine Kura cloth are sold in this market" (Shea 1975: 143).

15. Ahmadu Bello admired the Ansar ul-Islam association and its educational system (see Reichmuth 1993: 186; 1996).

16. Photographs of three important Muslim scholars from Ilorin (Abu Ikororo, Taj al-Adab, and Agbaji) were included under the heading "Awon Olutonisona Nipa Eto Lori Obinrin" (Those Leaders Who Guide Us on the Program/Behavior [*eto*] for Women) in a market booklet by Buniyamin Banire (2006: 8–9). Bamidele, who was born in Ekiti but trained in Ilorin and later taught in Ibadan, was also pictured.

17. *Saraki* is a Yoruba pronunciation of the Hausa word *sarki* (chief), suggesting that Agbaji was of Fulani descent.

18. Indeed, one of the local names for Jama'atu Tabligh, whose members also wear turbans, is the Lawani Group (Korede, interview by the author, April 5, 2013, Ikole-Ekiti). *Lawani* is the Yoruba word for "turban"; it is *rawani* in Hausa.

19. Danmole suggests that these groups may have had a common origin in Ilorin. Although some claim that the Zumratul Mumeenun was "an off-shoot of the Bamidele Movement in Ibadan, Ilorin sources deny this and say that the founder was a former pupil of Taj al-Adab" (1980: 234).

20. Anthropologist Abner Cohen noted the popularity of Tijāniyya in Sabo, the Hausa community in Ibadan: "The massive affiliation of the majority to the Tijāniyya order occurred after an important shaikh of that order had visited Sabo [Sheikh Ibrahim Niass publicly visited Kano in 1951 and again in 1952 (Gray 1998: 70)] and appointed local ritual

masters who initiated the men into the Order" (Cohen 1969: 11). Since many of the male residents of Sabo were traders with continuing connections to northern Nigeria, including Kano (where Muhammadu Sanusi I, who became the emir of Kano in December 1953, showed his strong support for Niass), it is likely that the acceptance of the teaching of Niass and the Tijāniyya brotherhood were influenced by the sheikh's tour and by Emir Sanusi's support (Gray 1998: 71). However, Yoruba Muslims who joined the Tijāniyya brotherhood around the same time were also possibly influenced by Muslim Yoruba traders from Ilorin (Danmole 1980: 232) or from Lokoja (Mohammed 1993: 120).

21. Conflict within the Ibadan group developed in the 1980s, based on differences between those with more advanced Islamic education and those with leadership positions. This dispute was settled in the late 1990s (Oladimeji 2005: 82).

22. Musa explains, "This is because it may possibly have happened that [the convert's] clothing has become dirty or it may be that he has used it for kneeling down before the orişa" (quoted in Ryan 1978: 252).

4   The Sardauna's Turbans

People with titles can wear any kind of turban—black, white, with flower patterns. But when you are about to be turbaned, the Emir will tie the white one. . . . After that the person can change the turban to any kind he likes. Wearing the white turban is a matter of choice, but people like white. . . . It's costly and has value. Even the horse the titled people are riding is different from the horses of their followers. . . . The black horse that has two white marks on its forehead and legs is *akawali biyu* but the one with one mark is *akawali daya*.

—Samaila Magaji, interview by the author, July 2012, Zaria

THE CONTINUING IMPORTANCE of turbans for Muslim identity is suggested by the dress of the followers of the Bamidele movement in Ibadan as well as in everyday ways, which may be seen in the painted illustration of the Arabic word for turban—ʿimāma—depicted on the wall of the School for Practicing Islamic Teachings in the Tudun Wada area of Kaduna (fig. 4.1). Indeed, the turban may be referred to in Hausa as the *rawani Sunnah* (the turban of Muslims) and is associated with the origins of Islam itself, as the description of Muhammad as "the wearer of the turban" suggests. Yet wearing turbans in particular styles—in terms of tying and materials—also reflects their use within the emirate system to distinguish individuals and groups by political and social rank as well as by geographical origin.

Ahmadu Bello, the Sardauna of Sokoto and premier of the Northern Region of Nigeria, was the grandson of Sultan Abubakar Atiku of Sokoto (Paden 1986: 73), hence he wore a turban tied in the style of Sokoto, with a single *kunne* raised from the back of the turban (fig. 4.2). Indeed, Ahmadu Bello was known not only for his Hausa embroidered robes but especially for his turbans—which ranged from pure white *harsa* turbans to blue-black ɗan Kura turbans to turbans with woven (*muwardi*) and printed (*atamfa*) patterns (fig. 4.3). The many photographs taken during tours of northern Nigeria, overseas travels, and attendance at government events document his predilection for wearing many different types of turbans (fig. 4.4). Yet why he wore these many different types of turbans is unclear—he did not write about them, at least in any extant documents. Others give several explanations for his behavior, which reflect their own perspectives as much as they explain the sardauna's actions.

Figure 4.1. The Arabic words عمامة ('imāma for turban) and النقاب (niqab for veil) on the front wall of the Makarantar Aiwatar da Koyarwar Musulunci (School for Practicing Islamic Teachings), Tudun Wada, Kaduna, March 1, 2011. (Photograph by the author)

Furthermore, these explanations are influenced by present-day concerns and changes in turban wearing more generally in northern Nigeria. For some, the association of turbans with emirs and their royal families (*sarauta*) has superceded the association of turbans with Islam. For them, the *hizami*—the "little turban" (fig. 4.5)—a head covering that consists of a cloth sash wound around a cap, mainly worn by religious leaders and scholars (*malamai*), is more representative of Islamic religious values (see chapter 7). For others, turbans are no longer fashionable, and, like the large embroidered robes (*babban riga*) that are being replaced with simply embroidered kaftans (*kaftani mai rumi*), turbans (*rawani*) are being replaced with caps (*hula*; see fig. 4.1) and, for some, with no head covering at all.

In this chapter, I consider the importance of wearing wearing of turbans (*rawani*), as well as embroidered robes (*babban riga*), and what they meant for Ahmadu Bello and political leaders in northern Nigeria during the colonial and early independence eras. Because of their significance in marking Islamic identity in relation to prevailing political regimes, turbans—exemplified by the distinctive styles of tying—underscore the importance of dress in reformist configurations of time and moral space. They thus provide useful insights into the historical processes involved in negotiating what sort of government should be in place and who has legitimate power and authority to rule.

Figure 4.2. On September 7, 1955, at Rawtenstall, United Kingdom, Premier Ahmadu Bello watches as J. C. Whittaker, director of David Whitehead and Sons, signs an agreement to establish the first modern textile mill in Kaduna. Ahmadu Bello appears to be wearing a machine-embroidered *babban riga* and a patterned turban tied Sokoto-style for the occasion. (Courtesy of David Whitehead and Sons Ltd. Archives, Parbold, Lancashire, UK)

Figure 4.3. Ahmadu Bello wearing a printed (*atamfa*) patterned turban in his office in Kaduna. (Arewa House Photograph Collection, courtesy of Arewa House, Kaduna, Nigeria)

Figure 4.4. Ahmadu Bello wearing a white turban with red dots, known as d́an India, while visiting on a tour of Iran. (Courtesy of the Kaduna State Ministry of Information, Kaduna)

Figure 4.5. Man wearing *hizami*-style "little turban" with blue pants and jacket with *mai rumi* embroidery under his robe (see chapter 6), Zaria City, June 11, 2011. (Photograph by the author)

Turbans during the Colonial Period

With the onset of colonial rule following the British defeat of caliphate forces in 1903, the wearing of turbans continued and possibly even increased, both because of the expanded availability of materials for use as turbans and because the system of governance, referred to as indirect rule, supported political administration through the emirate system (Last 1970). The turbaning of emirs, district heads, and other Nigerian political leaders in formal ceremonies reinforced local hierarchies of authority as well as distinguished (and exoticized) them as subjects of British colonial rule, which had its own system of hierarchical official dress (Cohn 1989). Even an outsider such as Martin Kisch, who served as an assistant resident in colonial northern Nigeria, observed the social distinctions indicated by the type of turban worn. For example, he describes men of political importance as those who "ride horses, and wear enormous turbans and beautifully embroidered trousers and *rigas*. They carry their money in the end of the turban that hangs down. They nearly all put part of the cloth [*amawali*] over their mouth" (1910: 100). In one sketch, he conflates the size of one man's social standing with the size of his turban: "The turban is blue, and being small, shows that the man is not a great 'blood.' Note the top of the native cap under the turban cloth" (141). Yet this turban appears to be made from shiny blue-black indigo-dyed *turkudi* cloth, which was associated with Muslim men's identity and allegiance to the Sokoto Caliphate (Shea 1975: 57). At the time of Kisch's writing, these shiny blue-black turbans, referred to as *bakin rawuna* or *ɗan Kura*, may have been made with machine-woven cotton broadcloth dyed with indigo and made shiny with indigo paste, rather than with narrow handwoven *turkudi* cloth strips, as in the nineteenth century. While less costly, *bakin rawuna* produced in the 1930s in the Kano area nonetheless were made with false seams in order to duplicate the seams formed by sewing the narrow *turkudi* cloth strips together (Kriger 1993: 365). For it was the appearance of narrow cloth strips, along with their metallic blue-black sheen, that constituted the value of these particular turbans.[1]

Photographs from the early 1930s taken by a colonial official, E. H. Duckworth, provide numerous examples of the types of turbans worn at that time as well as the place of their wearers within the prevailing political hierarchy. For example, the large white turban with a face veil (*amawali*) worn by the emir of Kano Alhaji Abdullahi Bayero, contrasts with the small white turban, tied simply and without face veil, worn by the Islamic scholar Sheikh Bashir (fig. 4.6) (*Nigeria Magazine* 1944: 30).[2] In another photograph, the retainer of the emir of Gwandu wears a large shiny blue-black turban, while the emir himself wears a large white turban with *kunne biyu* (two ears) along with an *amawali* face veil (fig. 4.7). Duckworth's photographs show a range of different types of turban styles although with the exception of a few *bakin rawuna* and one white turban with fine-colored stripes, all are white. Yet with the end of World War II and

Figure 4.6. Emir of Kano Alhaji Abdullahi Bayero (*left*), wearing a turban in Kano style, with the *kunne* toward the middle and back as well as an *amawali* mouth veil and *alkyabba* robe. The Islamic scholar with whom he is studying is "the Chief Professor at the Law School, Kano. Sheikh Bashir [*right*], wearing a turban in a different style, came from Gordon College, Khartoum" (*Nigeria Magazine* 1944: 35). (Courtesy of the Duckworth Collection, Melville J. Herskovits Library of African Studies, Northwestern University)

expansion of travel and trade, sources for and types of materials that could be used for turbans increased. This growth in global connections is reflected in the range of colored and patterned turbans worn by the Sardauna of Sokoto, Ahmadu Bello.

The Sardauna's Many Turbans

Alhaji Aliyu, Sarkin Mai Mota (the head of Ahmadu Bello's drivers), recalls his employer's different turban styles: "He used to wear a turban at his place of work, but it was different from the ones worn when there was any occasion. And he always wore green—his cloth completely, he used to wear green. The *rawani* he wore in the workplace was simple but during occasions, he used to wear *rawani* ɗan Sardauna, the big colored one" (interview by the author, July 10, 2012, Kaduna). The increased imports from Europe and India via British mercantile

Figure 4.7. Emir of Gwandu wearing a white turban with *amawali* mouth veil and striped silk *alkyabba* robe. His retainer, sitting behind him, wears a shiny blue-black indigo-dyed ɗan Kura turban. (Courtesy of the Duckworth Collection, Melville J. Herskovits Library of African Studies, Northwestern University)

trade houses, along with the continued production of locally handwoven and indigo-dyed textiles and textiles brought via the trans-Saharan trade routes to Kano (and subsequently Zaria and later Kaduna), provided Muslim men with a wide range of turban materials from which to choose. These materials included the fine, stiff, white netting manufactured in the United Kingdom known as *harsa* that was worn by Hausa emirs, as well as titled court officials, and was used in turbaning installation ceremonies. Men could also purchase locally made shiny ɗan Kura cloths dyed and pounded with indigo paste and several different types of patterned turban cloths called *muwardi*, which came from Mecca and India, the latter sometimes referred to as ɗan India turbans. Even before the twentieth century, pilgrims who had performed the hajj via an arduous overland journey brought back turbans and robes that marked their stay in Mecca; Emir Bayero himself had traveled by land to Mecca in 1936. With the advent of air travel by the mid-1950s and increasing numbers of pilgrims performing the hajj (Tangban 1991), additional types of turbans associated with Saudi Arabia, such as the Palestinian *keffiyeh* and Saudi *'aqal* (or *makawiya* and *kambu*, as they are called in Hausa), made their way into Muslim men's dress fashions in northern Nigeria (see fig. 6.11). Bello wore each of these types of turbans—and as his driver has observed, he preferred green, the color associated with the Prophet Muhammad—during ceremonial visits to events in northern Nigeria, when traveling abroad on trade missions, while attending commonwealth events, and when traveling to Mecca on the hajj.

For example, at the signing of the agreement to establish Kaduna's first modern textile mill on September 7, 1955, between the Northern Regional Development Corporation (NRDC), the Northern Regional Marketing Board, and the British textile manufacturing firm David Whitehead and Sons Ltd., Ahmadu Bello wore a *muwardi* turban with a woven pattern (see fig. 4.2). During the March 7, 1956, ceremony commemorating the building of that mill, Kaduna Textiles Limited (KTL), he wore a white *harsa* turban with a hand-embroidered *babban riga* (Maiwada and Renne 2013). He also wore shiny blue-black ɗan Kura turbans when attending state functions, such as a visit to greet the chief of Boro during a trip to Marwa, Cameroon, in December 1965 (fig. 4.8). During one trip to Iran, he wore a fine, white muslin turban with large, inlaid supplementary weft dots, known as ɗan India (see fig. 4.4); during a trip to Medina—probably one of his frequent trips to Saudi Arabia for the big and little hajj, he wore a patterned *muwardi* turban. His careful selection of turbans for particular colors and styles of robes suggested to some that he liked to dress well in traditional Hausa fashion and appreciated not only white garments but colored garments as well. Thus, in preparation for a trip to Niger in December 1960, government officials advised Ahmadu Bello about local dress practices: "*Dresses.* The Prime Minister, the Hon. Diori Hammani, his wife and some of his Ministers wear usually Western

Figure 4.8. Ahmadu Bello wearing a shiny blue-black *baƙin rawani* (ɗan Kura) turban and *alkyabba* cape to greet the chief of Boro during a trip to Marwa, Cameroon, December 21, 1965. (Photograph by Mr. Gombe, courtesy of the Kaduna State Ministry of Information, Kaduna)

dress while their traditional Chiefs especially Ministers without portfolio dress irreproachably in magnificent embroidered gowns, and beautiful oriental clothes 'Sardaunically'" (Ministry of Internal Affairs 1960).

"Sardaunically," of course, makes reference to the sardauna's preference for well-made and attractive Hausa Islamic dress. Ahmadu Bello's knowledge about different types of turbans and robes was evident from the attention he gave to the gifts to be given during his visit to Guinea, Morocco, and Libya in October 1963: he wrote in his characteristic green ink the names of two types of hand-embroidered robes (*aska biyu* [literally, two knives] and *malum malum*) to be given as well as a particular type of turban, *rawani* Mecca. Bello became so renowned for his attractive turbans that a particular type of turban made in India with woven designs became known as *rawani* ɗan Sardauna. Indeed, one man explained the sardauna's appeal in terms of his turbans:

> My father said that he loved the sardauna—above all the northern Nigerian leaders, the sardauna was the best.
> "Why do you say this?" I asked.
> "Because he wore beautiful turbans," he replied. My father later asked me to get him a turban like the sardauna wore, known as *rawani* ɗan Sardauna, and I did. (Mohammad Tahir, interview by the author, November 14, 2012, Samaru)

This exchange provides insight into why Bello took great care in selecting his turbans. His appearance not only attracted supporters from his Muslim Hausa-Fulani base but also attracted those practicing traditional religion, who were encouraged to convert during the sardauna's conversion tours in Katsina, Sokoto, and Zaria Provinces in 1964–1965 in part because of his dress (Abba 1981; *Nigerian Citizen* 1964, 1965a, 1965b, 1965c; Paden 1986: 569–575). "He wanted to 'put cloths on them [pagans],'" observed the Magajin Garin of Sokoto (Paden 1986: 269). According to one report, "at every place where he preached presents of clothings were distributed to the converts," and on a conversion tour in the early 1960s in Niger Province, he distributed books and clothing at the mosque in Kuta (Paden 1986: 575). Alhaji Aliyu, Sarkin Mai Mota, recollected the distribution of cloth on these tours somewhat differently: "Of course, Sardauna used to distribute robes to people but not on his tours. For example, on Saturdays and Sundays, he would give us robes, about one hundred to two hundred to give to people. He alone would go to Kano and would go to another place to distribute them. Whoever we saw, anybody, he could be a mad person or an *almajiri* [itinerant Islamic student]. Anyone, we would give them dresses. They would hold the madmen down and put the robes on them, even if some would tear them off later" (interview by the author, July 10, 2012, Kaduna). It is possible, however, that on some tours he distributed printed cloths as well as plain dyed cloths, which could be used as wrappers by women, along with simple robes, since tailored clothing was constitutive of Muslim men's identity (Kriger 1988). But Bello did not distribute turbans, which, while associated with Islam, were also associated with specific political positions and emirate affiliations.

The Distribution of Robes and Cloth as Sallah Gifts

In northern Nigeria, the Hausa term *Sallah* refers to the Muslim holidays of Eid-el-Fitr, which marks the end of the month-long Ramadan fast and the beginning of Sallah, and Eid-el-Kabir (also known as Eid al-Adha elsewhere in the Muslim world), which celebrates Abraham's willingness to sacrifice his son

(Newman 2007). Men spend months preparing new outfits for themselves that consist of elaborately embroidered robes and capes with turbans for participation in Sallah durbars (known as Hawan Daushe in Hausa; literally, horse riding after a religious festival). The emir and members of royal emirate families participate in these processions and displays of horsemanship. Families residing in towns such as Zaria, Katsina, and Kano dress in their new Sallah outfits, which include new veils, blouses, and wrappers for women and new dresses for young girls. Men and boys often wear new kaftans or robes, although not with turbans. Rather, they wear fancy new machine- or hand-embroidered caps, as Malam Alhassan Abdullahi, a trader at Kaduna Central Market in 2011 explained: "[The names of] some of the types of caps . . . sold [for Sallah] were Minister, Mai Geza, Kube or Zanna, Morofia, Dubai, Nek, Damanga, Pakistan, Dara [good], Mu Hadu A Banki, PTF [Petroleum Trust Fund], Mai Mangoro [Owner of mango], Mai AC [owner of air-conditioner], and Okadigbo among others. . . . Each of the caps . . . was of different grade, price, and design. For instance, . . . Minister was of four types with prices which ranged between N10,000, N3,000, N1,500 and N500" (Alabi 2011; see also Last 2014: 45).

Men, as well as boys and girls, line the streets of these towns to view the emir and riders, who likewise are wearing turbans of various types and prices, dressed in elaborate robes, with their horses sometimes adorned in matching trappings (fig. 4.9) (Renne 2013c). As discussed in chapter 1, the emir is expected to distribute robes to palace officials, emirate chiefs, and other community members as part of this celebration. During the nineteenth century, "presents" to the emir, such as handwoven, hand-embroidered robes, "were the form that much of the revenue which Sokoto received from the emirates took" (Last 1967: 105). Yet many of these gifts *cum* taxes were redistributed to scholars and the poor, particularly during the Sallah celebrations (103). Thus, not only were expensive, elaborately embroidered robes made with costly materials used by the political elite to distinguish themselves and enhance their prestige in precolonial Nigeria, these robes were also used to reward individuals for specific deeds and to solidify patron-client ties through gifts of quantities of robes to political followers.[3]

Another aspect of these robe distributions was the fact that the value of the robes varied, depending not only on the materials and density of the woven cloth used but also on "the method and quality of tailoring, the presence of lining, the materials used in the lining and its quality, the materials used in the embroidery, and the density and detail of the embroidery" (Kriger 1988: 56), as was the case with named embroidered caps described by the cap seller Abdullahi. While political allegiance was reinforced through robe giving, political ranking of individuals within the emirate was also represented. These sorts of discriminating choices made in the past are probably similar to those made by one district head, Malam

Figure 4.9. Malam Samaila Magaji, Sarkin Kwal-Kwali Zazzau (chief of decoration of Zaria Emirate), wearing *malafa* (*malfa*) hat over a *rawani* organdy turban during Hawan Daushe, Zaria City. (Courtesy of Samaila Magaji, Zaria)

Aminu Inuwa, in Zaria City during Eid-el-Fitr in 1991. He explained his choices to me in May 1995:

ER: How many robes were distributed?

AI: Ah, let me see, it was about fourteen. But in different categories.

ER: What were the categories?

AI: Ah, in the first place, there are important or more dignified people who are given the most expensive robes. Say, like the *aska biyu*. . . .

ER: So how many of the *aska biyu* did you distribute?

AI: One.

ER: Who did that *aska biyu* go to?

AI: . . . A friend to the district head in Zaria City. . . . All right, then *aska tara* [literally, ten knives] or, in other words, 'Yar Dikwa. I think the sewing of this type of robe originated from Dikwa in Bornu State. That is why it is called 'Yar Dikwa. This is my view anyway, but from the name.

ER: So how many of these were distributed?

AI: Three.

ER: And to which people were these given?

AI: One of the robes went to the district head's father-in-law, and then two—one was given to one of his village heads, a village head under him, and then one was given to a friend.

ER: These are *dinkin hannu* [hand-embroidered]?

AI: Yes!

ER: These are very costly.

AI: Yes! Very costly.

ER: There remain ten.

AI: Okay, there remain ten, *ko*? The rest are just *dinkin keke* [machine-embroidered], and they are two, three categories. One category was given to his subjects, his servants, some of his servants.

Robes are important, then, for maintaining a political hierarchy within an emirate—with the *sarkin* or emir as the head and the political offices of ranked district heads, titled chiefs, horsemen, guards, courtiers, and friends all visually distinguished by the miniscule details of their dress.

Some of the most costly robes, made of doubled material (referred to as *tokare*) and embroidered with the most elaborate patterns—such as 'yar Madaka and *aska biyu*, were produced by masters such as Alhaji Lawal Magaji, who lived in Anguwar Lalle and who embroidered robes for the emir of Zaria. According to Lawal Magaji, "the emir [was] buying robes [through his secretary] at any time, not just at Sallah or for turbaning ceremonies, but during Sallah he [bought] more. Last Sallah, [in 1996], he purchased both the small and large sizes of robes, more than one hundred, maybe two hundred. . . . He buys robes because of fashion ['addo], and it is a tradition for the emir to give robes at many times" (interview by the author, August 25, 1996, Zaria). Magaji estimated that in 1996 the cost of a *tokare* robe embroidered in the *aska biyu* pattern with the highest quality materials (Excelensa *shadda* and Anchor thread) was around N40,000, approximately US$465.

The demand for a range of embroidered robes produced by Lawal Magaji for the emir of Zaria, the refined distributions described by Aminu Inuwa, the Majidadin Danburan of Zaria, which measured the social and political worth of recipients as expressed in the fineness of a particular robe's embroidery, and the wearing of embroidered robes, were all part of the practice of appearing important, of *neman girma* (literally, looking for greatness). Titled turban-wearing emirate leaders who sought to enhance their prestige within their communities owned many robes, some of which they had commissioned and some of which they had received as gifts. Like them, Bello owned many *babban riga* as well as *alkyabba* capes (see fig. 4.8). However, he also owned many turbans—in many colors and patterns—many more than other officials.

Why Many Turbans?

Why did the sardauna wear such a range of colorful turbans when most of his contemporaries wore plain white turbans? People give several explanations. Many observe that he clearly liked to dress well. Indeed, he disliked British district officers who dressed poorly (Paden 1986: 226). As one professor and former director of Arewa House, Kaduna, explained: "Ahmadu Bello was a fastidious dresser and clearly he liked to dress well in traditional styles of garments—*babban riga*, *alkyabba*, and turbans. And he liked color. . . . Some people have preferences for certain colors—many like white, some like blue, but Ahmadu Bello liked patterned, colored turbans" (Karibu Chafe, interview by the author, August 14, 2012, Kaduna).

Another person I spoke with suggested that he wore patterned turbans because he liked to dress fashionably. Similarly, Samaila Magaji, the Sarkin Kwal-Kwali Zazzau, noted that "the Sardauna was somebody who was fond of colors. . . . It was because he liked colors, that was why he was doing turbans with colors" (interview by the author, September 1, 2012, Zaria). Alhaji Ibrahim

Dasuƙi, the former sultan of Sokoto, who became Bello's private secretary in 1953 (Paden 1986: 107n15) and served as secretary general of Jama'atu Nasril Islam (1971–1988), commented that the sardauna wore turbans and robes as a way of demonstrating his pride in Hausa culture (interview by the author, July 17, 2012, Kaduna). Thus, he wore a ɗan Kura turban at the constitutional convention in London in 1957 (Bello 1962: 203–208). Dasuƙi added, however, that Bello's wearing many different types of turbans was "simply a matter of taste, with no particular meaning or significance" (interview by the author, July 17, 2012, Kaduna). Another man I spoke with even suggested that he owned and wore many types of turbans simply because he had money and could afford to purchase them.[4]

While these explanations may be true to greater and lesser degrees, I suggest that there were political and religious aspects of Ahmadu Bello's turban wearing. Beyond what has already been suggested—that he wore beautiful turbans because they attracted followers and converts and that they demonstrated the richness of Hausa-Fulani culture to foreigners—his wearing of different styles of turbans of different provenance suggested a certain cosmopolitan experience, knowledge, and paradoxically, an appreciation of both tradition and modernity. He was involved in various international trade missions, both within Africa but also in the Middle East, Southeast Asia, Europe, and the Americas, where he not only observed other types of turbans but also had the opportunity to purchase them. In June 1961, for example, he traveled to Pakistan, Iran, Lebanon, Jordan, and the United Arab Republic (Paden 1986: 545). Following the establishment of the government-sponsored Nigerian Pilgrims Mission in 1958, Bello met regularly with Saudi royalty to discuss religious issues regarding the Nigerians' performance of the hajj (Paden 1986: 286–295). Similarly, as turbans have come to be associated with an Islamic identity for many, his wearing of turbans in many different Islamic communities—from Pakistan to Morocco—suggests a way of showing his support for global Islam and Muslim unity. And at the local level, the turbaning of traditional rulers, from emirs and titled court officials to district heads, represented for Bello the organization and unity of the north. As Last has observed, the political party that Bello supported, the Northern People's Congress (NPC), "tried to mobilize and reunite the traditional scholar class and through them the Muslim community for the first time since the Shehu's [dan Fodio] jihad. Heirs of the British administration, the NPC turned particularly to the defence of the traditional North as seen in Islamic terms" (1970: 352–353). While this form of political organization was both supported and undermined by the colonial policy of indirect rule, it has continued through the era of independence, along with the importance of turbans and robe distribution for some.

Turbans and Counterturbaning

Since independence and the establishment of the Nigerian state, with its capital first in Lagos and later, after 1991, in Abuja, large turbans have come to be associated almost exclusively with emirs and other important officials associated with the emirate council. As during colonial rule, these men are paid salaries by the Nigerian state, and in this sense they are subjects themselves of the nation-state. Thus, while they share political power with national, state, and local government political officials, they are not independent of them. As Ghali Na'abba (2011) notes, "Emirs prefer to be seen, not to be heard. To send this message, their elaborate turbans cover much of the face, including their mouth. They are usually surrounded by servants and guards that prevent any impromptu contact with the public. But they don't mind being sighted from afar in their fine regalia and other accompaniments of office. This adds to their mystique and gives meaning to their high titles. But despite this distance from you and me, it's not too difficult to know what's on their minds."

This tension between government and emirate officials was evident in September 2011 when Ado Bayero was asked to meet with Kano State governor Rabi'u Musa Kwankwaso during the Nasarawa Hawan Daushe procession. While the emir initially declined, he later reconsidered and met with Kwankwaso, wearing a white embroidered *babban riga*, a white *alkyabba*, and a white *harsa* turban with an *amawali* veil conspicuously covering his mouth, suggesting the social (and moral) distance between himself and the governor (Umar 2011).[5] Yet despite their politically subordinate position vis-à-vis the federal government, the wearing of turbans by Hausa-Fulani emirs, titled men, district heads, and their *dogarai* guards and followers at public functions and at the grand Sallah processions reflects the continuing importance of royalty in Hausa-Fulani social life. The "elaborate turbans" and the "fine regalia" evidenced at durbar processions in major emirates in the north reinforce people's pride in their history and culture. In 1975, for example, the installation of Alhaji Shehu Idris as the emir of Zaria was followed by a speech given by the military governor, Abba Kyari, after which he presented the staff of office and "two traditional flags presented [to Zazzau] by Shehu Dan Fodio" (North Central State Government of Nigeria 1975). Following a speech by the new Sarkin Zazzau, an elaborate durbar procession took place.[6]

The present emir of Kano, Alhaji Muhammadu Sanusi II, was first turbaned as the Dan Majen Kano by Emir Ado Bayero in Kano on June 8, 2012, while he was still serving as governor of the Central Bank of Nigeria (Giginyu 2012). Following the death of Ado Bayero on June 6, 2014, the Dan Majen Kano was turbaned as Muhammadu Sanusi II and subsequently received the staff of office as the emir of Kano on February 7, 2015.[7] Since that time, the new emir has attended many public functions such as Qur'ān reading competitions and school openings as

Figure 4.10. Alhaji Ado Abdullahi Bayero (*center*), emir of Kano, wearing a green and white turban and *amawali* mouth veil in honor of meeting with members of the ASUU. (Courtesy of Ya'u Tanimu, Zaria)

well as turbaning ceremonies, funeral observances for prominent Muslim leaders elsewhere in Nigeria, and important national political events, often wearing a white *harsa* turban, tied in Kano style. Wearing the appropriate turban for the occasion provides a means of expressing an emir's critical role in northern Nigeria political and religious life. Thus, when Ado Bayero met with national leaders of the Academic Staff Union of Universities of Nigeria (ASUU) wearing a green and white turban, he was signaling his acceptance of this all-Nigerian organization (fig. 4.10). What is also interesting about the meeting of this particular group is that, with the exception of the emir's *dogarai* guards standing behind him, none of the other men are wearing turbans or even *hizami*. Rather, as members of the academic community, they are wearing a range of caps (some of which indicate ethnic affiliation), and some men are even bareheaded.

Changing Turbaning Practices

The situation in which those associated with emirate rule continue to wear turbans (*rawuna*) and Islamic scholars wear *hizami* "little turbans," while other Muslim men in the north mainly wear caps or even no headcovering at all, suggests the political and religious changes that have taken place since the sardauna's time. One example of such a change is the recent order by the Agom Adara, the paramount ruler of Kachia Local Government Area in southern Kaduna State, that traditionally titled chiefs in the kingdom must replace their turbans with leopard skins, making reference to precolonial forms of chieftaincy in the area (Sa'idu 2012a). The order also pertains to Christian southerners wanting to distinguish themselves from Muslims who have dominated this area during the nineteenth century when the Sokoto Caliphate ruled, through the period of indirect rule of the colonial period, and during the independence period when Kaduna State government was led by Muslim governors. By insisting that his chiefs wear leopard skins, the Agom Adara is not only asserting the distinctive independence of his kingdom from long-standing Hausa-Fulani Muslim rule, he is also making an oblique criticism of Ahmdu Bello's conversion tours in the early 1960s. Yet for some of his chiefs, this order presents a dilemma: "in Kachia and Kasuwan Magani, . . . the district heads are Hausa/Fulani [while] the other two district heads in Kufana and Ankuwa are Adara by tribe but practice Islam" (Sa'idu 2012a). If these leaders were seen wearing leopard skins, they would not be allowed to enter a mosque to pray. In 2012, this issue had yet to be resolved, although there was some hope that individuals would be allowed to wear religious and ceremonial dress of their choice. Others, particularly those involved in emirate politics, support the continuation of a hierarchy of emirates, emirs, and district heads, all reflected in the types of turbans they wear in each other's presence. As one Zaria City man explained:

> When people come to the emirate to see the emir [of Zaria], the emir will come out with *rawani kunne biyu* and *alkyabba*. But the district head will only wear *rawani* with one *kunne* or none, and they will not wear *alkyabba*. And the same thing when they escort him somewhere. Anyone you see in Zaria with *rawani kunne biyu* is a sort of crown prince or king—whether the existing king or his children. Even if a person has money, he can only do one *kunne*. If he is the son of the emir, even if he has nothing, he will wear a turban with *kunne biyu*. You see that is a rule of the emirate council, anyone in the emirate has to follow that rule. Even the people who are from southern Kaduna, they have to follow this rule because they are under Zaria. If they come to greet the emir, they may do *rawani*. But in their places, they would just use a cap and put *hizami* around it. (Yahaya Muktar, interview by the author, June 2011, Zaria)

Nonetheless, turbans are used outside of this social ideal of royal prestige and political leadership. Turbans are familiar costume additions in Nigerian films made in Kano and may even serve as the center of a film's plot, as in the recent Kannywood film *Rawani*.[8] Indeed, the late Kannywood film star Kasimu Yero posed for a publicity photograph wearing a turban. When later asked if he had been turbaned—that is, if he held a traditional title—he said, "I just decided to take that picture to give an idea of my background and the background of my career. In fact, I come from a royal family in Zaria. So seeing me with royal garb is no big deal" (quoted in Ahmadu-Suka and Bivan 2017). However, those from other royal families in Zaria might not see it that way.

Governance and the Prestige of Turbans and Robes

During the nineteenth and into the first half of the twentieth century, many Muslim men living in the Sokoto Caliphate wore some sort of turban. Yet turban styles were not uniform. Shehu 'Uthmān dan Fodio favored simple dress and white turbans, while the emir of Kano introduced the distinctive *kunne* style of tying turbans, reflecting one aspect of the ongoing conflict over the basis of political authority—between religious leaders and kings, between austere and magnificent dress. This tension was observed by Imam Muhammad Ibn Abdulkarim al-Maghili, who advised, "Manifest your love of what is excellent, and of worthy people; show your hatred of corruption and corrupt people. Adorn your body, perfume your breath and make comely apparel with the adornments that are permissible without imitation or reducing the treasury to bankruptcy. Do you deck yourself out with gold, or silver, or voluminous silk that is shameful, ignoble and improper?" (quoted in Bobboyi 2011: 12–13).

While political authority of the emirs was sanctioned by royal birth, that of Islamic leaders was sanctioned by their scholarship.[9] In the administration of such a political hierarchy, difficulties such as conflict and corruption were bound to occur, as Shedu dan Fodio's son, Muhammad Bello, acknowledged (Last 1966). Ahmadu Bello, who showed his admiration for his great-grandfather in numerous ways,[10] made a similar admission more than a century later: "Corruption is a big matter and one which has given us a lot of anxious thought. . . . It is all very well to say 'abolish corruption' as though it was something that can be cut off by turning a tap or pressing a switch. No, it is a matter which springs from the very roots of human nature. Is there any country in the world which can honestly and convincingly claim to be absolutely free of corruption? I doubt it very much" (1962: 195).

Beginning with the nineteenth-century reign of the Sokoto Caliphate and continuing through the period of colonial rule, the tension between the authority of the Fulani Islamic scholars (*malamai*) and the kings of the seven Hausa-Fulani emirates (the Hausawa Bakwai) was increasingly evidenced by the distinctive turbans and robes worn by these groups. In public settings, emirs and titled men of the *sarauta* class wore large *rawuna* turbans and layers of embroidered *babban riga* made from yards of finely handwoven cloth or imported materials, while religious scholars wore simpler turbans made of plain white cloth. And along with prestige, the political power associated with robe and turban wearing is suggested by the metonymic use of the Hausa words for robes and turbans. David Heathcote (1979: 1:239) notes that the phrase *rigar sarki*, literally "robe of the king," is used to refer to the riders who accompany an emir, while the term *tuɓe*, literally "taking off of a garment," refers to deposing an emir (Bargery [1934] 1993: 1048). Similarly, "after the defeat of Kalembaina, the [chief/vizier] . . . gave his turban and gown to ['Abd al-Qadir bin] Gidado as a token of his relinquishing office and recognizing the new Vizier" (Last 1967: 70).

Under colonial rule, this political hierarchy and set of social-religious distinctions was reinforced by the imposition of indirect rule, particularly in the north where British colonial officials were loath to openly disturb prevailing religious mores and sought to suppress Islamic reform. Furthermore, the officials identified to some extent, based on their own system of royalty, with the idea of royal families as exemplars of political authority and wealth. Nonetheless, it was during this period of colonial bureaucracy that alternative forms of head coverings became prevalent, which included caps worn by the non-royal educated elite and smaller turbans worn by *malamai*. Ahmadu Bello, as sardauna and as a member of the royal house of Sokoto, wore many different types of turbans—large, expensive turbans for ceremonial functions and smaller, less costly *hizami* for office wear, and even embroidered caps at times. Yet he was also a strong supporter of Islamic unity, facilitating Nigerians' performance of the hajj, making many trips to Muslim countries, and supporting both Western and Islamic education—evidenced by his work with the founding of Ahmadu Bello University and numerous secondary schools in the north as well as Islamic schools in Kaduna. In a sense, Ahmadu Bello was a pivotal figure in that through his modernization efforts, by which he sought to strengthen the position of the north vis-à-vis other Nigerian polities, he was also maintaining Hausa-Fulani cultural traditions exemplified by turbans and robes.

Yet after independence, in his federal government position as premier of the Northern Region, Bello weakened the powers of the emirs, who continued to function but under the authority of federal and state governments. By wearing a variety of attractive turbans, he both emphasized a magnificent emirate past and muted his role in strengthening the position of officials of the Nigerian state. In this sense, Bello was an Islamic reformer who sought to establish a unified, technologically and intellectually modern Muslim North within the newly independent Nigeria without forgetting the past work of reformers such as dan Fodio. However, in his quest for Islamic modernity (*zamani*) and in his support for Sheikh Abubakar Gumi, one of the founders of the Islamic reform group Izala, discussed in chapter 7, Bello's position bridging the old and the new foreshadowed some aspects of the antagonism between Izala and the Sunni *tariqa* groups—Qādiriyya and Tijāniyya—which contributed to Islamic disunity in the north. As a follower of Qādiriyya, Ahmadu Bello, who was assassinated in 1966, did not live to see Gumi's criticism of Qādiriyya and Tijāniyya practices, some of which were described by Izala leaders as un-Islamic innovations.[11] Subsequent dissension within the Izala movement itself compounded this disunity, and in the late twentieth century, several Izala-based splinter groups emerged. Furthermore, as with earlier reformers such as dan Fodio, the distinctions between these Islamic groups have been visually expressed in types of turbans that their respective *malamai* wear. The *hizami* with a "tail" is associated with Izala, the tail-less *hizami* with members of the Tijāniyya, the full turban with a piece of cloth encircling the neck with Qādiriyya, and the round coiled turban with Shi'a Islamic Movement of Nigeria leaders. More recently, members of the Salafiyya group led by Sheikh Muhammad Auwal Albani, who stressed the importance of Western and Islamic education, often wore embroidered Hausa caps, while the leader of Boko Haram, Mohammed Yusuf, and his followers wore turbans that they associated with "the time of the Prophet."

Conclusion

In northern Nigeria, large turbans are now almost exclusively worn by members of royal Hausa-Fulani families and their retinues, and even then, mainly during ceremonial functions, particularly turbaning proceedings and Hawan Daushe processions. As Dasuƙi observed, turbans are no longer considered fashionable by younger Muslim men in Kaduna and Zaria. This situation may be related to a more general process, evidenced in the Middle East and discussed by Bruce Ingham—namely that "in the early twentieth century dress was far more elaborate than it is now" (1997: 51). He attributes the reduction of variety of cloaks, robes, and head coverings to post–World War II modernization efforts that supported "simpler and less exotic designs" (51).[12] While this situation may also be seen in everyday Muslim dress in northern Nigeria in the late twentieth and early twenty-first centuries, the elaborate turbans, beautifully embroidered robes, and lavish horse decorations worn during Sallah (Id-el-Fitr and Id-el-Kabir) processions held throughout the north suggest that the competitive tension between the authority of Nigerian state officials and the emirs and their councils continues, if not openly, then sartorially. Thus, while some, like dan Fodio, disapproved of this ostentatious dress, which they considered to be un-Islamic and even backward, others, such as Ahmadu Bello, saw such displays as a means of celebrating an Islamic identity and past: "The immense prestige of their office is thus harnessed to the machine of modern progress and cannot, I am sure, fail to have a notable effect in bringing the country forward. To remove or endanger this prestige in *any way*, or even to remove any of their original trappings, would be to set the country back for years" (1962: 229). As this statement suggests, Ahmadu Bello sought to merge these distinctive dispositions and bases for political authority by combining the wearing of his many beautiful turbans, the distribution of *babban riga*, and conversion tours with his support for Western innovations—which included the first Western university in northern Nigeria and textile manufacturing establishments in Kaduna, Zamfara, Zaria, and Gusau. Through this seemingly dichotomous behavior, he sought to bring prosperity and unity to the north. Another seeming dichotomy—the wearing of turbans by men and veils by women—which has had implications for the structure of political authority, is considered in chapter 5.

Notes

1. These ɗan Kura turban cloths are now made with machine-woven broadcloth, and some are imported from China.

2. Sheikh Bashir came from Gordon College, Khartoum, to become the chief professor at the Muslim Law School, Kano (*Nigeria Magazine* 1944: 35).

3. According to Alhaji Aliyu, "During Sallah, we would go to distribute money and dresses to people. He didn't give *rawuna* turbans, only robes. Also, he didn't give *akoko* [white, unpatterned cloth] out because it's used for wrapping the dead. He would give them *atamfa* [patterned cloth] because there is a textile factory that makes *atamfa* with the sardauna's name and the party name. He also distribute[d] watches and earrings with the party sign. And he gave wrappers to everyone—not just party supporters" (interview by the author, July 10, 2012, Kaduna).

4. Turbans are expensive. In 2011–2016, turbans ranged from N2,000 to N20,000, depending on the type and size:

> *Rawani* organdy, imported: N2,000
> *Rawani* ɗan Kura, imported from China: N7,000 for 6 yards
> *Harsa*, imported from UK: N10,000–20,000
> *Harsa*, imported from China: N3,000
> *Rawani* ɗan Sardauna, imported from India: N7,500
> *Rawani tessala*, made from *saki* cloth, "the real one": N7,500

5. The position of his *amawali* cloth would not be lost on viewers, who would have seen it as a way that the emir expressed his displeasure.

6. Following this display, the military band played the Nigerian national anthem, thus the federal government had the final say.

7. Sanusi was suspended from office by former Nigerian president Goodluck Jonathan in early 2014 after Sanusi announced that US$20 billion was missing from the Nigerian National Petroleum Corporation, funds that had disappeared during the Jonathan regime. After the government prohibited Sanusi's travel abroad and officials seized his passport at the Lagos airport (Mutum 2014), Sanusi returned to Kano. Following the death of Ado Bayero, Jonathan used police and secret service operatives to block Sanusi's entrance into the emir's palace, but public pressure forced him to allow the new emir to enter a week later, on June 13, 2014 (Mudashir, Muktar, and Yaya 2014). This example of a former government minister using his hereditary position to stymie the political machinations of the head of the federal government suggests the ways that the moral authority of emirate political-religious leaders may prevail under certain circumstances.

8. The film was directed by Ahmad Aliyu Tage and produced by Isa Abacha. I purchased a DVD copy in Zaria in March 2016.

9. However, some emirs, such as the Sarkin Zazzau Muhammad Sambo and Aliyu Sidi, were also known for their Islamic scholarship.

10. "[Muhammad] Bello, and not the Shehu, was the explicit model for the Premier, and he named schools and institutions after him; Bello's tomb in Wurno and his mosque in Sokoto were given priority in the big construction programme during which the tombs and praying places of all those connected with the jihad were rebuilt in concrete" (Last 1970: 353).

11. Ahmadu Bello was assassinated in Kaduna on January 15, 1966, on the same day that Prime Minister Abubakar Tafawa Balewa was assassinated in Lagos. Both men were killed as part of a military coup that led to the Nigerian Civil War, which began in July 1967.

12. However, as anthropologist Bernard Cohn (1989) has observed in the context of colonial and postcolonial India, turbans and other garments associated with the Mughal court dwindled as British colonial officials sought to restrain Mughal rulers' authority and autonomy. While British colonial rule in northern Nigeria differed in many ways from what transpired in northern India, the practice of indirect rule and the formation of the nation-state, as well as the modernization of trade and industry, had consequences for the dress of men and women living in northern Nigeria.

5   Veiling, Gender, and Fashion

Veiling was and is a practice that is deeply embedded in the cultural system. Perhaps the whole issue should be reframed. Is it the same "veil" that is being documented throughout the millennia?

—Fadwa El Guindi, *Veil: Modesty, Privacy, and Resistance*

June 16th [1921] On Thursday the 10th of Juldandu a messenger arrived from the Emir of al Yemen bringing me a considerable quantity of goods—24 veils for women, two ordinary gowns, a large gown, a black turban and trousers.

—Hamman Yaji, quoted in James Vaughan and Anthony Kirk-Greene, *The Diary of Hamman Yaji*

IT IS INTRIGUING to imagine what the "24 veils for women" received by Hamman Yaji, the emir of Madagali (fig. 5.1), consisted of, where they came from, how they were worn, and by whom. Were they made of imported silks or printed cottons or of finely handwoven cotton cloths, worn as head and body coverings by the Muslim wives and concubines of Hamman Yaji? Were these coverings, translated generally as veils, used to distinguish elite Muslim women—wives and concubines—from nominally Muslim servants and slave women? It is difficult to say, based on Yaji's diary (Vaughan and Kirk-Greene 1995), although travelers' narratives from the nineteenth century and colonial accounts from the early twentieth century suggest that such cloths may have been used in these ways.[1] However, what is particularly interesting about the use of textiles as face and head coverings in northern Nigeria is that women *and* men have worn permutations of both—in fact, some men wear face veils while many women do not. Thus, the stereotypical association of veiling with particular gendered Islamic practices, such as women's seclusion, modesty, and forms of dress that encompass the entire body, is complicated by men's use of face veils and by similar ideals of Muslim men's comportment in public—for example, dressing with reserve and averting one's eyes (Lemu and Heeren 1976: 25). As Reina Lewis has suggested, "The veil was part of a system of gender seclusion that impacted more than the rich than the poor, more on the urban than the rural and that co-opted men into reciprocally modest behaviours" (2003: 10).

In addition to the twenty-four women's veils, Yaji also noted receiving a black turban (*bakin rawani*), possibly made from shiny indigo-dyed *turkudi* cloth (fig. 5.2), which with turbans made from lengths of fine undyed *turkudi* cotton cloth were

Figure 5.1. Hamman Yaji, the emir of Madagali (*left*), wearing a turban with an *amawali* mouth veil (here only covering his chin), with a village chief. (From Strümpell 1912, opposite p. 87)

associated with Muslim men's identity (Shea 1975: 1:57). Paul Staudinger ([1889] 1990: 2:205), traveling in western Hausaland in the 1880s, noted Hausa-Fulani men wearing such turbans. He also observed that some women wore *turkudi* cloth, either undyed white or possibly indigo-dyed, as a cover cloth that was at times used as a veil: "Wealthy and highborn women and girls wear in addition something like a stole about their shoulders, a so-called women's cloth ([Hausa] *turkedi*). This they often pull up from behind over their heads and the few women who are not allowed to show their faces in the street, *usually only the wives of some kings*, also use this garment to veil their faces by leaving only a narrow gap" (206–207; emphasis added).

Staudinger's description suggests an overlap not only in the materials used for men's and women's dress but also in the ways that class and rank intersected with gendered forms of head, face, and body coverings. Murray Last notes this as well: "In pastoral Fulani society, as in the pagan peasant societies of the Hausa and

Figure 5.2. Emir of Kano Alhaji Abdullahi Bayero (*left*), wearing a white *harsa* turban and *amawali* veil covering his mouth, with court officials, all wearing turbans with *amawali* veils but with mouths uncovered; the official sitting second from right is wearing blue-black *rawani* ɗan Kura, 1938. (Photograph by Stanhope White, courtesy of the Bodleian Libraries, Oxford)

Bambara, women were free to work and play outside the house. In contrast, women of the Muslim communities before the jihad had been distinguished by wearing veils" (1974: 24). Indeed, slave women were not allowed to wear veils or cover their heads (Last 1967: 234), while slave men could not wear turbans (Last 2014: 44).

These distinctive configurations of gender and dress, coverings, and class were also in evidence when Hausa women who had received titled offices of the emirate were given turbans as part of investiture proceedings. The rarity of this practice, however, is underscored by the saying "*Kallabi tsakanin rawuna*" (the headscarf among the turbans), referring to the exceptional seventeenth-century ruler of Zaria, Queen Amina, and proving the rule of men's political leadership. Women were associated with headscarves, not turbans, which were almost exclusively associated with the political authority of men.

Men's veiling was similarly unusual, and with the exception of those discussing Tuareg men's veils (Murphy 1964; Rasmussen 1991), little has been written about what the use of interconnected but distinctive forms of veiling might mean

Figure 5.3. Photographs of the wives of the emir of Kano wearing a range of *mayafi* veils, from the collection of Hajiya Rabi Wali, whose grandmother is shown in the lower right corner, June 16, 2011. (Courtesy of Hajiya Rabi Wali)

in terms of gender and political and religious authority. The material from northern Nigeria is especially useful for taking this approach because of the complexity of the head and face coverings used—some men and some women veil, some women and some men wear turbans. In this chapter, I examine the historical contexts of the meaning of face, head, and body covering as material expressions of piety, status, and class, which reflect processes of cultural negotiations over gender, social, and religious roles in Muslim society in northern Nigeria. Just as the simplistic dichotomy of veiled/unveiled as equivalent to subordination/freedom is an unsatisfactory approach to understanding gendered relations, so the sexual dichotomy of male/female hardly captures the fluid permutations

Figure 5.4. Sarkin Zazzau, Ja'afaru Dan Isyaku (*center*), 1937–1959, wearing a *rawani* turban with *amawali* face veil and *alkyabba* cape, with members of his court wearing robes and turbans, Shika, 1938. (Photograph by G. H. Gibbs, courtesy of the Bodleian Libraries, Oxford)

of gendered social and religious identities, variations of which are expressed through these cloth coverings in Hausa Muslim society.

While women *and* men have historically worn veils in urban Muslim communities in northern Nigeria, they have done so in visually distinctive and socially significant ways. Until recently, veiling for women consisted of a range of head coverings and shawl-like body coverings that revealed their faces (fig. 5.3). Men's veils consisted of an extension of their turban cloth—referred to as an *amawali*—that was tied in such a way to provide enough cloth to cover the lower half of the face, particularly the mouth and nose; *amawali* were mainly worn as face coverings by emirs (fig 5.4, fig. 5.5). Other royal men, while they wore turbans with *amawali* veils, generally did not use them to veil their faces.[2] Clearly, Fadwa El Guindi's admonition to consider whether it is "the same 'veil' that is being documented" is relevant here (1999: 12). Furthermore, the different styles and meaning attributed to men's and women's veils within Hausa society provides an interesting means for a consideration of how ideas about gender have changed and have also underwritten critical aspects of successive Islamic reform movements there. Yedida Stillman's observation concerning changes in Muslim women's veiling practices has relevance for Islamic reform movements in northern Nigeria:

Figure 5.5. Sarkin Zazzau, Aliyu Dan Sidi, 1904–1920, wearing an *amawali* face veil with a turban tied with *kunne biyu*, which refers to the spelling of Allah in Arabic, ﻪ ﺪ ﺪ ﺍ: the turban end draping down signifies ﺍ, the two *kunne* signify ﺪ ﺪ, and the encircling of the turban around the face signifies ﻪ. He is also holding *carbi* prayer beads. He was deposed by British colonial officials in 1920. (Courtesy of Yahaya Muktar)

> One important force contributing to reveiling in one form or another has been the Islamist movements, both militant and non-militant. These movements . . . represent an alternative to secularism on the one hand and institutional Islam on the other. Irrespective of their political activities, all of these groups advocate a return to a holistic Islamic way of life and to Islamic traditional values, which include inter alia a traditional code of modesty and gender differentiation. One of the primary external markers of the latter is *al-zayy al Islami* or *al-zayy al-Shari'i* [Islamic or Shar'i attire]. (2000: 158)

Thus, the different meanings associated with veiling—as an assertion of moral Islamic and, at times, political authority; as a form of protection; as a marker of social status; as a sign of sartorial expertise; and at times as subversive disguise—underscore the ephemeral ambiguity of this particular form of dress, the import of which is likely to continue to change in different contexts and eras.

Veils and Islamic Reform

Redefining the respective roles of women and men is often a critical aspect of Islamic reform movements. Prior practices relating to their gendered roles in social

Figure 5.6. Wives of the emir of Katsina wearing *mayafi* veils, with the visiting duchess of Aosta wearing a pith helmet and veil. (Photograph by C. J. Chaytor, courtesy of the Bodleian Libraries, Oxford)

life may be seen as un-Islamic, prompting the need for change. How women's positions as daughters, wives, and mothers are perceived are reflected in Islamic texts written by scholars such as Shehu 'Uthmān dan Fodio. They are also reflected in prescriptions concerning dress, particularly veils and veiling practices. These roles, and the types of dress historically associated with them, are distinguished from the meanings associated with ostensibly similar forms of dress—in this case, veils worn by male political leaders, specifically emirs. Maintaining or reassessing these gendered distinctions through the use of textiles and dress is an aspect of Islamic reform often associated with the establishment of a new moral order.

During the Sokoto Caliphate, royal and commoner women incorporated quantities of locally handwoven and imported manufactured textiles into their head and body covering repertoires. This practice continued during the colonial period, with royal women wearing large cover cloths called *mayafi* as veils (fig. 5.6)—some made use of the very narrow-strip handwoven *turkudi* cloths as

Figure 5.7. Women selling onions at Kano market with *dankwali* and *lullubi* head coverings. Some women face the photographer, while one woman (*seated, third from left*) has covered her head and face with her *mayafi* cloth veil, Kano, 1938. (Photograph by George Howard Gibbs, courtesy of the Bodleian Libraries, Oxford)

well as imported textiles—while commoner women used ordinary handwoven wrappers as cover cloth veils (fig. 5.7) and imported cotton kerchiefs (*kallabi* or *dankwali*; fig. 5.8) as headscarves.

With independence in 1960 and increased travel to Mecca for the hajj, the shift toward wearing of a range of imported veils made from manufactured textiles increased. By the 1970s, the meanings associated with veiling changed again as a new style of head covering from the Middle East—the *hijab*, specifically associated with women—was introduced by Nigerian Muslim leaders associated with Izala (see chapter 7). Presently in northern Nigeria, Hausa-Fulani Muslim women wear a range of textiles as veils—some locally made, some imported from the Middle East, China, and Europe—to cover the head, face, and at times, the entire body. Reflecting ideals of proper bodily comportment, these different styles of veils have reinforced particular interpretations of male and female bodies. Yet what constitutes proper veiling practice has been continually reassessed, renegotiated, revised, and replaced, which reflects the political, social, and economic context in which religious reform and piety have been framed.

Figure 5.8. Woman outside of Kano spinning cotton, a woven cotton strip displayed at her side. She is wearing a printed *kallabi* headscarf and handwoven cotton wrapper. (Photograph by George Howard Gibbs, courtesy of the Bodleian Libraries, Oxford)

Gendered Configurations and Material Expressions of Piety and Status

When the jihād that led to the foundation of the Sokoto Caliphate began in 1804, dan Fodio instructed Muslim men to wear turbans and Muslim women to wear veils (dan Fodio 1978; Ogunbiyi 1969). Yet the many uses of lengths of cloth associated with head covering sometimes accentuated social distinctions while blurring specific gendered ones. The veils worn by emirs are related to specific types of turbans, which by color and material, distinguish royalty (*sarauta*) from commoners (*talakawa*), as discussed in chapter 4. In his *Dictionary of the Hausa Language*, Charles Henry Robinson clearly makes this distinction in his inclusion of the term *rawanin sarauta*, translated as "the badge or insignia of royalty," which is often described as white (1913: 291). Similarly, the *amawali*, translated as "a veil, worn over the mouth and hanging down in front, [a] loose fold of turban hanging from mouth over chest" is also white (14). Robinson further notes, "If white = a sign of royalty" (1913: 14). However, the color white is also prescribed as proper Muslim dress (Kriger 2006). Photographs from the early twentieth century show royal men such as the emirs of Kano, Gwandu, and Zaria wearing *amawali* covering their mouths (see fig. 2.4, fig. 5.4, fig. 5.5). While women veiled as well, they wore large cloths over their heads and bodies known as *lullubi* (*lulube, lilibi*) and defined as "a long veil reaching to the feet" (Robinson 1913: 235).

According to later dictionary definitions by G. P. Bargery, only women wore the *lullubi*, which he defined as "a woman's covering her head and shoulders with a cloth" ([1934] 1993: 731).[3] Nonetheless, while women might have worn large cloths of fine silk and cotton as a body veil and men might have worn the fine *turkudi* or imported white muslin cloths as turbans with *amawali* cloths covering the mouth, these two forms of veiling also distinguish Muslim elites from the poor and royals from the commoners, indicating a social system in which social and class rank intersected with gendered identities that underscores cultural rather than biological differences.[4]

Veiling and Social Distance, Veiling and Modesty

Another way of considering these permutations of gendered and social associations with veiling is to examine the different explanations given for the use of veils and the contexts in which they are worn. While Robinson's and Bargery's dictionaries provide different terms for veils,[5] they do not provide specific information about the men and women wearing them, nor why they did so. Examining explorers' accounts of the nineteenth and twentieth centuries and more recent autobiographies of Hausa-Fulani women and men provides some possible explanations for their uses of veils.

Colleen Kriger (2006: 82) suggests that the men's face veil, or *litham*, made of very narrow handwoven cloth strips (*turkudi*), some dyed blue-black, may have reached Hausaland through trans-Saharan trade networks and specifically through Wangara traders, since several groups of North African men wore such face coverings.[6] Indeed, in Tuareg-speaking areas in Niger and Mali, Tuareg men's use of blue-black cloths as turbans with folds of cloth that may cover the nose and mouth has evoked considerable documentation and discussion (Lamb and Holmes 1980: 90–94; Murphy 1964; Picton and Mack 1979; Rasmussen 1991). Until recently, only Tuareg men, not women, regularly veiled. Robert Murphy argues that Tuareg men's veiling—which was not restricted by rank or class[7]—reflected a generalized social distancing in a society where the possibility of encountering men of senior status and certain women kin led to a preference for wearing turbans with sufficient cloth that could be manipulated to cover the mouth and nose, with different degrees of covering reflecting distinctive social relations (1964: 1266, 1273; see also Lhote 1955: 308–309). The mouth and its hidden recesses are a potential source of "sentiments of shame and pollution" (Murphy 1964: 1271), related to the dangers of eating and speaking as well as to suggestions of sexuality and mortality.

Covering the mouth may also be seen as a way of showing reserve. In Hausa, the term *kawaici* (reserved) may be used to refer to a reserved man—*yana da kawaici*; literally, he has reserve. However, one may also refer to this manner by saying *ba ya shiga mutane*, literally, that one may not enter a man, meaning that a reserved person does not allow outsiders to engage him personally or know his personal inner thoughts. This prohibition of entry suggests that showing reserve by covering the mouth with a face veil may also be a form of protection from the dangers that high status may entail (Murphy 1964: 1259; see also Last 2014). It also suggests the prohibition *ba shiga*, which is sometimes painted on entrances to family compounds, warning that unrelated men should not enter them in order to maintain the *kulle* (secluded) status of household women within.

Along with use of the face veil as an expression of reserve and rank through social distance, the importance of covering the mouth may best explain men's face veiling by Hausa-Fulani political leaders. In the early 1940s, the sultan of Sokoto, Siddiq Abubakar III, was photographed wearing a fine white cotton face veil and turban (fig. 5.9). The social flexibility of the *litham*, or face veil, described by Murphy (1964) and Henri Lhote (1955) is suggested by the message written on the back of this postcard by an unknown British colonial official: "He has a delightful smile and charming manners. Face usually uncovered." However, whether this lowering of the veil reflected a relaxed relationship between these two men or was done for some other reason is unclear. Younger members of the court, such as the ciroma, the emir of Kano's son, would normally wear turbans, indicative of Islamic faith and of their royal status, without covering the mouth or face (fig. 5.10).

Alternately, until recently Muslim women in northern Nigeria, both royal and commoners, did not cover their faces (and mouths) with veils, although the types of head coverings and cover cloths that they have worn may be referred to as forms of veiling. There are several examples of this behavior in nineteenth-century explorers' narratives. During their travels in 1830, Richard and John Lander attended a royal durbar in Kiama (part of the Borgu kingdom to the southeast of Sokoto), where "a few of the women on the ground by the side of the king wore large white dresses, which covered their persons like a winding-sheet" (1854: 217). This description, while vague, suggests that these women wore large cloths, *lullubi*, that entirely covered their heads and bodies. Staudinger described women's cover cloths in the 1880s, such as the blue-black ɗan Kura *turkudi* cloth that they used to cover their heads and faces, as veils. He also mentioned the use

Figure 5.9. Postcard of the sultan of Sokoto, Siddiq Abubakar III, wearing a white *darsa* turban and fine white gauze *amawali* face veil. A message written on the reverse side by a colonial official refers to the face veil covering the sultan's face, ca. 1940. (Courtesy of the Duckworth Collection, Melville J. Herskovits Library of African Studies, Northwestern University)

Figure 5.10. The ciroma of Kano, son of the emir of Kano, wearing a turban with the *amawali* cloth lowered. (Courtesy of the Duckworth Collection, Melville J. Herskovits Library of African Studies, Northwestern University)

of headscarves and other imported textiles: "In contrast to the men, women like more colourful and striped cloths and frequently wear materials of European manufacture. For the stoles of wealthy women magnificent materials are often used, and they set a great store by their finery and their hairstyle. . . . Often the women tie a kerchief about the head and red ones in particular are very becoming to these dark-eyed beauties. Such a piece of material, about the size of a pocket handkerchief, is called *alfuta* in many areas" ([1889] 1990, 2:206–207). Robinson defines *alfuta* as "a handkerchief used by women to bind round the head" (1913: 10); the Arabic attribution of this term suggests that these textiles may have been imported via the trans-Saharan trade (Johnson 1976).

The use of veils and cover cloths as part of women's practice of modest comportment was also mentioned in nineteenth-century narratives. Eduard Flegel describes Madugu Mohamman Mai Gashin Baƙi's encounter with a young, un-married woman in 1872: "On this day our Madugu was riding out with his Mai-unguwa, that is, the chief of his quarter of the town. . . . Mai-unguwa invited him to accompany him to visit one of his mothers-in-law, who had just returned from Nupe, having been captured in war by the ruler of Birni-n Guari [Birnin Gwari]. She was still young, beautiful, and a first rate housewife. But of all this Madugu could see nothing as following the custom of the country she knelt, wholly cov-ered by her cloth and with her eyes averted, before the lordly visitors" ([1885] 1985: 17). In 1886, Staudinger made a similar observation: "In the evening we had an interesting visitor. A princess of royal blood, daughter of the king of Zaria, came to see us under the pretext of wishing to buy beads. . . . And after the manner of Hausa women she kept her face modestly averted and the head partly veiled by the wrap thrown over part of the head, but gradually her manner lost its shyness" ([1889] 1990, 1:189).

In these examples, the maintenance of social distance comes into play. However, the reasons for this behavior, reserved avoidance and protected mod-esty, and the means for accomplishing it—face veils, large cover cloths, and headscarves—have a specific gendered cast.[8]

Concepts of Modesty in Northern Nigerian Society

As these nineteenth-century accounts suggest, the concept of modesty—*kunya*—was (and continues to be) associated with proper Hausa Muslim women's comportment, which included the use of various types of face, head, and body coverings. As previously mentioned, the extent and types of covering depended on one's social status, class, and Islamic practice. This situation was particu-larly the case during the nineteenth century with the establishment of the So-koto Caliphate, when Muslim women's veiling was prescribed by the caliphate's founder, Shehu dan Fodio. In addition to a modest demeanor, he also advocated women's education (Ogunbiyi 1969: 55–56). His daughter Nana Asma'u estab-lished a system of Islamic education for women during the years of the Sokoto Caliphate that continued into the twentieth century (Bivins 2007; Boyd and Last 1985; Ogunbiyi 1969). The women *jaji* teachers whom she trained covered them-selves with large handwoven cloths and wore special *malafa* (or *malfa*; see fig. 2.3) hats tied with bands of red cloth, indicative of their authority as they went about the city of Sokoto and its environs to instruct other women in knowledge of the Qur'ān: "The *malfa* hat, a type of hat associated with the political authority of the Inna of Gobir and introduced to women religious teachers in Sokoto by Nana Asma'u in the mid-19th century. A red strip of cloth, called the *nadi*, was tied around the hat's brim and the handing over of the red cloth to women paralleled the turbaning ceremony (*rawani*) marking the political authority of men" (Boyd 1989: 50–51).

Additionally, in her writings during the mid-nineteenth century, Asma'u discusses the importance of women's dress (Mack and Boyd 2000: 83). While Asma'u and women *jaji* teachers worked in the area around Sokoto, Islamic education for girls and women was not pursued in many other parts of the caliphate during the nineteenth century. Thus, in the emirate of Zazzau (Zaria) to the south of Sokoto, Asma'u's influence on women's education appears to have been less widely felt. Judging from interviews of older Zaria City women in 2001, while Muslim women were conscious of the importance of covering themselves in public, many women could neither recite verses from the Qur'ān or hadith nor read Arabic or *Ajami* script, and there was no special dress associated with women's Islamic education. Nonetheless, the increasing consciousness of covering and proper Muslim dress led to an increased demand throughout northern Nigeria for various types of imported cloth, which included cloth brought from Tripoli on trans-Saharan trade routes and handwoven cloths from Kano as well as from Nupe and Yoruba areas, particularly when they became part of the caliphate.

Early Twentieth-Century Women's Head Coverings

The existence of the Sokoto Caliphate as an independent political entity ended with the establishment in 1903 of British colonial rule as the Protectorate of Northern Nigeria, which continued until Nigerian independence in 1960. Photographs taken by British colonial officers in the first half of the twentieth century evidenced the range of veiling styles during this period. E. H. Duckworth, for example, made a tour of Kano, Zaria, and Bida from December 1931 to May 1932 and photographed many sorts of textiles used as head coverings by women and young girls, which suggest a mix of imported and locally handwoven cloths described in travelers' accounts. In a picture taken in a hospital at Zaria, one woman appears to be wearing a dark cotton wrapper (*zane*), possibly of imported industrial cotton cloth that has been locally dyed, with a headscarf (*dankwali*) of imported printed material (*atamfa*), and a handwoven cotton cover cloth (*lullubi* or *mayafi*) draped over her head and shoulders. Two other women in the photograph wear large head ties made of printed material, coiled and knotted in the style referred to as *adiko*, with cover cloths of either printed or handwoven materials (see Renne 2013b: 62). Also, in a series of pictures taken at a girls' primary school in Kano, two young pupils—one of whom is the emir of Kano's daughter—are wearing large head ties with outfits of imported plain and printed cotton cloth (fig. 5.11).[9]

However, none of these photographs from the 1930s show women wearing large head ties made of stiff, synthetic imported material known as *saro* (or as Jubilee or Hayes cloths), which became popular in the 1960s, and it was probably

Figure 5.11. Daughter of the emir of Kano (*left*), whose social status is underscored by her wearing an *adiko*-style head tie and a tailored dress with satin cloth inset, Kano, ca. 1930s. (Courtesy of the Duckworth Collection, Melville J. Herskovits Library of African Studies, Northwestern University)

at this time that married women transitioned from wearing *adiko* head ties made with imported plain and printed cotton materials. Several private collections of photographs taken by professional and family photographers, mainly in Zaria during the oil boom years of the 1970s, show women wearing *saro* head ties in a general style known as *gwagwaro* (fig. 5.12). The lighter weight *gyale* veil, also imported, was sometimes draped over the *gwagwaro* head tie.[10] While some older women continued to wear cover cloths or *gyale* over *gwagwaro* head ties, some urban Hausa Muslim women during this period wore large head ties alone. These twentieth-century changes in head and body coverings reflected the increasing range and availability of imported textiles. They also reflected the sense of optimism and modernity that came with Nigerian independence and the growing affluence associated with increased revenues from oil sales in the 1970s.

Figure 5.12. The woman in this studio photograph of a couple in Zaria City is wearing a *gwagwaro* style of head tie made popular by Victoria Gowon, wife of former Nigerian president Yakubu Gowon, ca. 1970s. (Photograph of photograph by the author)

New Forms of Veiling and the Twentieth-Century Islamic Reform Movement Izala

Women in Zaria have continued to wear these newer styles of head coverings and veils, particularly the combination of *gwagwaro* head ties covered by *gyale* veils, as depicted in photographs from the 1970s. However, a combination of political, economic, and religious factors contributed to the emergence of the twentieth-century Islamic reform movement Jama'atu Izalat al-Bid'a wa Iqamat al-Sunna (Movement against Negative Innovations and for Orthodoxy), also known as Izala (see Kane 2002; Loimeier 1997; Umar 1993). In some ways echoing the reformist Fulani jihād of the nineteenth century, Izala leaders argued that northern Nigerian Muslims needed to reform Islamic practice, and they saw Islamic education for married women (as well as for girls) as part of this reform. And, as in the nineteenth-century jihād, women's involvement with Islamic education also entailed specific changes in dress. Married women in Zaria City began to wear the *hijab* when attending the newly established *Islamiyya Matan Aure* classes for married women. As with other aspects of Izala reforms, which became internalized as proper Islamic belief and practice by the movement's followers, some, but not all, Zaria City women began to reevaluate what was considered proper, pious Muslim comportment in their community, which included covering oneself with a *hijab*.

The Introduction of *Hijab* to Zaria City

When Izala classes for married women were introduced in Zaria City (Birnin Zazzau, the old walled section of the large town of Zaria), they were considered revolutionary by some women and men who felt that breaking the prevailing rules of seclusion would lead to immorality and dissent in the home. This situation was complicated by the implicit (and at times explicit) criticism of the two prevailing Islamic groups in northern Nigeria, the Qādiriyya and Tijāniyya orders, by Izala leader Sheikh Abubakar Gumi and his followers. While following Gumi's advice to seek Islamic knowledge to better themselves as proper Muslim wives and to better train their children, married women attending *Islamiyya Matan Aure* classes faced considerable criticism. These classes were generally held at night, initially in private houses and later in Islamic and primary schools in the area—in other words, outside family compounds. While women had been covering themselves with *gyale* cloths by that time, by wearing the more body-encompassing *hijab*, women sought to protect themselves and their respectability when entering public spaces to attend Islamiyya classes:

> When the *hijabi* was first introduced, people said a lot of bad things about it. I can give you an example [from my own experience]. I have a *hijabi* that

goes to my feet, when people saw me with it they said a lot of bad things, some will say *tazarce* [like the long robes worn by the former president Sani Abacha (Renne 2004a)], some will say *takunkunmin Gumi* [shackles of Abubakar Gumi] some will say *rakata jahannama* [it will escort her to hell], and many bad things. . . . This kind of thing happened to those who are wearing *hijabi*. (interview by the author, June 10, 2001, Zaria)

Despite the antagonism, women attending Islamiyya classes persisted in practicing what they were taught, as one married woman in Zaria City explained, "*Hijabi* is a protection a person covers her body with. Now if I am wearing a *hijabi*, you don't know the type of dress I wear. God instructs us to wear *hijabi*, is it not the Prophet who said we should wear it? If a person wears a *hijabi*, especially the one that goes down to the ground, it [provides] protection and respect that will not be with the person who wears *gyale*" (interview by the author, April 25, 2001, Zaria).

While initially wearing *hijab* allowed married Muslim women to extend their mobility by delineating what constituted a moral space outside of their homes in order to be taught by Izala teachers (Renne 2012), it was also seen as a material symbol representing Izala's critique of Qādiriyya and Tijāniyya orders, which had not widely supported women's education outside their homes. For others, it was seen as contrary to Hausa culture, as women had been using the shawl-like *zane* or *mayafi* prior to the introduction of the *hijab*; even the *gyale* veil was considered to be a modern introduction by some (interview by the author, July 22, 2001, Zaria).

These different readings of and reactions to women's wearing the *hijab* contributed to the initial conflict over the *hijab* in Zaria City. These clashes were sometimes generational, sometimes between spouses, and sometimes among women themselves:

Yes, I do wear *hijabi* because it is what Islam religion brings to us, since from the Prophet Muhammad's—*salla Allah alaihi wa sallam* [may Allah's peace and blessings be upon him]—time up till now. I started wearing *hijabi* since when I was at home; I think it is twenty years [ago] when I started. Yes, at that time there was a problem because it is not all people who were wearing the *hijabi*, even in our house. [Among] our parents, there were seven men—my father, really, the senior among them, didn't like *hijabi* at all. Some of us are teaching him, making him to understand; our brothers are telling him [it is] because . . . we are going to Islamiyya. [On account of this] we didn't wear *hijabi* until we went out because he didn't like them. (interview by the author, July 29, 2001, Zaria)

However, despite such initial confrontations, women persisted in wearing the *hijab* in public, when attending Islamiyya classes, and when praying in their houses. Indeed, as women became accustomed to wearing the *hijab*, they became less and less comfortable wearing the *gyale* head cover/shawl, and some women rejected the *gyale* altogether.

* * *

According to Hajiya Rabi Wali, women in Kano prefer to wear *gyale*, not *hijab* (interview by the author, June 16 2011, Kano; see also Lubeck 2011: 273). However, by the late 1990s, *hijab* came to be associated with a generalized Muslim identity and have become commonplace in Zaria and Kaduna. The fact that *hijab* as well as *gyale* (and *hizami*-style turbans) were brought back as *kayan* Mecca, for gifts and personal use, by pilgrims who had completed the hajj (Liman 1996), contributed to this general acceptance. Presently, *hijab* are worn as school uniforms by young girls in primary and secondary schools and, since 2002, as nursing uniforms in Ahmadu Bello University Teaching Hospital at Shika, to the northwest of Zaria. Members of the Nursing and Midwifery Council of Nigeria made this decision at the general meeting held in November 2001. They noted that Nigerian nurses were to be distinguished by uniform color and style of sewing and, additionally, "female nurses should wear either a Nurse cap or shoulder length hyjab [*sic*]" (Ndatsu 2002).[11]

Nonetheless, not all Hausa Muslim women wear *hijab*, particularly elite women who prefer to dress in modest but more stylish *gyale*. This distinction in types of head and body coverings by rank and class was clearly in evidence among participants in a family support program event conducted in Zaria City on December 12, 1997. Elite women, including the Kaduna State governor's wife, wore *gwagwaro* head ties covered with *gyale* veils, while several of the local women participants from Zaria City wore *hijab*, a reminder of the intragender variability in material expressions of religious identity and status.[12] Yet the status distinctions expressed through *gwagwaro-gyale* styles of veiling and *hijab* have been blurred by *hijab* fashions introduced by presidents' wives. There has been a long-standing precedent of presidents' wives setting fashion trends—for example, Victoria Gowon and Maryam Babangida both inspired head-tie styles that were named for them (see fig. 5.12). More recently, Turai Yar'Adua, wife of the late president Umaru Yar'Adua, began wearing a particular style of *hijab* that was likewise named for her.

Veiling Fashions in Twenty-First-Century Northern Nigeria

Initially, the long *hijab* was prescribed by Izala teachers as the most appropriate form of covering for Muslim women when going out in public. Indeed, the cloth itself was to be sufficiently thick and opaque (Abdullah 2005: 32) so that it "would not show the form of the woman's body" (Ibrahim, n.d.: 10). These *hijab* were only made in neutral or dark colors, which would not attract attention to their wearers, in what might be described as a form of unattractive antifashion (Heath 1992). Yet because of their drab plainness, some women preferred to wear the more fashionable and attractive *gyale* to certain social occasions, as one woman explained:

> If I will pray, I do wear *hijab* and [also] if I will go to school. Sometimes [I will wear it] if I am going out, but not all the time. For example, if I am going to a wedding if it is in the evening and I am feeling hot, I have a big *gyale*. I will take it and cover my body. Sometimes if you go to a wedding with *hijab*, they will look down on you [because] you should dress beautifully and put on your shoes and cover your body. You are trying to do that for that day. If you are going to relate with men, you should wear *hijab*. If it is only women and inside the house, you can cover your body with *gyale*. The *gyale* is brought from Mecca, and we are still buying it. (Interview by the author, May 1, 2001, Zaria)

However, changes in the styles of *hijab* available have enabled women to wear them to special occasions *and* be "in fashion." These new styles, referred to as fashion *hijab*, emerged in early 2008 and were said to have been initially introduced by women on hajj bringing them back from Mecca. Full-length *hijab* were made with synthetic fabric, often in floral designs such as the *flowa* print fashion *hijab* (fig. 5.13). Subsequently, some married women made shorter fashion *hijab* in lighter nylon fabrics (known as *mai roba*—referring to their stretchy, rubbery quality) in a range of patterns and colors that mark a fashion-conscious difference. While many older women prefer plainer, patternless *hijab* made with plain-weave or suedelike cotton materials, some elderly matrons may wear the patterned fashion *hijab* according to their inclination. Yet as is the case with fashion, even these geometrically and floral-patterned fashion *hijab* of 2008 were considered old-fashioned by 2009, as one middle-aged women explained: "I do wear the fashion *hijabi* but not the small one—it is long. I do it because I want to be in fashion (*ana yayinshi*). But now, if you give me the material for a fashion *hijabi*, I won't do it [for myself], I will do it for my daughter. Because I don't like it now, it's much too common" (interview by the author, June 11, 2009, Zaria). For this fashion-conscious woman, the latest *hijab* are made with solid-colored, textured, synthetic materials in two styles, which include those made with a synthetic crinkly material as well as the *gyale-hijab*, made with two flaps of fabric that are thrown across the neck (fig. 5.14).

These changing preferences in *hijab* styles reflect the shifting social and religious identities of women in Zaria, whereby wearing the *hijab* is no longer exclusively associated with a reformist Izala identity but rather with being Muslim more generally. Indeed, "it is upon these collectively, sometimes historically recurrent identity instabilities that fashion feeds," as Fred Davis (1992: 17) has

Figure 5.13. *Flowa* print fashion *hijab*, Zaria City, June 11, 2009. (Photograph by the author)

Figure 5.14. The style of *hijab* known as *gyale-hijab* is worn here by the late Rashida Muhammed, Zaria City, 2009. (Photograph by the author)

noted. The most recent styles of *hijab* worn in Zaria aptly reflect this fluidity of social identities. For women who initially rejected the *hijab* and its association with Izala, the new styles of fashion *hijab*—which, as the name *gyale-hijab* implies, are a hybrid of the *gyale* veil and *hijab*—provide the means for these women to express their identities as modest Muslim women while eschewing religious connections with Izala, reflected in its initial advocacy of drab, full-length *hijab* made with thick, heavy cloth.

By 2012, some *hijab* began to be made with extensions for the arms, which provide both mobility and modesty. One style, known as *hijab alkyabba*, referring to the *alkyabba* robe worn by royals, consists of a long *hijab* with sleeves and is decorated with silver brads (*mai silva*) at the wrists and forehead. It is also called *mai wuya* (literally, owner of the neck), referring to the cowl-like extra fabric encircling the neck (fig. 5.15). Two other recent styles of fashion *hijab* particularly popular with young, unmarried girls include the shoulder-length *hijab mai flowa*, which includes a large coquettish flower (fig. 5.16) and the "come and look" *hijab* with a revealing slit in the back.

This process of changing Islamic dress was taken a step further in the period from 2000 to 2003, when identification with the Middle East was strengthened by the buildup to the US-led invasion of Iraq and the subsequent invasion. At this time, some Muslim women in Kaduna and Zaria began wearing the *niqab*—a type of veil that covers the face, except for the eyes, which they associated with Saudi Arabia and with Middle Eastern dress more generally. One woman living in Kaduna explained why she began wearing the *niqab* and how she learned about its importance for Muslim women:

> Really, I can't remember the time I started wearing *hijabi*, because at first, if I'm going to travel outside the house, I didn't go without it. But I think I started wearing *niqab* in 1999. I started wearing it all the time in 2000. The reason why I wear *niqab*—there was a time we went out to do prayers. At one place, they said we could not go and pray without the *niqab*. We asked them why; they told us one verse in Suratul Azab in which God said to his Prophet to tell their wives and children and companions and women who believe in the Prophet [that] they should cover themselves. Because that is what is right for them. Because it will not harm them. . . .
>
> I have known about the *niqab* [for some time], but I think it started from Saudi Arabia because I used to see it on TV. I don't know who introduced the *niqab* to Nigeria because I don't have that history, but I've been seeing *niqab* worn by some Shi'a women before Izala women. But later on, the Shi'a women stopped wearing it, maybe because they wanted to distinguish themselves from Izala women. And wearing *niqab* is a great thing; that is why Izala people are the main people wearing it in Nigeria. (Interview by the author, April 2003, Kaduna; see also Renne 2013a: 99)

Figure 5.15. *Hijab mai silva* refers to silver brads on the head piece, Zaria City, May 15, 2012. (Photograph by the author)

Figure 5.16. Fashion *hijab* in the style known as *mai flowa*, Zaria City, August 29, 2012. (Photograph by the author)

Thus, while not all Muslim women in northern Nigeria wear the *niqab* with the *hijab*, those who do have internalized a similar sense of being exposed and uncovered and of being a proper Muslim woman, as was the case for those who began wearing the *hijab* in the 1970s.

Negotiating Gendered Identities, Political Rank, and Religious Reform

The previous discussion of various examples of the gendered and ranked permutations of veils and face and head coverings is reflected in the definition of the word *nade* (to roll): "*Nade*, commonly pronounced *nede*, to roll, roll together, used of twisting yarn in spinning, also to put on a turban; *ta yi nede kaman namiji*, she wore a turban like a man. *nade* also denotes to put on the royal turban, i.e., to be crowned as king" (Robinson 1913: 273–274).

The sentence given to illustrate *nade*'s usage, "she wore a turban like a man," suggests two aspects of turbaning. First, women could literally wear turbans like men when they took titled offices such as *magajiya* [woman chief of brothels], as described by Baba of Karo in an incident around 1890: "I remember when I was about ten years old, after my mother died, a prostitute was chosen to be Magajiya and she was installed in front of the Chief of Zarewa's palace; we went and watched. The prostitutes all danced in the morning, then they went to the house of Sarkin Zarewa, where he gave her a turban and appointed her Magajiya" (M. F. Smith [1954] 1981: 64).

Second, women's head coverings may be tied in ways that resemble turbans, hence a woman may wear a turbanlike head covering that, while not designating her as a chief, may indicate another sort of ranking. In another example given by Baba of Karo, for the period 1904–1907, she describes a portion of a Hausa wedding: "He comes to the door of the compound . . . , the *kawa* [bride's best friend] brings a cloth like a turban and ties it round the bride's head, then out they come for playing and drumming" (M. F. Smith [1954] 1981: 89). More recently, in the 1970s, the large women's head covering (*gwagwaro*) known as *saro* could be shaped in a particular way that looked like a turban because it was made of a stiff, synthetic textile. These turbanlike head coverings may be given names that refer to political leaders, such as *soro* Iliya, named for the way it is tied to resemble the arched ceiling (*soro*) of a Hausa home's entry room (*zaure*) and a former title holder named Iliya (fig. 5.17). Similarly, one large *gwagwaro* head tie made of printed cotton cloth (*atamfa*) was identified as *olu gwagwaro*, referring to a Yoruba king, *Olu* (interview by the author, June 25, 2009, Zaria). Thus, while women's state titles were largely abandoned during the colonial period, the ranking of women's social status continues to be expressed by turbanlike head coverings in some cases.

Figure 5.17. Studio photograph of women wearing *soro*-style head ties that resemble turbans, Zaria City, 1970s. (Courtesy of Samaila Nabara)

Conclusion

Barbara Cooper (1997: 192) notes that Hausa women in Maradi, Niger, used various strategies to retain their modest respectability while expanding their agency and alliances as Muslim women. It is unclear whether Muslim Hausa women in Zaria and in northern Nigeria, more generally, consciously used headdresses tied in ways that represented forms of cultural diplomacy to assert their continued authority, if not in traditional politics, then in the domestic sphere—as women heads of households, as grandmothers with many children and grandchildren, and as mothers-in-law. In the case of the *hijab*, this use of a material thing, which eventually came to be seen as appropriate head and body coverings by many Hausa Muslim women in northern Nigeria as symbols of religious identity and gendered status, became part of a process of negotiation of women's agency in moving outside their homes in order to acquire Islamic education. As such, the *hijab* has been both a form of accommodation and protest. By enveloping their heads and bodies (but not their faces) with dark-colored cloth, they projected a protective space in which their bodies were hidden and at the same time asserted their rights as Muslim women to move in public spaces and pursue Islamic knowledge. These rights have since expanded to include the increased attendance of Muslim women at secondary schools and universities and to work as nurses and primary school teachers.

Veils and turbans worn by men underwent a different, though not unrelated trajectory. Turbans worn by Muslim scholars, which in the past would have included many emirs, evolved in ways that reflected the increasing political authority of kings over religious scholars. In nineteenth-century Zaria, the simple robe of the emir of Zazzau, Sarkin Sambo, suggested pious simplicity and Islamic learning favored by some Hausa rulers, while his dark blue veil also suggested both social distancing and modest behavior. By the twentieth century, emirs regularly wore turbans with *amawali* face veils, which were most commonly white rather than the dan Kura *turkudi amawali* that was probably worn by Sarkin Sambo. Yet for present-day emirs in northern Nigeria, wearing a turban and veil has become more a mark of political authority and rank rather than Islamic scholarship, while sheikhs and *malamai* continue to wear turbans of varying styles. As with women who wear *hijab* and *niqab* as an expression of their Muslim piety, religious scholars wear turbans—more often, the smaller *hizami*—which serve a similar purpose.

That Hausa women's *hijab* and men's *hizami* may be associated with representations of Islamic reform, as well as with political and/or moral authority, raises the question of why, in terms of social analysis, men's and women's veiling are treated so differently. Returning to Murphy's discussion of men's veiling as a way of maintaining social distance, one might question why women's wearing of veils such as *hijab* are not conceptualized as a form of social distancing as well. (Murphy attributed Tuareg women's infrequent veiling to the fact that they held a

Figure 5.18. Emir of Kano Alhaji Muhammadu Sanusi II, participating in the traditional Sallah procession known as Hawan Daushe and when he paid a Sallah visit to his mother (Zuwa Babban Daki) in Kano. He is wearing a purple-dotted turban and fashion *amawali* made of the same material rather than all-white *harsa* or ɗan Kura cloth. His robe is made of handwoven cloth strips with leno weave patterning, Kano, July 8, 2016. (Photograph by Abdulkarim DanAsabe, courtesy of Alhaji Muhammadu Sanusi II)

subordinate position within a patrilineal social system, and hence no such marking of distance was necessary.) However, that women in Zaria City thought of *hijab* as a means of maintaining social distance was clear from their explanations of why they began to wear this sort of head/body covering—to keep men from approaching them or looking lasciviously at them in public. While one could certainly argue that their need to do so reflects their subordinate position in Hausa society, one might also argue that the social distance of veiled emirs represents, despite their enormous political power, a form of protection from their precarious and vulnerable position as leaders of political bodies, for as P. J. Dixon (1991) has noted, "uneasy lies the head." Yet their use of *amawali* veils to cover or uncover the face was also a way to indicate displeasure, reserve, or friendly openness (see fig. 5.9). Moreover, just as Muslim women have taken to wearing more decoratively patterned and styled fashion *hijab*, this tendency toward fashionable distinction may also be seen, for example, in the *amawali* veil with large purple dots worn by the emir of Kano during the Hawan Daushe procession in Kano on July 8, 2016 (fig. 5.18). Despite their different social positions, the dynamics of Muslim women and northern Nigerian emirs' wearing of veils share some common threads.

Some of the permutations of gendered identities expressed through dress can be clarified by looking at precisely how men and women in northern Nigeria wear turbans (or turbanlike head coverings) and veils (or veil-like face coverings). Indeed, individuals and groups have used head coverings and dress to complicate the symbolic representations of identities—not only when *'yan daudu* ["feminine men"] dressed as women (Gaudio 2009: 8) or when women *bori* dancers dressed as chiefs (M. F. Smith [1954] 1981)[13] but also in the more quotidian ways that head and face coverings have been used in strategic, gendered ways to reinforce moral, if not political, authority. Rather than focus exclusively on the veil and on the women who wear them, the fact both women and men may wear veils in northern Nigeria speaks to the complexity and contingencies of situations in which changing forms of religious piety and permutations of gendered social identities are assessed, negotiated, and materially expressed. The prescriptions that women cover their heads (but not faces) with veils and men uncover their heads during the state of *ihrām* when performing the hajj suggests another system of dress and gendered distinction, which is considered in chapter 6.

Notes

1. Precolonial traveler accounts include Barth 1857; Clapperton 1829; Denham, Clapperton, and Oudney 1831; Flegel (1885) 1985, 1985; Lander and Lander 1854; Staudinger (1889) 1990; and Robinson 1897. There are several colonial accounts: for example, Kisch 1910, Kumm 1910, and Niven 1982.

2. This restricted use of *amawali* veils by Hausa emirs and royalty suggests a different social dynamic from that practiced by Tuareg men, who uniformly wore a type of face veil.

3. One such women's cloth was collected at Eggan (in central Nigeria) during the Niger expedition of 1841. It was attributed to Nupe women handweavers and consisted of a "narrow, striped headcloth made of fine silk and cotton that would have been worn by the wives or concubines of prominent Muslim men" (Kriger 2006: 53).

4. For example, in her history of Islamic dress, Stillman notes that in the early Mamluk period in Egypt, "an edict was issued forbidding women to wear turbans, although this probably means male-style turbans since women had worn and continued to wear compound turban-like headdresses for centuries, all the way up to early modern times" (2000: 80). She also argues that one aspect of women's use of turbanlike headdresses was to attract men who, as part of court life, were more inclined to be attracted to other men.

5. This abundance of terms may reflect the importance of turbans in late nineteenth-century social life, although more frequent interchanges of these expatriate men with Hausa men due to conventions of seclusion and restrictions on conversations with women may have affected the extent to which terms relating to women's headcoverings were collected. In a supplement to the second edition of Bargery's Hausa-English dictionary compiled in the early 1980s, Neil Skinner added two terms associated with women's veiling, the *gyale* and *hijabi*, which had come into use during the intervening years.

6. According to Nehemia Levtzion and J. F. P. Hopkins, "the king of the town of Kawkaw is an independent ruler. . . . He has many servants and a large retinue, captains, soldiers, excellent apparel and beautiful ornaments. . . . The clothing of the common people of Kawkaw consists of skins with which they cover their nudity. Their merchants [Wangara] wear chemises (*quadawir*), mantles (*aksiya*) and woollen bands rolled around their heads (*karazi*). . . . The nobles and eminent persons among them wear waist-wrappers (*uzur*)" (cited in Candotti 2010: 189). See also Lovejoy 1978 regarding the impact of Wangara traders on the development of Hausa textile production.

7. Men who could not afford the expensive blue-black turban veils would wear ordinary blue or white cloth (Murphy 1964: 1263).

8. In the case of Tuareg society during 1959–1960 when Murphy (1964: 1264) carried out fieldwork in Niger, he noted that while women did not wear face veils as did men, they might nonetheless cover their faces with their cloths as a sign of respect and modesty particularly toward certain individuals—for example, a father-in-law. To explain why it was more important for men to maintain social distance through veiling, Murphy argues that women did not need to do so because of their lesser standing—both in terms of political leadership and kinship relations. Their position within Tuareg society reduced the possibility of social infractions and the need for the greater social distancing that veiling provided. Twenty years later, Kel Ewey Tuareg women had taken up covering their heads with head kerchiefs, which they wore in public, although Susan Rasmussen (1991: 113) argues that this shift cannot be explained either by increasingly strict Islamic observance or by conventions of modesty. Rather, Tuareg women have begun wearing headscarves during periods of social transition—from young, unmarried girls to adult, married women and from adult, married women to elderly women dependents, in which the headscarf provides a protective extension of the tent (113).

9. In these photographs from the Duckworth Collection taken at the Kano girls' school (see fig. 5.11), the girls' dress suggests their social status; the foreign photographer and camera presumably also affected their dress and presentation (see Steiner 1985). In the early 2000s,

I was told that young, unmarried girls in Zaria only wore headscarves (*dankwali*), while the large head ties (*adiko*) worn by the Kano schoolgirls in figure 5.11 were now worn only by married women (interview by the author, June 18, 2009, Zaria).

10. Judging from Skinner's vocabulary supplement in the early 1980s to the Bargery ([1934] 1993) dictionary, the important lightweight shawl-like veil, *gyale*, probably came into use during the oil boom years, when there was a surge in textiles imported into Nigeria. Skinner notes that the word *gyale* has a Yoruba derivation (from the Yoruba word *gele*, for head tie), and was adapted by Hausa speakers. It is possible that these veils were introduced by Yoruba women who came to the north during the 1970s for school and work or by Yoruba traders from southern Nigeria who brought imported textiles for sale in the north.

11. A controversy arose at Ahmadu Bello University Teaching Hospital in March 2009 when a nurse was dismissed for wearing a *hijab* that was longer than the prescribed shoulder length. The nurse, Safiya O. Ahmad, insisted that the breast-length *hijab* that she was wearing was the same as the one she wore during nurses' training (Sa'idu 2009b). Several people in the Zaria community saw her dismissal as anti-Islamic, while others argued that the hospital had accommodated Muslim women's request to wear a *hijab* as part of the nursing uniform. In April 2009, Ahmad was reinstated and allowed to wear her breast-length *hijab* (Sa'idu and Yusuf 2009).

12. This distinction in type of veils and head coverings also reflects urban-rural differences. Hauwa Mahdi (2013: 180–182) observes that rural Hausa women who farm wear *dankwali* rather than *hijab* veils. Urban women, particularly those working in public spaces, favor wearing *hijab* on religious grounds and for protection.

13. According to Rudolf Gaudio (2009: 8), *'yan daudu* are often associated with homosexuality. *Bori* dancers are members of the *bori* cult—a polytheistic Hausa religion whose followers believe in a range of spirits known as *bori*.

6 Performing Pilgrimage
Worship and Travel, Textiles and Trade

Because travel brought them, through suffering, into learning as a way of life, Muslims saw it as a figure for metamorphosis, coupled with an experience of the painful.

—Houari Touati, *Islam and Travel in the Middle Ages*

One of the most important objectives of the Hajj is for us to learn how to do without all the lawful comforts and luxuries that we are accustomed to indulging in. This is why a pilgrim wears the sparest of clothing—a waistcloth and a shoulder cloth without any decoration or embellishment.

—Salman bin Fahd al-Oadah, *Alleviating the Difficulties of the Hajj*

As the ninth-century Muslim scholar and judge Abū ʿUbayd ibn Sallām, who had traveled to Mecca, prepared to leave for Bagdad, he dreamt that he saw the Prophet "seated on a rug and surrounded by chamberlains." The next morning he decided to remain in Mecca (Touati 2010: 210). Traveling to Mecca to perform the hajj has also been a dream of many Nigerian Muslims. The pilgrimage to Mecca reflects various aspects of social life in northern Nigeria, which include piety, sacrifice, travel, trade, and just as importantly, dress, as Patricia Baker (1995) has observed. Indeed, a number of the new types of Islamic dress—styles of veils and turbans as well as *jellabiya* gowns and *alkyabba* capes—are now worn in Nigeria because of the hajj: Nigerians see other pilgrims wearing them and can easily purchase them from the many shops in Medina and Mecca.

Several themes are evident from these journeys. The first and most obvious is the exposure to new forms of knowledge and practice associated with Islam, as Houari Touati (2010: 1) suggests in the chapter epigraph. For Alhaji Jaʾafaru Musa of Hunkuyi, a town in Kaduna State, his study with an Islamic scholar in Sudan expanded his knowledge of Islam and of the work of the popular Tijāniyya sheikh Ibrahim Niass, depicted in the famous poster in Musa's house (fig. 6.1). For Alhaji Umar Falke, his study with several Tijāniyya scholars from various parts of Nigeria, which included Malam ʿAbd as-Salam (from Lokoja) and Sharif Muhammad b. Ahmad Zangina (from Kano) (Mohammed 1993: 123), expanded his knowledge of Tijani texts, promoted his place in Tijani leadership in Kano,

Figure 6.1. Alhaji Ja'afaru Musa Hunkuyi (*far left*) with family members in his home in Hunkuyi, in northern Kaduna State. He is a follower of Sheikh Ibrahim Niass and traveled on foot to Mecca in 1987. Posters of various important figures in the Tijāniyya order adorn the room's walls, Hunkuyi, March 5, 2014. (Photograph by the author)

and enabled his trade connections throughout southwestern Nigeria. For Alhaji Ahmadu Abdullahi (fig. 6.2), the *mai rumi* embroidery that he learned in Tunisia has a long history in North Africa and is associated with proper Muslim dress—which both covers the body and is beautiful to behold. Second, all three men shared with their families the new practices and knowledge that they had learned, which contributed to their families' well-being and strengthened family relations. Finally, more recent hajj practices associated with air travel have altered these journeys of practice. Learning new embroidery techniques takes time. Alhaji Abdullahi spent approximately six years from the time he left Zaria until he returned, acquiring *mai rumi* embroidery skills along the way. When his grandson performed the hajj, he went by plane, spending only two months away from Zaria. He did not return with new embroidery skills but rather with different types of textiles purchased in Mecca and Medina. He later used these materials in garments that incorporated his purchases—machine-embroidered lace and sequined velvets—with embroidered cotton damask (*shadda*) using *mai rumi* motifs. Similarly, while Alhaji Musa studied with a Tijāniyya scholar in Sudan on his way to Mecca, he was not able to continue his studies on his way back to Nigeria, as he returned by air rather than on foot. Thus, the opportunities

Figure 6.2. Abdullahi family calendar commemorating those
who have performed the hajj. Alhaji Ahmadu Abdullahi's
photograph is on the top left corner, Anguwar Limanci Kona,
Zaria City, March 22, 2013. (Photograph by the author)

for the study of new texts with Islamic scholars in North Africa as well as in
Sudan—associated with pilgrimage by road—have been reduced.

Earlier pilgrims from Nigeria journeyed on foot, carrying out the pilgrimage
over a period of months and, at times, several years (Yamba 1995). One of the
earliest pilgrims from northeastern Nigeria was "Dunama, the second Muslim
king of Kanem to adopt Islam, . . . [who] performed the hajj in the twelfth century
A.D. In his lifetime, he went on pilgrimage to Mecca three times and perished
in the Red Sea in the third attempt" (Tangban 1991: 242). One gets a sense of the
arduousness of this journey from a description by Herman K. W. Kumm, who
accompanied missionaries from the Sudan Interior Mission first to the Bight of
Benin in southern Nigeria and then north to Lokoja. He subsequently traveled
northeast through Keffi, Garoua, and Bussa to Fort Archambault (in what is now

Chad) and then on to Khartoum in northern Sudan in 1908–1909. During his travels, Kumm met up with small groups of pilgrims walking to Port Sudan, where they would take a ferry across the Red Sea to Jeddah, in Saudi Arabia:

> We passed a small Kirdi village, and later skirted a considerable swamp, going along the edge of a *fadama*, when we came up with a Hausa caravan. The leader of this caravan had three days previously asked my permission to accompany me from Fort Archambault to the Anglo-Egyptian Sudan. It consisted of some 60 people who became merged in my own following.
>
> These good pilgrims had a special claim on me [as a British citizen], as they came from our own territory of Northern Nigeria. Most of them were Kano people, one or two had their homes near Sokoto, and a few were from Kontagora and Zaria. With almost all their money gone, the provisions eaten, and only some half-a-dozen partly-starved donkeys left, they were in a pitiable state. . . . Their caravan included five old men, fifteen young men, twenty women, four or five young girls, a dozen boys and half-a-dozen infants. (1910: 147)

In this chapter, I examine three aspects of the pilgrimage travels of northern Nigerians—by road and by air—in order to consider the intersection of Islamic practice, travel, and trade as well as textiles and dress associated with the hajj experience. Pilgrimage by road, considered most efficacious in terms of *barka* (blessings), was also the most arduous, and the examples cited indicate the numerous difficulties that pilgrims faced. However, pilgrimage by road, as noted above, enabled travelers to take breaks from their journey in order to study with famous Islamic scholars and also work at a range of occupations, which included hand embroidery and farming, to buy provisions to continue their travels.[1] This section also considers the related connection between pilgrimage by road and the expansion of the reformed Tijāniyya brotherhood associated with Ibrahim Niass in northern Nigeria. The three men performing the hajj discussed in this chapter—one from Kano, one from Zaria, and one from Hunkuyi—were all adherents of the reformed Tijāniyya brotherhood. Specifically, I consider why Tijāniyya religious leaders in Nigeria—such as Malam Muhammadu Salga (Umar 2000) and Niass (Gray 1998; Mohammed 1993)—had such a strong appeal to these men.

By the mid-1950s, discussions between Premier Ahmadu Bello, British colonial officials, and government representatives in Saudi Arabia and Sudan led to more pilgrims traveling by air (Paden 1986; Tangban 1991). The second section of this chapter examines the establishment of state pilgrims welfare boards, which were initially operated by region and most recently by the National Hajj Commission of Nigeria (NAHCON), which has state branches. While the shift to air travel reduced scholarly learning and trade along pilgrimage routes, it did enable many more Muslim men and women from northern Nigeria—and from a range of Islamic groups—to perform the hajj, although various travel and

Figure 6.3. Kaduna State *hajiya* pilgrim wearing a *hijab* made from the cloth used during the 2008 hajj, Shika, Kaduna State, June 22, 2009. (Photograph by the author)

housing difficulties in Mecca remained. In northern Nigeria, the expansion of a hajj-related bureaucracy (Weber 1946) began with the formation of the Nigerian Pilgrims Mission in 1958, instituted by Prime Minister Abubakar Tafawa Balewa in consultation with Bello, who then served as the mission's chairman (Paden 1986: 286). This action began the routinization of the hajj, which included providing informational booklets, pilgrimage training camps, travel documents, and specific pilgrimage textiles, discussed in the chapter's third section. With many more people performing the hajj, each state provided pilgrims with printed cotton textiles for garments, which, along with government flags, identified them (fig. 6.3), at least when they were not in the spiritual state of *ihrām*, at which time men uniformly wore untailored white *ihrām* (Hausa, *harami*) dress and women wore loosely tailored white *jellabiya* gowns (Okenwa 2016a). After completing the final stages of the hajj, Nigerian pilgrims were free to visit the many shops at Mecca and Medina, where they not only saw but were able to buy garments, prayer rugs, and *zam zam* water (holy water). They were also exposed to pilgrims from around the world with their own styles of Islamic dress. As discussed in chapter 5, this exposure contributed to the expansion of *hijab* fashions in northern Nigeria and also introduced new styles of men's head coverings (Heathcote 1972). Some of these things from Mecca, *kayan* Mecca (literally, the load from Mecca), were brought back as gifts for family and friends as well as for personal use (Kenny 2007; van Santen 2013).[2] Adapted by craftsmen, tailors, and seamstresses in northern Nigerian cities, these garments served to link people there with the blessings of Mecca in their daily lives. Some had studio photographs taken of them wearing these garments on their return, further reinforcing this link. Today, pilgrims use smart phones and take digital photographs to document their travels and dress. Along with online hajj visa applications, airline ticketing, and communications, these digital practices are "generating new spatial and temporal orientations" (Strassler 2010: xv) and new ways of being in the world.

Pilgrimage by Land: Scholarship, Worship, and Work

There are several examples of northern Nigerian men who traveled by road to Mecca in the twentieth century, all of whom used their knowledge of embroidery, medicine, and farming—and generous contributions by hosts along the way—to support their travels. They also combined scholarship with their journey, staying for weeks, months, and even years with Islamic teachers in Sudan, Chad, Egypt, and North Africa. The stories of three such men—from Kano, Zaria, and Hunkuyi—that follow describe both the challenges and the benefits of making the journey to Mecca by road.

Alhaji Umar Falke

The first example comes from a manuscript written by Falke (1893–1962), who began his pilgrimage to Mecca in 1946. Earlier, in 1921, he had traveled from Kano to Ilorin, where his father worked and where Falke learned the robe embroidery business.[3] He amassed funds from his embroidery of *babban riga*, specializing in the pattern embroidered around the back and front of the neck opening known as *kwaɗo da linzami* (literally, frog and harness) (Mohammed 1978: 54; Heathcote 1972: 15). He also worked as a healer, which included the practice of divination (*hisab*) and the making of protective amulets (*layoyi*), folded pieces of paper with writings from the Qu'rān enclosed in leather packets (Hassan 1992; Heathcote

1974; Rubin 1984). After leaving Kano by train in 1946, he arrived in Jos, where he stayed with Alhaji Na-Mallam, who along with others contributed funds for his journey. Traveling by truck with a group of fellow pilgrims, he went through Potiskum and Damaratu (in present-day Yobe State) to Fort-Lamy (N'Djamena), Chad, then on through Sudan, entering the Darfur area at Junainah and traveling east along the road to Al-Ubayyad and El-Fashr (see Yamba 1995: xiv). Falke describes part of his journey:

> We arrived at Junainah at noon. We rented the house of a Sudanese Arab and spent two days there. On Monday we passed on. Alhaji Salih of Damagran, the Sudanese, insisted we should pay 250 pennies which is the equivalent of two and one half Egyptian pounds. This was the lorry fare to al-Ubayyad. The distance from Junainah to al-Ubayyad was a six day journey in a good and reliable car because the road was extremely rough, rugged and difficult. It was very sandy and hilly. We arrived around sunset [July 11, 1948]. We alighted there said our prayers and prepared our provisions. We broke our fast at sunset and slept.... On the 19th [day] of Ramadan [July 15, 1948] ... [we] started again for Fashr. We drove through the mountainous region near "Kura" mountain. (Mohammed 1978: 232–234)

While Falke did not trade in robes during his travels, he did put his knowledge of *hisab* divination to good use. When detained by Egyptian quarantine agents, this knowledge secured his release and that of his fellow pilgrims; he was also able to increase his funds through the practice of *hisab* for clients as he traveled (Mohammed 1978: 62). Along with his preaching and scholarship, Falke was active in the reformed Tijāniyya brotherhood associated with the leadership of Niass. Also, possibly due to living with his father in Ilorin and reinforced by his training in Lokoja with the Tijani malam 'Abd as-Salam (Mohammed 1993: 123), he learned to speak Yoruba fluently, which facilitated his teaching throughout southwestern Nigeria. As Abdullahi Mohammed has noted, "Through the life and library of Umar Falke, the depth and breadth of Islamic learning in Hausaland, and the close connections among travel, trade, and learning [may be seen]. It is in this respect that Umar Falke is 'typical,' i.e. he combined skills in Islamic learning with trade, and was part of a larger socio-economic-religious network associated with a [Tijani] Sufi brotherhood. To that extent, his life mirrors hundreds of Hausa trader-scholars" (1978: 158).

Alhaji Ahmadu Abdullahi

Unlike Falke, who was already a member of the reformed Tijāniyya brotherhood before traveling to Mecca, Ahmadu Abdullahi (see fig. 6.2), an earlier pilgrim from the Gidan Koko compound in Anguwar Limanci Kona, in Zaria City, became a member of the brotherhood only as a result of his pilgrimage journey. However, like Umar Falke, he practiced the hand embroidery of large *babban riga* before his departure. During his travels, he also learned a new embroidery technique known as *mai rumi* in Zaria. (*Rumi* refers to the type of *abawa*, loosely spun silk or rayon thread, commonly used in this embroidery work.[4]) Perhaps because he performed the hajj on foot, as was the practice in the early twentieth century, and by necessity had to earn his way as he went, Abdullahi was able to take more time to study along his way to Mecca. During his travel along the trans-Saharan trade route from Kano to North Africa, he stopped in Tunisia to study and work. It was there that he learned to embroider in the *mai rumi* style, which was used to decorate the front and necklines of garments.[5] When he returned home, he subsequently taught members of his family how to sew this type of embroidery, and they continue to specialize in making kaftans embroidered in this style to this day (fig. 6.4).

Family members associate Alhaji Abdullahi's six-year travel to Mecca and back with his introduction of *mai rumi* embroidery (Vogelsang-Eastwood 2010). According to Alhaji Abdullahi's grandson, Yakubu,

It was almost one hundred and twenty years [ago] that our grandfather came back from Saudi, [where] he went for hajj. The time our grandfather went for hajj, he walked there. On his way going, he stopped at some countries like Sudan, Morocco, and Tunisia. The main thing he brought from hajj was the *ḍinkin mai rumi* and the Islamic education he got. You know, some of the history [of his trip] we don't know because what he told our fathers, they didn't tell us much. . . . The only thing that they told us was that on his way, he learned things and that he brought the work—*ḍinkin mai rumi*. (Interview by the author, March 22, 2013, Zaria)

The *mai rumi* embroidery that Abdullahi brought back from Tunisia has a long history in Africa. This embroidery technique, a form of couched stitching also known as *passementerie*, originally came to North Africa from Turkey sometime during the period of the Ottoman Empire (fig. 6.5) (Vogelsang-Eastwood 2010). Turkish embroidery techniques influenced work in much of the Middle East and North Africa. In Morocco, this type of embroidery was used to decorate men's kaftans (particularly necklines) and women's hooded *jellibiya* (Vogelsang-Eastwood 2010: 111). Presumably, these styles of embroidered garments, very similar to a type of *mai rumi* embroidery now done in Anguwar Limanci Kona in Zaria City, were also made in Tunisia, where Abdullahi learned this work.

Presently, both men and women in the Abdullahi compound embroider kaftans, vests, and jackets with *mai rumi* patterns, although some men have begun to do machine-embroidered *mai rumi* work (known as *ḍinkin polis* or *ḍinkin kon* in reference to the brand of sewing machines that they are using). Women, however, only do certain types of hand-embroidered *rumi* stitches. For example, Umma Abdullahi does the straight stitching along

Figure 6.4. Hajiya Umma Abdullahi displaying a kaftan with *mai rumi* neck decoration, which she sewed. The *mai badji* (badges) circular decorations were sewn by men; Anguwar Limanci Kona, Zaria City, March 22, 2013. (Photograph by the author)

the necklines of kaftans, while men embroider the decorative figures (in this case, *mai badji*, see fig. 6.4). Thus, *mai rumi* embroidery reflects gender distinctions of work in Zaria City social life—men may work outside the home, using embroidery machines in the market, while women do hand embroidery within their family compounds. Nonetheless, as the Abdullahi family calendar suggests (see fig. 6.2), both men and women from this family have performed the hajj. I asked Abdullahi's grandson Yakubu about some of

Figure 6.5. Turkish soldier of the Ottoman Empire wearing a uniform with *passamenterie* embroidery on sleeves, neckline, and pants pockets. (Courtesy of the Textile Research Centre, Leiden)

the names of embroidered work that needed clarification. In the process of asking about *zabuni* (a jacket embroidered with *mai rumi* work; fig. 6.6), I also asked whether his grandfather was a member of Tijāniyya prior to leaving for Mecca; Yakubu told me he was not but "converted along the way" (interview by the author, March 13, 2016, Zaria).

Alhaji Ja'afaru Musa Hunkuyi

Alhaji Ja'afaru Musa Hunkuyi (see fig. 6.1), from the village of Hunkuyi located along the road from Zaria to Makarfi, traveled to Mecca by foot in 1987, which was unusual as most Nigerian pilgrims had begun going by plane in the early 1960s. Alhaji Musa spent almost two years in Sudan, where he worked to

Figure 6.6. Machine-embroidered *mai rumi* jacket (known as *zabuni*) made by Yakubu Abdullahi, Zaria City, July 19, 2010. (Photograph by the author)

make sufficient cash to pay for his several attempts to reach Mecca, first from Sudan, then from Libya and Egypt. While in Sudan, he studied with Sheikh Sabir, who instructed him in Islamic texts and also taught him how to properly perform the hajj. This sheikh was most likely a member of the Tijāniyya order, as was Musa himself even before leaving for Mecca. When Musa returned to Hunkuyi, he brought his new learning based on the texts that he had studied, which he passed on to his sons, who are also members of the reformed Tijāniyya brotherhood.

Alhaji Musa's journey to Mecca took him to first to Chad, where he traveled through N'Djamena, Halbashi, Atiya, and Aga'in (see Mohammed 1978: 221–234; Al-Naqar 1972: 139). On entering Sudan, he stopped in the town that he called

Aluba (al-Juba?), where he stayed with Sheikh Sabir, who gave him a room in his house for nine months. Musa read with this sheikh and also learned how to perform the hajj from him. According to Alhaji Musa, "I have the books that I got from Sudan, but I don't know where they are now. The malam would put people in groups, and each group would read one book only. If you were reading *Aziya*, the whole group would read and finish *Aziya*. When they finished, they would go to another book again" (interview by the author, March 5, 2014, Hunkuyi).

Aside from reading with Sabir, Musa also took note of his surroundings and local dress: "The dress that I bought at this place were long like *jellabiya* [long kaftan-like garments] but there were so many things that looked like our own *babban riga*, embroidered in the *malum malum* pattern. And they wore turbans, the only difference being that their turbans were bigger than our own" (interview by the author, March 5, 2014, Hunkuyi).

During this period, Musa bought some land and began farming to support himself and raise funds for his subsequent efforts to get to Mecca. After staying a year and a half in this town, he sold his farmland and traveled to Ethiopia, where he got a passport and intended to travel to Mecca:

> I was about to go but there was fighting between Eritrea and Ethiopia. . . . I was staying with one man, his name was Abdullahi. He was not Hausa, he was Ethiopian. I stayed with him for three months. Since I found that it was not easy to go to Mecca through Ethiopia, I returned to Sudan.
> I was told that if I went to Libya, I could easily get to Mecca, so I went to Libya and spent twenty-seven days there. I didn't read when I was there, I just stayed with Hausa people there [in the large Hausa community called Anguwar Dan Daura, referring to Daura in Katsina State] and earned enough to go to Mecca. When I found I couldn't go through Libya, I went to Egypt. . . . I spent thirty-one days in Masar [Cairo], I stayed with a man named Abubakar—a Nigerian—and the place where I stayed, they were all Hausa, no Arabs there. They called the place Anguwar Magwane. When I learned that I could not go to Mecca unless I stayed three years to get an Egyptian passport, I returned to Sudan. There I got one man to help me get a [Niger] passport so from Ba Sudan, I went by boat to Mecca. (Ja'afaru Musa, interview by the author, March 5, 2014, Hunkuyi)

For Musa, one of the main obstacles was obtaining a passport that would enable him to travel safely to Mecca. Since then, more recent political problems in Sudan have discouraged others from traveling to Mecca by foot despite the additional blessings (*barka*) that this hardship bestows on pilgrims.

Tijāniyya in Northern Nigeria: Zaria and Kano

Both Musa and Farke were members of the Tijāniyya brotherhood before they left for Mecca, a reflection of the connection between the emir of Kano and Niass, who first visited Kano publicly in 1945.[6] However, the history of this order in northern Nigeria, as was the case for *mai rumi* embroidery, suggests its relationship with North Africa. Tijāniyya Islam was founded by Sheikh Ahmad al-Tijani, who later established a *zawiya* (prayer group) in 1781 in Fez, Morocco (Mustapha and Bunza 2014: 61). Tijāniyya doctrine later spread to northern Nigeria through the teachings of al-Hajj 'Umar al-Futi, who first visited Sokoto in 1825 on his way to and from Mecca (Hiskett 1984: 251). While al-Hajj 'Umar traveled elsewhere in Hausaland, it was probably the later teachings of Malam Umaru Wali who attracted Tijāniyya followers in the mid-1880s in Zaria (Hiskett 1980). It is also possible and perhaps even more likely that Musa's family had joined the Tijāniyya brotherhood in the early 1920s when *zawuya* were first established in Zaria and Kano by several North African Tijani scholars (Umar 2000: 334). For example, in Zaria, one North African Tijani scholar, Malam Sayyidi Muhammad, resided in a house provided by the emir of Zaria, Aliyu Dan Sidi (see fig. 5.5), although he later moved to Lokoja (Mohammed 1993: 122). While the history of Musa's acceptance of Tijāniyya practice is unknown, his family was also influenced by the teachings of Niass, which may have affected Musa's belief and practice, particularly the sheikh's emphasis on "modelling one's life on that of Prophet Muhammad" (Clarke 1982: 207) and on "a doctrine which vindicates or justifies good fortune by making it clear that material success is a gift of God" (208). As Peter Clarke notes, "The Niass branch of the Tijāniyya, like the Muridiyya, probably attracted many people who were either alienated by the colonial system or who suffered from changes in family life brought about by urbanization and socio-economic change . . . in Kano. . . . [M]any of those who joined his branch of Tijāniyya were economically deprived . . . [yet] as [Mervyn] Hiskett points out, support for Niass's branch of Tijāniyya is not limited to the disadvantaged but includes wealthy merchants, businessmen and professionals" (1982: 208).

Certain aspects of the teachings of Umaru Wali, Sayyidi Muhammad, and Ibrahim Niass suggest why Musa decided to go to Mecca on foot rather than by plane, which was a fairly well-established practice by the late 1980s when he left Hunkuyi to perform the hajj. In the Zaria area, the Tijāniyya order attracted followers from the *talakawa* working-class population, which included craftspeople and farmers. The outlook of this group of Muslims contrasted with the *sarauta* royalty class, who supported Qādiriyya practice there. Followers of Tijani scholars and teachers saw themselves as members of the Tijāniyya brotherhood and as recipients of an "absolute guarantee of salvation" (Mohammed 1993: 117), regardless of their background or training, thus countering what Max Weber has referred to as the "status privileges" of others (1946: 288). Their working-class background also contributed to the preference of some Tijāniyya followers—either by conviction, necessity, or both—to travel to Mecca by foot. Not only was it less costly than air travel—pilgrims could work along the way—but it was also seen as the true hajj, performed "the hard way" (Polly Hill, cited in Yamba 1995: 129).

Other aspects of the Tijāniyya practice would have made it an appealing form of Islamic worship to traders and craftspeople in Zaria and Kano. For example, Ahmed Mohammed notes that for members of the Tijāniyya brotherhood, "intellectualism is not the basic criterion for deserving one's upward mobility spiritually" (1993: 117). For those unable to read or write in Arabic, English, or even Hausa, such a dispensation would be important. Furthermore, initiation through *tarbiya* (a ritual that consists of a series of questions and answers concerning the relationship of God and man) (Mohammed 1993: 131) reinforced the non-elitist character of this order. In addition, the importance of the *zawiya*, a place of group worship, for the *zhikr* ritual, which could include the use of a white *wazifa* cloth, had a performative aspect—worshipping with the physical presence of the spirit of the group's founder, Al-Tijani. This practice was particularly attractive to Muslims whose life revolved around doing things related to family and farm, travel and trade (Houtman and Meyer 2012). The resident of Zaria described the *zhikr* ritual in 1925:

> With reference to your Confidential Memorandum No. C. 368/94 of the 9th inst. I have enquired further into the significance of the "white sheet" which is spread out during the Tijani séances. . . . It was explained to me that after the "Mainyan [Manya] Masu-Yi," i.e., the actual participants, as apart from the spectators and audience, had walked round the sheet a number of times—the number varying with the number of spectators—the Prophet is supposed to be present in spirit on the sheet to listen to their prayers. I am told it is not a symbol of the Mahdi who will arise. (E. H. D. L. 1925)

Hiskett, in his discussion of the continuing practice of *zhikr*, suggests a variation on this explanation: by "spreading a white cloth on the floor of the mosque, around which the Tijanis sit to perform *dhikr* [Remembrance]," they do so "because they believe that the founder, Ahmad al-Tijani, or sometimes the *Gwawth* [reformer] of the day, is present at the *dhikr* in spirit; and the white cloth for him to sit on symbolizes his presence" (1980: 131).[7] Indeed, in Zaria, Tijāniyya members continue to use white *wazifa* cloth in this way in *zhikr* sessions during Friday mosque. Preferably, the cloths themselves come from Mecca, although they may also be obtained from Senegal in association with the *ziwaya* of Niass at Medina-Kaolack or from the shrine of the sect's founder, al-Tijani at Fez, Morocco. Alternatively, the *wazifa* cloth may be white cloth obtained in local markets; there is no stipulation that the cloth be made of handwoven cloth strips (Yakubu Abdullahi, interview by the author, March 13, 2016, Zaria).

Aside from the importance of the promise of salvation associated with Tijāniyya recitation of *salat al-fatih* prayers (Mohammed 1993: 117) and the practice of *zhikr*, the Tijāniyya order was also attractive to wealthy merchants who combined religious travels with trade. As Mohammed (1978: 123) notes, Tijāniyya scholarship in Lokoja attracted students from many parts of Nigeria, which contributed to ethnic collaboration as was the experience of Umar Farke, who later went on to teach and trade in Lagos. Finally, Tijani recognition of the acquisition of wealth as a blessing from Allah reinforced the work of wealthy traders. Furthermore, by performing the hajj, trader-scholars such as Farke met potential partners, leading "to the kind of confidence and trust necessary for business partnerships" particularly important for those associated with long-distance trade (Mohammed 1978: 63).

Indeed, on his return from Mecca in the late 1940s, Farke sought to improve the practice of the hajj by going into partnership with Alhaji Baba Dan-Bappa and Alhaji Mahmud Dantata, both wealthy Kano businessmen. Dantata was serving at the time as the managing director of the West African Pilgrims' Association (Mohammed 1978: 63), which had been established to facilitate Kano pilgrims' travels to Mecca. This organization was subsequently superseded by the Nigerian Pilgrims Mission, which was established in 1958 by the prime minister of Nigeria, Alhaji Abubakar Tafawa Balewa, based on a report received from the delegation headed by Premier Bello.

Pilgrimage by Air: Routinization of the Hajj

Beginning in 1955, Ahmadu Bello annually performed the hajj—flying from Kano to Jeddah—until his death in 1966. He played a significant role in expanding northern Nigerians' participation in the hajj through his efforts to expand Nigerian Muslims' participation in global Islam. In 1955, he traveled to Saudi Arabia under the sponsorship of the Northern Nigeria Regional Government to assess the situation for Nigeria pilgrims there (Tangban 1991: 242).

In February 1958, he traveled with the emir of Kano and Alhaji Adegbenro to Khartoum and Jeddah to meet with political leaders to discuss ways of improving Nigerians' performance of the hajj. In subsequent correspondence to Bello, Balewa commented on the group's report and their suggestions for improving relations with Saudi authorities to facilitate Nigerians' hajj experiences:

> I was very glad to receive the eagerly awaited Report on your Mission to the Sudan and Saudi Arabia.
> The uncertainty that has marked the arrangements for the pilgrimage this year has been dispelled by your work in both countries. We can now proceed with confidence to organize the necessary arrangements in the knowledge that our plans are based on fact and no longer as before on a series of rather conflicting reports. You have established the basis of cordial relations between these two countries which will benefit us in many ways not only in those connected with pilgrimage matters.
> I am studying your recommendations carefully and have given instructions that those requiring urgent attention should be examined forthwith.

Figure 6.7. Pilgrims boarding the first Nigerian flight to Mecca from Maiduguri. (Photograph by Hamo Sassoon, courtesy of Bodleian Libraries, Oxford)

I am particularly anxious about the question of the payment of Mutawif fees [paid to hajj guides in Saudi Arabia] and hope that we shall arrive at a suitable arrangement, acceptable to all concerned, in a very short time.

The decision to send a delegation to these two countries, with yourself as head, has therefore been fully justified by the results that were achieved. On behalf of the Federal Government, I send you, the Emir of Kano and Alhaji Adegbenro, my deep appreciation for all you have done.

I gladly accept your suggestion that the Federal Government thanks the two Governments for all the help they gave to your Mission. (Balewa 1958)

Later in 1958, Balewa set up the Nigerian Pilgrims Mission "to negotiate many of the pilgrimage arrangements in Sudan and Saudi Arabia as well as the status of large numbers of Nigerians who settled in those countries" (Tangban 1991: 243). Aside from payments to *mutawwifs* (hajj guides), one sticking point between Sudanese and Saudi officials was the issue of the many undocumented Nigerian pilgrims, known as *tikaris*,[8] who had overstayed the hajj period and were working in Mecca, Medina, and Jeddah (Liman 1996: 39; Peters 1994: 96).

The idea of using travel certificates in lieu of passports was broached as Saudi officials sought to establish tighter controls over hajj pilgrims from West Africa (Paden 1986: 288–289). With the passage of the Nigeria Travel Agencies Control Law of 1958, the Northern Region Travel Agency Licensing Board was established, which was responsible for "issuing licenses to pilgrim agents and their sub-agents" to facilitate hajj travel (Tangban 1991: 244).

The efforts of Ahmadu Bello and Tafawa Balewa to regularize the annual performance of the hajj exemplify the complicated connections between what are considered to be religious tradition and government practice, connections that are reflected in the relationship between the hajj, air travel, and the proliferation of *kayan* Mecca. While the performance of hajj has a long history in West Africa as one of the five obligations of Muslims who are able, very few could fulfill this requirement until the advent of air travel (fig. 6.7). This development enabled Usman Liman to fulfill his dream of going to Mecca: "By Hajj season of that year in 1987, the idea had finally taken root in my mind that I wanted to go to Mecca at the earliest opportunity" (1996: 1). In other words, modernity facilitated the perpetuation and fulfillment of a traditional ideal.[9] Consequently, a succession of government agencies, each utilizing expanded bureaucratic measures, have been established over the years to handle the increasing numbers of Nigerian pilgrims.

Nigerian Hajj Organization

Following the formation of the Northern Region Travel Agency Licensing Board in the late 1950s, the Nigerian National Pilgrims Welfare Board was instituted, with regional offices in Kano, Sokoto, Kaduna, Ilorin, and Maiduguri, in 1975 (Tangban 1991: 247). More and more Nigerians sought to perform the hajj in the 1970s—from 28,000 in 1971 to 78,043 in 1980 (Tangban 1991: 248), and the Pilgrims Welfare Board was replaced by the Nigerian Pilgrims Commission in 1990. The act (Cap. 321, L.F.N. 1990) that authorized this commission was subsequently repealed in 2006, when the National Hajj Commission of Nigeria (NAHCON) was established.

Beginning in the mid-1960s, intending pilgrims followed a series of steps before traveling to Mecca. They first obtained medical and vaccination certificates, after which they met with approved hajj agents (or their sub-agents) to pay and receive receipts for their transport costs (by road or air). After these documents were obtained, pilgrims were given passports and visas for their travel. When traveling by air, they were expected to come to Kano airport a few days before the flights were to depart, where they stayed in a transit camp located at the airport grounds (Tangban 1991: 246). There they received printed materials and further instruction in hajj procedures.

Pilgrims' dress, distinctively prescribed for men and women, was one of the topics covered in this orientation. During the period of *ihrām*, male pilgrims were not allowed to wear sewn garments but rather changed into the two-piece waist and shoulder cloths known as *ihrām* (*harami* in Hausa) dress, along with open sandals (Okenwa 2016a). According to the author of a Saudi-produced booklet, *Alleviating the Difficulties of the Hajj*, which was distributed to Nigerian

Figure 6.8. Alhaji Yusuf Abdullahi at Mount Arafat, east of Mecca, wearing *ihrām* (*harami*) dress, with tents in the background, 1966. (Courtesy of Yusuf Abdullahi, Kaduna)

pilgrims: "The basis for the prohibition of wearing of sewn articles of clothing is the hadîth where a man asked the Prophet (peace be upon him) what a pilgrim must wear in the state of ihrām, to which he replied: 'He should not wear a shirt, nor a turban, nor pants, nor a cloak. He should not wear cloth that has been dyed with *wors* or saffron'" (al-Oadah 2006: 35).

Indeed, for many men pilgrims, the removal of tailored, sewn clothing and the donning of white *ihrām* dress was "what truly meant hajj for us" (Hammoudi 2006). And even while the white *ihrām* cloth might be made with several different types of textiles (except silk), in various states of repair, its association with one's presence in Mecca among Muslims from all over the world dressed in the same simple way was a moving experience for many (fig. 6.8).

There are no such specific prescriptions for women pilgrims' dress, except that they should cover their heads and bodies, without a veil touching their face. As Dr. Saleh Okenwa (2016a) notes in his essay, "Practical Steps in Performing the Hajj Rites," published on the NAHCON website, "A woman can wear whatever she likes as long as it does not display her adornments or resemble men's clothing." In Kano in the 1980s, as part of Aminu d-Din Abubakar's efforts to improve Muslim women's education and to foster Islamiyya education for married women, he organized training programs for women preparing to

Figure 6.9. Beginning in the early 1980s, Kano women participated in hajj training classes. An imitation of the Ka'aba is behind them on the right. (Courtesy of Hajiya Rabi Wali)

perform the hajj. This training even included practice walks (*tawaf*) around a model of the Ka'aba (fig. 6.9). Information available from NAHCON and other websites advises women on how to properly perform the hajj and what to wear while at Mecca. For example, in the article "Common Mistakes Women Make during Hajj or Umrah" (Shameem 2011), questions about appropriate dress are addressed. Women pilgrims from northern Nigeria dress modestly, wearing white garments, often *abaya* and veils, which do not cover their faces.

Once pilgrims are no longer in the state of *ihrām*, they may wear tailored clothing, which includes outfits that are sewn from printed cotton cloth (*atamfa*) given to them by their state Pilgrims Welfare Board (see fig. 6.3). These outfits represent another aspect of the regularization of hajj procedures for pilgrims as well as the organization of the increasing numbers of Nigerians traveling to Mecca. According to the current Kaduna State Pilgrim Welfare Board overseer, Alhaji Habib Umar Mahmud, earlier *atamfa hajji* (printed hajj) cloths were produced by some of the textile mills in Kaduna, such as Arewa Textiles, Finetex, and United Nigerian Textiles Limited (interview by the author, March 7, 2016, Kaduna). Since the closure or reduced productivity of these mills by 2010, the board has ordered these cloths from African Textile Manufacturers Ltd. in Kano. While the date printed on the cloth and colors differ, the main patterning is essentially the same, which helps Nigerian pilgrims to find each other among the many other pilgrims performing the hajj.

These distinctive uses of cloth by pilgrims during the performance of the hajj are paralleled by the specific uses of textiles in clothing the Ka'aba, as this practice is sometimes called: "The textiles of the Ka'ba comprise a number of different elements, including an overall covering (*kiswa*) and a belt (*hizam*) placed at about two-thirds of the height of the wall of the Ka'ba. Over the door is a curtain (*sitara* or *burqu'*). Inside the Ka'ba are other textiles: a curtain to the door leading to the roof known as Bab al-Tawba, and red and green textiles with chevron designs on the inside walls. Within the sanctuary, the Maqam Ibrahim was also covered with a textile" (Porter 2012: 257).

The *kiswa*, the famous black silk cloth hand-embroidered with verses from the Qur'ān in gold and silver thread (Baker 1995: 18–19), refers to the Arabic word for "robe," thus reinforcing the idea of clothing this most sacred shrine. Indeed, Venetia Porter notes that "the tradition of covering the Ka'ba with textiles has pre-Islamic origins, part of an ancient tradition of veiling sacred places out of respect" (2012: 257). Because of its close association with the Ka'aba, the *kiswa* cloth used during the period of hajj, which will be replaced in the following year, is afterward cut into pieces that are distributed to important religious and political pilgrims. Ahmadu Bello, who received a piece of the *kiswa* after his 1958 pilgrimage, observed that it was "a great honour" to be given this most precious example of *kayan* Mecca (Paden 1986: 295).

Kayan Mecca

If one aspect of the hajj experience is the profound spiritual rebirth through participation in the circling of the Ka'aba at Mecca and attendance at the Prophet's mosque at Medina, another is the desire to purchase things from Mecca. *Kayan* Mecca—things from Mecca—not only serve as gifts for family and friends but also represent mementos that will remind pilgrims of their performance of the hajj once they are back home. This need is satisfied by the numerous shopping opportunities at extensive markets and air-conditioned malls surrounding the holy areas of these cities. While many pilgrims partake of this sort of travel tourism, several recent pilgrims have noted the alternating spiritual and commercial aspects of the hajj experience, some with considerable consternation (Hammoudi 2006; Liman 1996).

Stocked with many items, from clothing to jewelry to prayer mats, shops offer a range of hajj souvenirs, from inexpensive headscarves to costly watches. Thus, there are myriad material ways of documenting one's presence in Mecca and Medina—namely by purchases that may be given as gifts or kept for one's own personal use. While small bottles of *zam zam* holy water, prayer beads (*carbi*), and *hijab* are the most frequently given gifts—both because they refer to the religious basis of the hajj and they are inexpensive—more costly things

Figure 6.10. Young boys wearing *kambu* head ropes (*'aqal*) given to them as gifts from a family member who had recently performed the hajj. (Courtesy of Aishatu Yusuf)

such as fine robes and gold jewelry are also for sale. As Kenny (2007) notes in her discussion of gift giving associated with pilgrimage, performing the hajj incurs social obligations to those who remain at home. Pilgrims must make careful calculations of appropriate gifts to be given to senior and junior relations, as well as to work mates and friends, if they are to be respected as a proper *alhaji* or *hajiya*. These gifts from Mecca can be quite meaningful to recipients, as Kenny learned from a Guinean woman: "A woman explained the significance of her prized white scarf from Mecca to me: These gifts are very special because they come from the holy place. This is the place you're supposed to go if you are able according to the ideas of the religion. It doesn't mean you'll go to heaven! It is the holy place, chosen by God, where all sins are forgiven" (2007: 372).

Gifts of clothing are also distributed to family and friends in Zaria. Similarly, *zam zam* water from Mecca (Porter 2012: 246) and a special sand from Medina known as *d'ebimu* are highly prized gifts because they are believed to have special healing properties. One woman I spoke with who participated in the 2010 hajj had purchased bracelets, seven *abaya* gowns, *zam zam* water, and *d'ebimu* sand for gifts. Another woman from Zaria who traveled to Mecca in 2004 brought back several types of Islamic dresses for herself and for family members. For herself, she bought a floral-patterned white and blue *abaya* with a large stole that she wears when praying as well as a light-blue satin brocade *abaya* with metallic machine embroidery around the neck, cuffs, hems, and center seam. She also bought several Indonesian-style *hijab* (or *jilbab*, as they are known in Indonesia), which she distributed to women relatives, keeping one for herself. By wearing these foreign styles, the women situate themselves beyond what may seem to them as local

Figure 6.11. Alhaji Samaila Nabara at Mecca wearing a *keffiyeh* headdress provided by a professional photographer, 2008. (Courtesy of Samaila Nabara)

and parochial, outdated Islamic practices and within the larger Islamic world. Wearing new styles of veils obtained while on hajj reinforces this sense of being in step with current Islamic belief and behavior. Of equal importance, however, is the fact that these garments have come from Mecca, hence the use of these garments for prayer, which imbues them with the spirituality and blessings associated with having performed the hajj. Thus, these things from Mecca both reinforce relationships among family members and suggest a continuing physical connection between pilgrims who have returned to Nigeria and Mecca (fig. 6.10).

Hajj Photographs

Just as more people have gone to Mecca to perform the hajj as a result of improved techniques of travel, new forms of photographic techniques have led to a range of possibilities for photographs commemorating people's pilgrimage to Mecca. As was popular practice for studio photographs taken in the 1970s and 1980s, some photographers provided dress props for pilgrims wanting to further authenticate their hajj experience. Thus, one man who went on hajj in 2008 had several pictures taken of himself and fellow pilgrims by a commercial photographer who also provided the *keffiyeh* used in one photograph (fig. 6.11). Abdullah Hammoudi (2006: 209) mentions seeing photographers providing camels for pilgrims' photographs. Another way of documenting this connection is through studio photographs that pilgrims had taken when they returned from Mecca, depicting themselves wearing some of the things they obtained while on hajj (fig. 6.12). More recently, pilgrims use their smart phones to keep images of their pilgrimage at hand (Renne 2015: 18).

Figure 6.12. Studio photograph of Alhaji Yusuf Abdullahi and his parents on their return from Mecca. His mother is dressed in brocade fabric and wears a necklace, both purchased there. His father wears garments and a turban from Mecca while holding a book with a print of the Black Stone of Mecca on the cover. The phrase written at the top represents a transcription of the Arabic phrase that means "Glory to God Who Does Not Die." Photograph dated November 5, 1966, taken in Kaduna, Nigeria. (Courtesy of Yusuf Abdullahi)

One should note, however, that the purchases portrayed in these photographs and listed by Zaria pilgrims above are small compared with those of some pilgrims after completing the *hajj*, as described by Usman Liman at the conclusion of his pilgrimage in 1991: "The first thing that struck me was the amount of luggage. Luggage of all shapes and sizes could be seen. There were some that looked like mini-containers meant for shipment. A meandering queue of the luggage stretched for several hundred metres" (1996: 77). The hajj presents pilgrims with many experiences—of religious solemnity, austerity, and honesty; of a sense of unity with fellow Muslims; of the excitement of travel and of living outside of the bounds of one's quotidian life as well as the pleasures of purchases and consumption associated with tourism. Indeed, the sacred practices associated with performing the hajj, which are framed by the profane practices of commercial consumption, mirrors the idea of Mecca as being both the place on earth closest to paradise, the ultimate home of Muslims, and being, nonetheless, materially grounded in this transient and everyday world.

Conclusion

In describing their experience of the hajj, people often noted both spiritual and mundane aspects of their travel to Mecca. Several people remarked on the emotion that the closeness to the Ka'aba evoked, reminding them of the Prophet Muhammad's presence there and of all the people who have followed in his path. Others remembered the difficulties finding pilgrims from their area and the long wait in Jeddah before their flight departed for Nigeria. Yet these challenges pale in comparison with those associated with earlier forms of pilgrimage to Mecca, some of which are described earlier in this chapter. Indeed, these distinctive forms of travel have parallels with other aspects of hajj performance and textile use—the different configurations of piety, travel, and textiles relating to the hajj suggest the ways that they have changed over time.

For example, travel by foot enabled interactions with Islamic scholars, which encouraged some, such as Abdullahi from Zaria City, to join the Tijāniyya brotherhood. It also supported handwork—for example, embroidery or farming—which made the trip financially and officially feasible. While official written travel documents were useful, they were not mandatory. Alhaji Umar Falke, who traveled by road to Mecca in 1948, was incensed by colonial officials' and customs officers' insistence on such documentation as he viewed hajj travel as a religious endeavor that superseded other, more mundane bureaucratic aspects of pilgrimage travel (Mohammed 1978: 145). Yet travel by road or sea began a process whereby customs and immigration officials as well as travel agents became increasingly involved in processing pilgrims' travel documentation, bookings, and physical needs. Writing and associated technologies of printing—travel brochures, typewritten documents, and health cards—contributed to the development of a formal application to the Nigerian government, which negotiated the number of pilgrims allowed by the Saudi government in any given year. This dynamic intensified with the increased numbers of northern Nigerian Muslims who sought to perform the hajj and was reflected in the succession of hajj-related government agencies that were established to handle pilgrimage requests. The most recent agency, the National Hajj Commission of Nigeria, represents the current technologies associated with performance of the hajj, which includes an instructive website that provides digital information on the performance of the hajj (e.g., "Tips on the Performance of Umrah (Lesser Hajj)," by Saleh Okenwa [2016a, 2016b]). The Pilgrims' Registration Form is also available on this site, which includes sections on pilgrims' state affiliation and passport information, financial support, health records, and if the pilgrim is a woman (*mahram*), the name of a guardian who will travel with her. Once this document is completed, signed, and submitted, the information is entered into computers after which a printed receipt will be issued. Yet even with modern technologies, expanded oversight, and improved accommodation, the challenges of maintaining the well-being of pilgrims in Mecca and Medina persist.[10]

A similar pattern of technological development, travel, and textiles may be seen in the establishment of industrial production in Kaduna and Kano. Indeed, Falke was a founding member of the Kano Citizens' Trading Company, one of the first textile manufacturers in Kano. It was established in 1949 (DanAsabe 2000: 56), shortly after Falke returned from Mecca. While this particular textile mill as well as others that began production in the 1960s were ultimately short-lived, the presence of industrial textile manufacturing in northern Nigeria represents a particular technological regime. Related to ideals of industrialization, education, and urban uplift more generally, these goals were also reflected in the emergence of new Islamic reform groups, which were related to increasing connections with Mecca through the performance of the hajj, with Saudi Arabia through support for the establishment of Jama'atu Nasril Islam (Association for the Support of Islam), and with the wider Muslim world. The connections between Islamic reform and textile production in Kaduna are considered in chapter 7.

Notes

1. C. Bawa Yamba notes that because "in Sudan, Hausa pilgrims prize the caps and embroideries from Hausaland above all else . . . some of the landlords of the pilgrim-immigrant establishments count the importation [and sale] of embroidered cloths from Hausaland among their economic activities" (1995: 141).

2. Erin Kenny (2007) discusses how some pilgrims used the pilgrimage as a means of trade.

3. "Throughout his life he combined his scholarly interests with long-distance trading (hence his byname Falke—*falke* or *farke* means travelling trader in Hausa; Newman 2007: 58) that took him to Lagos and Takoradi [Ghana]" (Hunwick and O'Faley 2016).

4. *Rumi* is defined as "a collection of silk [or rayon] thread of assorted colours" (Bargery [1934] 1993: 867), while *abawa* is "loosely spun cotton thread used in embroidery and also in the weft of weaving" (2).

5. David Heathcote refers to garments embroidered in this style as "'Mecca' type garments [that] reflect arabesque and plant shapes common to Islamic decorative art in North Africa and the Middle East" (1972: 19).

6. Roman Loimeier notes that Niass visited Kano privately in 1944 at the invitation of Emir Abdullahi Bayero and publicly the following year, when Niass met with the emir and selected Tijani scholars. The first large public appearance of Niass in Kano took place in 1951, when "thousands of followers of the Tijâniyya from all over Northern Nigeria had come to Kano to meet him" (1997: 40).

7. Hiskett continues: "Or others say that Shaykh Ahmad al-Tijani used to place a white cloth on the ground in front of him while praying, in order that people should not pass in front of him and distract his attention. They have continued this practice out of respect for him. Yet others maintain that the Prophet himself is present at their *dkhirs/zikiris* and that the white cloth is for his use" (1980: 131).

8. E. E. Peters cites eighteenth-century explorer John Lewis Burckhardt's discussion of African pilgrims in Sudan, whom he refers to as Takruri (singular) and Takayrna (plural), noting that the singular name was believed to have derived from a country called Takrur. However, "the singular of this name is not derived from a country . . . , but from the verb *takurrar*, to multiply, renew, to sift, to purify, to invigorate, i.e. their religious sentiments, by the study of the sacred book, and by pilgrimage" (1994: 96). Nonetheless, the word *tikari* has come to have a pejorative cast.

9. Some, however, such as Shehu dan Fodio's son Muhammad Bello, questioned the basis of the pilgrimage during times of military threat and social insecurity (Al-Naqar 1972: 55–61).

10. Two disastrous incidents occurred during the 2015 Hajj. The first concerned the collapse of a large construction crane on September 11, 2015, which killed many pilgrims praying in the vicinity of the Ka'aba (Muhammad 2015). Thirteen days later, on September 24, there was an inadvertent stampede during the performance of Jamarat (symbolic stoning of the devil) in Mina by panicked pilgrims, which led to the death of 309 Nigerians. As of November 2015, forty-seven Nigerian pilgrims officially remained missing (Jimoh 2015c).

7 Marks of Progress

Islamic Reform and Industrial Textile Production in Kaduna

> Until the completion of the school, Gumi made his garage at his house in Kaduna available for the teaching of the first classes, whereas the Pakistani businessman Yusuf Gardee [majority owner of the Northern Nigerian Textiles Mill] donated 12,000 copies of the Qur'ān.
>
> —Roman Loimeier, *Islamic Reform and Political Change in Northern Nigeria*

IN HIS MEMOIR, *Where I Stand*, Sheikh Abubakar Gumi recounted his consternation during the 1962 hajj after seeing some Nigerian pilgrims beating the *jamra* (the image of Satan) with their shoes rather than throwing small stones as prescribed (Gumi 1992: 104; see also Loimeier 1997: 136). On consulting with the then premier of the Northern Region, Ahmadu Bello, whom he had accompanied on hajj, they determined to improve Islamic education in northern Nigeria. Upon returning to Kaduna later that year, they brought together northern Nigerian Islamic leaders to discuss the establishment of a new organization, Jama'atu Nasril Islam (JNI), to foster Islamic unity in the north as well as to provide resources for the building of new mosques and schools to improve Islamic education in the region. In Kaduna, Gumi began classes in the garage of his house, with teachers initially paid by Bello and Gumi (Gumi 1992: 105). Through support from local businessmen and their connections with Saudi and Kuwaiti donors, JNI subsequently was able to sponsor the building of numerous schools and mosques, as well as the building of its headquarters in Kaduna.[1]

While Ahmadu Bello was deeply concerned with spiritual development, he was also interested in the material development of the north (Paden 1986: 529). In the 1960s, the growth of Kaduna as a center of Islamic learning was paralleled by its growth as a center of textile manufacturing in northern Nigeria, which was largely due to his efforts. Beginning in the mid-1950s, Bello worked with officials from the British textile manufacturing firm David Whitehead and Sons Ltd. to establish the first modern textile mill in Kaduna, which opened in November 1957 (Maiwada and Renne 2013). Kaduna Textiles Limited (KTL) began production of

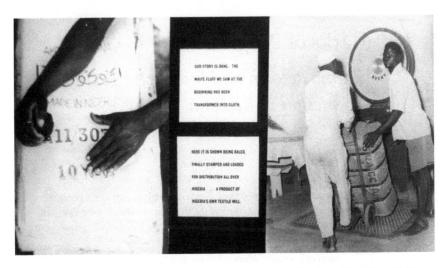

Figure 7.1. KTL cotton baft (*akoko*) shipments displayed in the "Made in Nigeria" exhibition, Kaduna, May 1959. (Courtesy of David Whitehead and Sons Ltd. Archives, Parbold, Lancashire)

plain cotton cloth (baft; *akoko* in Hausa; fig. 7.1) for which there was great demand in northern Nigeria, and which could be manufactured with locally grown cotton. Bello's interest in strengthening northern Nigeria's economic position underwrote his concerns with textile industrialization, which had been resisted by government officials during British colonial rule. This position coincided with colonial policy to increase exports of Nigerian cotton to Great Britain in order to supply the Manchester textile manufacturing industry.[2] Referred to as "cotton imperialism" (Johnson 1974), this program was ultimately unsuccessful, and cotton production was later directed toward the Nigerian textile industry.[3] During the period beginning in 1955 and ending with his death in January 1966, Bello was involved in encouraging cotton production and the establishment of six textile-related mills in Kaduna.

The development of the textile industry had several consequences for the practice of Islam in Kaduna and elsewhere in northern Nigeria. Work opportunities in the mills drew people from rural areas throughout the Northern Region to Kaduna. Before 1913, when Kaduna was selected to be the capital of northern Nigeria by Frederick Lugard, the governor-general of Nigeria (1914–1919), it consisted of rural savannah that was home to the Gbagyi people (Paden 1986: 318). By 1950, it had grown to be an administrative center with an approximate population of 52,000; in 1965, its population was estimated to be around 150,000 (Paden 1986: 579). Rex Niven, the resident of Jos and, at times, acting lieutenant-governor of Kaduna, described this postwar transformation in relation to textile production:

"After the war Kaduna changed dramatically, from a small country capital to a bustling city. An industrial area was opened to the south of the Junction station. The first to arrive was the textile factory, covering six acres. This was the beginning of a Government enterprise aimed at making as much of local produce as possible; Nigeria grew plenty of good cotton; why send it to Lancashire [UK] to be made into cloth for subsequent reimportation?" (1982: 233).

In Kaduna, new urban social relations associated with textile manufacturing contributed to an expansion of Islamic schools and hajj-related education. Furthermore, the introduction of industrial textile manufacturing supported the expansion of both Western and Islamic higher education with the establishment of Departments of Industrial Design, Textile Technology, and Islamic Studies at Ahmadu Bello University as well as the Department of Textile Technology at Kaduna Polytechnic.[4] Finally, as more cloth became locally available, more options for styles of Islamic dress—particularly veils but also for *ihrām* dress worn during the hajj (see chapter 6)—became possible. Also, quantities of dyed and printed cloth were distributed during Muslim religious holidays as well as during Bello's conversion tours in northern Nigeria (Abba 1981). As Shirley Lindenbaum has noted regarding periods of transition from colonial to national rule elsewhere, "Cloth was the visual representation of a grammar of politics in which actors invented and improvised in response to a vast rearrangement of power relations" (quoted in Schneider and Weiner 1986: 181).

However, these parallel developments of textile manufacturing and Islamic education shifted as different sets of power relations reasserted themselves after the military coup and assassination of Ahmadu Bello in 1966. Disunity among various Islamic groups led "each in his own way [to try to] instrumentalize the JNI for his own religious and political aims" (Loimeier 1997: 145). This situation was reflected in a related inclination for dress or uses of cloth that would distinguish members of these different groups. Thus, in Kano and other northern Nigerian cities where the reformed Qādiriyya-Nasiriyya was established, uniforms, "often of modern para-military design" (fig. 7.2) (Mustapha and Bunza 2014: 60), were sewn for leaders and important members participating in the Maulidin Abdulkadir [celebration for the birthday of the Prophet]. In Kaduna and Zaria, followers of the reformed Tijāniyya group under the leadership of Sheikh Ibrahim Niass used the white *wasika* cloth when performing *dhikr* [Remembrance] (Hiskett 1980: 131; see chapter 6). The range of Nigerian-manufactured plain, dyed, and printed cotton fabrics, which were inexpensive and easily obtainable, facilitated the emergence of these different dress styles and religious practices.

In addition to these reformed *tariqa* groups, the Islamic reform movement Izala was established in Jos on February 8, 1978.[5] Sheikh Isma'ila Idris, with Gumi's support, sought to counter the practices of the Qādiriyya and Tijāniyya brotherhoods, some of which they viewed as "bid'a [innovations] which are not

Figure 7.2. Members of the reformed Qādiriyya-Nasiriyya group wear paramilitary-style uniforms—white trousers and jackets with black belt and narrow shoulder-to-waist sash—in all their festivities, such as the weekly *zhikr* remembrance ritual shown here at Qādiriyya House, Kano. (Photograph courtesy of Abdulkarim DanAsabe)

in concordance with the Sunna of the Prophet" (Loimeier 1997: 229, see also 142–148; see also Kane 2002: 85–87; Umar 1993). Gumi was viewed as the spiritual leader of this movement in Kaduna, where it became known for its Islamiyya schools and its support of women's Islamic education. Because of its importance, Gumi argued that "as long as a man's wife covers her body properly, well, there's no problem" with her leaving her home to attend Islamiyya classes (Christelow 1987: 233). In order to cover their bodies properly, married women attending Izala Islamiyya classes began to wear the *hijab*; the growth of textile manufacturing in Kaduna facilitated the availability of inexpensive colored and printed cotton fabrics that seamstresses could then sew into different styles of *hijab*. This connection between religion and textile manufacturing, exemplified by women wearing *hijab* while pursuing Islamic education, was reinforced indirectly by the Pakistani businessman Yusuf Gardee, who was both a majority shareholder in Northern Nigerian Textiles Mill Ltd. (NNTM) of Kaduna (Maiwada and Renne 2013: 178) and an active participant in the JNI, as will be discussed.

Along with attending Islamiyya classes for Islamic education, women intending to perform the pilgrimage to Mecca were encouraged to take classes that taught them basic Muslim prayers and proper practices of Muslim pilgrims. For the performance of the hajj, women were expected to veil. Furthermore, members of different state hajj contingents were given six to ten yards of cloth (*atamfa hajji*) specifically printed for each hajj year (see fig. 6.3). This cloth was produced in Kaduna textile mills for the Kaduna State Muslim Pilgrim Welfare Board. Thus, distinctive Islamic identities associated with wearing particular types of cloth and dress expanded, just as Islamic education, the performance of the hajj, and textile manufacturing in Kaduna grew after Nigerian independence in 1960. This chapter examines how this interlinked expansion of Islamic reforms, which include women's education and training in the performance of the hajj, and textile manufacturing (of a range of branded cloths) relate to the growth of and later rifts within the Izala movement. In Kaduna (and to some extent in nearby Zaria), these developments underscore how the material and religious marks of progress associated with these processes reinforced one another. The chapter concludes with a discussion of the political-economic context that led to the closure of most of the textile mills in Kaduna and Kano by 2005 and an upsurge in political and religious violence associated with the emergence of the radical Islamic group Jama'atu Ahlus-Sunnah Lidda'Awati Wal Jihad— known as Boko Haram—after 2006 (Anonymous 2012; Maiangwa et al. 2012; Mustapha 2014).

The Beginnings of JNI and Izala

In January 1962, several northern Nigerian Islamic leaders met in Kaduna to discuss plans for the establishment of Jama'atu Nasril Islam (JNI), with the aim of promoting unity among different Muslim groups in northern Nigeria (Loimeier 1997: 135). Some, such as Shehu Galadanci (Paden 1986: 565ff., cited in Loimeier 1997: 158), have argued that were it not for the assassination of Bello on January 15, 1966, JNI would have continued in its ecumenical position of openness to all Nigerian Muslims, which had been Bello's original intention (Kane 2002: 64). As a descendent of Shehu 'Uthmān dan Fodio, he was not in a position to quarrel with the leaders of the Qādiriyya, nor would he have been dispositionally inclined to do so. Furthermore, Bello sought to strengthen the position of Muslims in northern Nigeria through religious unity, making him more tolerant of different Islamic practices. Yet his close ties with Gumi, with whom he regularly traveled on hajj, suggests that while he was a conciliator, he also had political differences with various northern Nigerian Muslim leaders, which included the sultan of Sokoto himself (Loimeier 1997). Furthermore, he was impressed with Gumi's Islamic learning and Arabic fluency as well as with his close ties with Saudi religious leaders.

After Bello's death in 1966, JNI continued to grow under Gumi's leadership. His connections with Saudi patrons contributed to the expansion of Islamiyya schools and mosques (Loimeier 1997:157), while his appointment in 1975 as the Amir al-hajj (the head of the hajj) reinforced his earlier resolve, along with that of Ahmadu Bello, to train northern Nigerians as proper Muslim pilgrims. However, Gumi's education in Sudan and his close connections with Saudi religious leaders led him to support the development of a particular form of Islamic reform associated with Salafi beliefs and practices, which stressed fundamental texts, the Qur'ān and hadith (see also Brigaglia 2012). Indeed, as the name of the new movement, Jama'atu Izalat al-Bid'a wa Iqamat al-Sunna, or Society for the Removal of Innovation and the Reinstatement of Tradition, suggests, Gumi sought to eliminate practices associated with Sufi groups—Qādiriyya and Tijāniyya in northern Nigeria—which were seen as deviations from the teachings of the Qur'ān and hadith. As Muhammad Umar has noted, "It should be acknowledged that anti-Sufism is a protest—specifically against Sufism but more generally against many other things: traditionalist non-capitalist values, the religious authority of Sufi orders, and perceived corruption of religious beliefs and practices" (1993: 165). Thus, practices such as using sand ablution, *sha rubutu* (drinking the ink washed from boards [*allo*] with written passages from the Qur'ān), bowing down to emirs, visiting the shrines of Muslim saints, and the making and use of protective amulets (*layoyi*) exemplified what Gumi and his followers considered to be innovative practices not prescribed in the Qur'ān that should be stopped (Loimeier 1997: 152). Prayer beads (*carbi* or *tesba*; fig. 7.3)[6] were also forbidden: "Izala condemned the use of the *tesba*, claiming it is of Buddhist origins. It was also argued that the Prophet prayed by counting on his fingers" (Mustapha and Bunza 2014: 66; see also van Santen 2012). Thus, some Izala members use small digital counters strapped to one finger (fig. 7.4), while others use handheld counters, which may also include a compass for determining which direction is east so that they can pray facing Mecca.

The denunciation of these practices reflect a more general theological position of Izala leaders who both sought to eliminate *skirk*, or associationism, such as the worship of saints as a form of worshipping God, and to accuse other Muslims of *takfir*—of being unbelievers (Kane 2002: 125). Thus, spiritual connections with God made through trance-prayer as performed by Sufi mystics were condemned by Gumi. For followers of Izala, knowledge of the Qur'ān and hadith served as the fundamental basis for Islamic belief and practice as may be seen in other Saudi-derived Salafi/Wahhabi reform movements elsewhere in West Africa (Kaba 1974). The Qur'ān, hadith, *tajwīd*, *tawhīd*, *fiqh*, and *sirah* as well as the Hausa Ajami text *Hanjjojin da suka hana bin dan tariqa salla daga alkur'ani da hadisi manza Allah* (Kane 2002: 130–136) were taught at the expanding network of Izala-based Islamiyya schools in Kaduna and nearby Zaria, which included classes for children, young men, and single and married women.

Figure 7.3. Young boy wearing a *rawani* turban of *harsa* materials and an embroidered *riga*, with prayer beads (*carbi*) in GMC Studio photograph, Pada, Zaria City. According to Abdul Raufu Mustapha and Mukhtar Bunza, "the Tijāniyya have the most elaborate rosaries [*carbi*] of all" (2014: 66). (Courtesy of Safiya Jafaru)

Figure 7.4. Examples of the prayer counters that Izala members strap to a finger. These *carbi* were sold by street vendors in Kano and have become part of young Muslim men and women's fashionable wear, Kano, March 5, 2016. (Photograph by the author)

Dress Associated with Izala

Aside from these major doctrinal differences, followers of the Izala movement, particularly *malamai* and married women, could be identified by their clothing. While personally exhibiting very different dress preferences, Ahmadu Bello and Abubakar Gumi exemplified some of the basic differences between the dress of followers of *tariqa* and Izala movements. Bello favored *babban riga* and a range of turbans, with their elaborateness depending on the occasion (e.g., see figs. 4.2, 4.3, and 4.8). However, wearing turbans was and continues to be associated with the *sarauta* (royal) class and with traditional rulers, who are generally followers of Qādiriyya or Tijāniyya. Thus, even while he worked to circumscribe the role of traditional rulers in the federal government, Ahmadu Bello supported the institution of traditional rulers as a way of strengthening the political position of a unified Northern Region. Yet by forcing the resignation of the emir of Kano, Muhammadu Sanusi I, in 1963 (fig. 7.5), Bello sought to consolidate his position of power as the premier of Nigeria's Northern Region over traditional rulers—the emirs—with the goal of making the north "the strongest force in the Federation" (Loimeier 1997: 119, 122).

Gumi, however, supported state and national political leaders in northern Nigeria, partly as a way of strengthening the political position of northerners vis-à-vis the Nigerian state. His position lacked the ambivalence of Bello in his support of traditional rulers, not only because of their *tariqa* affiliations but also because of what he saw as their opulence and profligate behavior. According to Gumi, "[The emirs] had brought back to life all the corrupt practices against which Sheikh dan Fodio went to war with the former Hausa rulers. They had become kings with big palaces full of servants and courtiers, and required other people to bow down before them. They kept concubines and did not really fear God's anger. Were all these not what Sheikh dan Fodio despised and wrote extensively against in his books?" (1992: 108).

Gumi sought, as well, to distinguish himself in the simplicity of his dress. He often wore a plain cotton kaftan and a *hizami* "little turban" with the tail draping down the back or over the shoulder (fig. 7.6).[7] This particular style of turban not only distinguished Izala members from the *sarauta* class but also separated Izala *malamai* from Tijāniyya *malamai*, who would also wear *hizami*-style turbans, although the end could be brought under the chin or tucked in at the back.

This move toward simpler dress styles, particularly wearing caps and little turbans as well as simple *kaftani* outfits rather than large *babban riga* styles, was an aspect of Izala's rejection of costly ritual practices. As Roman Loimeier observes, "Ceremonial expenditures meant a considerable strain for family heads. The religious arguments of the 'Yan Izala provided them with the necessary reasons for stopping or reducing these expenditures or to entirely renounce their affiliation with their respective *tariqa* without necessarily acquiring a bad conscience on account of this behavior" (1997: 256–257; see also Kane 2002: 136).[8]

Figure 7.5. Ahmadu Bello (*left*), wearing a *rawani* ɗan Sardauna, and the emir of Kano, Muhammadu Sanusi I, at a garden party, perhaps in Kaduna. (Arewa House Photograph Collection, Arewa House, Kaduna)

Figure 7.6. Sheikh Abubakar Gumi (*center*), wearing a white *hizami* and kaftan, accompanies Ahmadu Bello (*left*), who is wearing a more decorative *rawani* with an *alkyabba* cape, on a trip to North Africa. (Arewa House Photograph Collection, Arewa House, Kaduna)

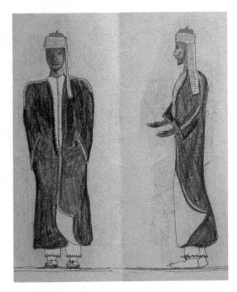

Figure 7.7. Sketch for a robe commissioned by Rex Niven for the president and speaker of the House of Chiefs, made by Ede and Ravenscroft Ltd., Robe Makers and Tailors, London, in honor of the 1956 visit of Queen Elizabeth II to Nigeria. In a memo dated November 20, 1955, Niven described the robe, cap, and turban: "I . . . think a dark green 'jabba' with gold trimmings with a small 'Bornu type' cap with tight gold or silver turban . . . would be very effective" (Niven 1982: 252). (Courtesy of the National Archives of Nigeria, Kaduna)

Thus, expenditures for fancy *babban riga* dress and turbans at special events could legitimately be reduced. The popularity of the *hizami* turban among Izala scholars and teachers reflects, in part, their relatively low price when compared with large *rawuna* turban.[9] However, the association of *hizami* with Saudi Arabia also made them attractive. As one man explained to me, "*Hizami* came to us from a long time ago, and it came from Saudi Arabia . . . and is for the *mala-mai* [Islamic teachers]." For Izala Muslim teachers who wanted to identify with Gumi, the fact that he had close ties with Saudi Arabia and also regularly wore a *hizami* made the style attractive to Izala adherents. Based on evidence from the Duckworth photographs, *hizami* were not common in the 1930s. They became somewhat more evident in photographs from the 1950s, when they were incorporated into official colonial uniforms, both for government officials and for soldiers. For example, Niven, the speaker of the House of Chiefs, commissioned new robes for two government officials to be worn at Lugard Hall during the visit of Queen Elizabeth II to Nigeria in 1956. The design consisted of a robe and small *hizami*-style turban and cap (fig. 7.7). Photographs from the 1970s show some Islamic scholars wearing *hizami*-wrapped caps with and without tails. By the 1980s, wearing a white or colored (patterned or red) cap with a *hizami*, with a tail hanging down over the left shoulder, came to be associated solely with Izala Islamic scholars and teachers. It was the Izala *malamai* wearing "little turbans" who were instrumental in teaching married women to read and write in Arabic in *Islamiyya Matan Aure* classes for married women.

Islamiyya Matan Aure: Islamic Classes for Married Women

The importance of Islamic education for women, specifically knowledge of the Qur'ān and hadith, was a key aspect of the Izala movement and was an important factor that contributed to its success in attracting followers, as discussed in chapter 5. Indeed, Loimeier has noted that "as a result of the efforts to promote education for Muslim women, the 'Yan Izala have cultivated a huge reservoir of potential supporters and at the same time exerted increasing pressure on the Sufi brotherhoods to follow suit" (1997: 251). In parts of Kaduna such as Tudun Wada and in the nearby city of Zaria, married Muslim women were encouraged to attend Islamiyya classes if they were properly covered, which, as Gumi noted, was prescribed in the Qur'ān (Renne 2012). These classes were usually held at night, when women had finished domestic chores and when the cover of darkness—as well as the *hijab* they wore—hid their identities. While some classes were held in the garages or outer rooms of homes of *malamai* instructors, later on, *Islamiyya Matan Aure* classes were held in schools that had been built for Izala students or in public schools used only during the day. Classes for married women are usually offered four or five days a week from approximately 8:00–10:00 p.m. In Zaria City, as in Kaduna, *Islamiyya Matan Aure* classes were generally well attended. The following excerpt from my journal, recorded on February 20, 2001, captures the atmosphere of one such class: "At the night school for Matan Aure in Kan Fagge/Limanci, after climbing some steep winding steps, we were shown six classrooms filled with married women reading or discussing the Qur'ān and various Islamic books. There wasn't light, so the rooms were illuminated with lanterns and candles. . . . Some women, they are very serious, and [their attendance is] the consequence of considerable effort—simply getting there after a long day. And the importance of reading the text of the Qur'ān . . . for women's self-esteem shouldn't be underestimated."

While there was no set curriculum for these classes in Zaria, school *malamai* instructed women in learning fundamental Islamic texts such as the Qur'ān, hadith, *tajwīd, tawhīd, fiqh, sirah,* and Arabiyya (and at some schools, Hausa and English). In studying the hadith, for example, students were expected to know the *40 Hadith* (An-Nawawī 1991), both how to read and write them. In their class sessions, teachers explained the meanings of these hadith to students so that they could explain them to others. While women in Class 1 were first taught using *ajami* (Hausa written in Arabic script) instead of Arabic, they were expected in Classes 2 through 4 to learn how to read and write the Arabic alphabet in order to read basic Arabic texts. Through oral and written examinations, women who mastered these materials were promoted to the next class (Renne 2012: 69). One woman who was visiting a Class 6 session in February 2001 was impressed with the way it was conducted, explaining to me, "The malam for the class was very good, and I even asked some questions myself—about the Four Questions one will be asked at death. There were twelve women present—two were absent having just delivered [babies]; some others weren't there—but the ones in attendance were very serious and could read quite well. The teacher also tested students, asking one to take up [reading] where he'd left off, and if the student hadn't been paying attention she'd be caught out."

Afterward, the visitor was advised by the students that she "should wear a *hijab.*" This advice reflected what women students themselves had been told, that to attend *Islamiyya Matan Aure* classes, it was necessary for women to be covered (i.e., to wear the *hijab*). Indeed, for many Muslim women in Kaduna (and Zaria), the introduction of the *hijab* as proper Islamic dress is associated with the beginnings of Izala (Umar 1993) and its support for women to attend newly established Islamiyya classes for married women there in Kaduna beginning in the late 1970s and early 1980s.

When initially introduced, Izala classes for married women were considered revolutionary by some, who felt that breaking the prevailing rules of seclusion (see chapter 5) would lead to immorality and dissention in the home. This situation was complicated by Gumi's (1992) criticism of the Qādiriyya and Tijāniyya orders. Heeding Gumi's advice to seek Islamic knowledge in order to better themselves as proper Muslim wives and to better train their children, some married women attending *Islamiyya Matan Aure* classes faced considerable criticism. While Muslim women in Kaduna, Kano, and Zaria had been covering themselves with *gyale* cloths at that time, women sought to protect themselves and their respectability when entering public space to attend Islamiyya classes by wearing the more body-encompassing *hijab*, despite the antagonistic behavior of some: "I started wearing a *hijab* at the time [Shehu Usman Aliyu] Shagari became head of state [1979]. It is at that time that I entered Islamiyya. . . . When people saw me with *hijab*, they were saying it is not good. There was a time we wore black *hijab* and children were chasing us. There was even a time we went to one village and they stoned us. But there is not this problem now, because it is now popular. [This is the] effect of the *hijab* in the respect of a woman [*mutunci mata*]" (interview by the author, March 18, 2001, Zaria).

Izala *malamai* encouraged married women coming to their classes to wear the *hijab* because of their teaching of Qur'ānic verses (e.g., Sura 24:31) on modesty. This change reflects the tendency of religious reformers to represent themselves as purifying past practices (El Guindi 1999), in this case, by ridding Islam of innovations (*bid'a*) that were not clearly outlined in the Qur'ān and the hadith (Kane 2002). Yet the shift from wearing the *gyale* to the *hijab* was taken up more widely, not only by women followers of Izala but by other Muslim women as what was considered proper modest Muslim comportment was reevaluated.

As discussed in chapter 5, the *hijab* not only came to be accepted as respectable dress for entering the public sphere, it also came to be seen as part of being beautifully dressed, of being fashionable. The range of *hijab* styles that became fashionable in the late twentieth and early twenty-first centuries reflected the growth of the textile manufacturing industry in Kaduna and Kano, which offered women a range of textile materials. Fashion *hijab* were made possible by the availability of an assortment of printed and dyed fabrics produced in Kaduna.

Textile Manufacturing and Economic Uplift of the North

Just as improved religious education was part of Ahmadu Bello's larger agenda for northern Nigeria, the industrialization of cloth production and associated improvements in the cultivation of cotton were vitally important to him as well. In the mid-1950s, Bello, in conjunction with members of the Northern Regional Marketing Board and the Northern Regional Development Corporation, met with officials from the British textile manufacturing firm David Whitehead and Sons to discuss plans to establish the first modern textile mill in Kaduna (see fig. 4.2) (Maiwada and Renne 2013).

Once KTL began production in October 1957, company officials attended to various processes that facilitated its early success with Nigerian consumers. First, the quality of the cloth needed to match their expectations. Gordon Hartley, a former employee of David Whitehead and Sons and the commercial manager at KTL, met with buyers in trading firms in Manchester and Liverpool, whose agents would be distributing KTL's products in Nigeria: "I remember various samples coming through from Kaduna. . . . The first sample got me no further than UAC [United Africa Company]. The grey cloth buyer there, Steve Goulding, almost laughed at what I showed him. It did, indeed, resemble a limp piece of rag. He showed me what he wanted—a fabric heavily filled with starch and calendered so that it almost shone. We sent the sample to Kaduna and eventually we had a product which I could confidently take around Manchester and Liverpool. . . . Once full production was achieved I was able to sell six months' production within a morning's stroll around Manchester and a brief visit to Liverpool" (Hartley 2012). Mill management and workers successfully produced increasing amounts of quality baft cotton cloth, which was attractive to agents from major textile firms operating in Nigeria and to Nigerian customers.

Next, the presence of company trademarks, which were stamped or printed on the fabric edge, was also important to Nigerians, who might wear a cloth in a particular way so that this mark was evident to viewers. Initially, KTL officials needed to confirm that trading firms—such as Paterson Zochonis Ltd. (fig. 7.8), which bought KTL products—would allow KTL to use their company trademarks ("chop marks") on the textiles that were sold to these firms. Nigerian traders who

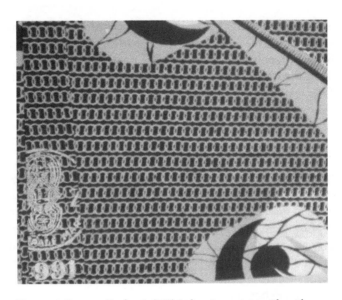

Figure 7.8. Paterson Zochonis (UK) Ltd. cotton print textile with sandal trademark, manufactured for the West African market in June 1964. (Photograph by Jaclyn Kline, courtesy of the Museum of Science and Industry, Manchester, Paterson Zochonis Collections)

bought cloth from trading firms such as Paterson Zochonis wanted to see these marks, although eventually KTL developed its own trademarks.

Aside from these company efforts, the Nigerian government also provided tariff protection, which fostered KTL sales by keeping its prices low in comparison to textile imports. When KTL began production in 1957, customs tariffs instituted by British colonial officials prevented other European and Japanese textile manufacturers from flooding the Nigerian market with their products. As a result, Hartley noted, locally produced cloth manufactured by KTL had a significant advantage: "We did have an important starting advantage in that there was a customs tariff for textile products entering Nigeria which amounted to eight pence per square yard. In pre-Naira currency we planned to sell our baft at seventeen shillings and sixpence per ten yard piece (twenty-one pence per yard), which gave us a substantial advantage over the imported product. The West Africa merchants knew that, given a satisfactory product, they would have to deal with us" (Hartley 2012). This tariff of approximately 45 percent for less expensive textiles such as plain baft, piece-dyed, and printed cotton textiles remained in place until 1977, when a ban on imported textiles was implemented that replaced the tariff system altogether (Onyeiwu 1997: 243).

Figure 7.9. Ahmadu Bello and Harold Macmillan (*third and fifth from left, respectively*) at the "Made in Nigeria" exhibition, Kaduna, May 1959. (Courtesy of David Whitehead and Sons Ltd. Archives, Parbold, Lancashire)

KTL's early success was highlighted in the Kaduna "Made in Nigeria" exhibition, which opened in May 1959. Colonial officials were also anxious to show positive efforts toward self-governance, modernization, and development—which KTL represented—in anticipation of Nigerian independence in 1960. This approach, which attempted to negate earlier colonial opposition to industrialization, was reflected in the showcasing of KTL. Ahmadu Bello and the British prime minister, Harold Macmillan, attended the opening as did many Kaduna residents (fig. 7.9). Walking through the exhibit, they viewed a series of exhibit booths with accompanying explanatory panels that illustrated the textile production process from cotton field to cotton bales and finally to bales of woven baft cloth stamped with KTL marks (see fig. 7.1).

With the increasing demand for KTL cloth, the mill was expanded in 1960–1961 to include mill 2 specifically for making a bleached cotton shirting (Nich Rutherford, interview by the author, June 11, 2011, Minchinhampton, UK), while mills 3 and 4 were added in the early 1970s. Several other textile mills were opened in Kaduna in the 1960s, including Nortex (Nigeria) Ltd., a mill partly owned by the NRDC, Northern Nigeria Developments Ltd., the Sudanese financier E. Seroussi, and local businessmen, which opened in 1963 (Paden 1986: 515). United Nigerian Textiles Limited, a large integrated textile mill that included spinning, weaving, dyeing, and printing was established in 1964 with backing from Hong

Figure 7.10. Sarkin Zazzau, Alhaji Muhammadu Aminu (*left*) and Sardauna of Sokoto Alhaji Ahmadu Bello (*center*) in 1960 during a United Nations Organization visit to Giwa Market in Zaria Province. (Arewa House Photograph Collection, courtesy of Arewa House, Kaduna)

Kong–based CHA Textiles group, while the United Africa Company–backed cotton spinning factory Norspin opened in 1963. Arewa Textiles Ltd., which had backing from ten Japanese cotton spinning firms, opened in 1965 (Onyeiwu 1997: 241). While all these firms were built and operated in conjunction with foreign backers, Bello participated in various aspects of their operation, at groundbreaking ceremonies, at meetings with mill workers, and in the development of local cotton as sources for mill production (fig. 7.10) (Paden 1986: 264). Hartley (2012) notes Bello's involvement in Kaduna textile mills' success: "If we knew that any distinguished visitor was coming to Kaduna we would expect a call. If Fred Fuller [David Whitehead and Sons production manager] was on site Sir Ahmadu would want him to conduct the party through the mill; in fact, I believe that after a time the Sardauna was so familiar with the place that he could have shown them round himself." These mill-related efforts reflected the optimism of the early independence years as well as the perception that Nigeria—with its growing population and petroleum resources, which presaged its future affluence—was a good financial investment.

This optimism was checked by the Nigerian Civil War, which began in July 1967 following the military coup and assassination of Ahmadu Bello and the Nigerian prime minister Abubakar Tafawa Balewa in January 1966 and the counter-coup and killing of Major General Johnson-Ironsi in June 1966. General Yakubu

Gowon was subsequently installed as head of the military government of Nigeria, and he presided over the ending of the civil war in January 1970. During the war, KTL and the other textile mills in Kaduna operated under constrained conditions; some, such as Arewa Textiles, were put into the service of the federal government to produce khaki material for military uniforms (Muhammed Buhari, interview by the author, July 8, 2010, Samuru). According to Hartley (2012), the war affected the company in other ways as well:

> At the outbreak of the Biafra War we immediately lost about a third of our workforce, who volunteered overnight. I went down to the railway station and saw huge numbers boarding special trains. Some of the poor chaps wore only flip-flops on their feet and none appeared to have uniforms. I don't know where they were headed to be initiated to the army . . . presumably to Lagos. When I went to the mill we had a crowd of people at the factory gates ready to take over from the missing people. Jonathan Gomwalk was our Personnel Manager at the time and soon sorted out a replacement force. I don't remember there being a severe loss of production, though efficiency suffered greatly for a time. What I do remember is being required to provide truckloads of cloth for the burial of bodies after the various massacres. Army lorries turned up and the cloth was covered over by tarpaulins. It was the dry season, so I assumed that the reason was to prevent causing further panic.

However, with the end of the war and increased oil revenue from petroleum resources from the Niger Delta region, Nigeria entered what is referred to as the oil boom years of the 1970s. This boom led both to greater government expenditure on federal projects seen as part of national development and to increased spending by Nigerian consumers (Panter-Brick 1978: 3). The strong national currency, the naira, also made purchases of foreign equipment for improvements in production possible.

Two additional mills were built in 1970 with the intention of producing *zauwati*, bleached baft, which could be used in the production of a line of printed textiles under the KTL name. An agreement between KTL and the NNTM in 1974, encouraged by the Northern Regional Development Corporation, made this merger possible.[10] Gardee, the mill's majority shareholder, decided to donate his majority shares (74 percent) of the mill to JNI when he left Nigeria (fig. 7.11) (Loimeier 1997: 144; Maiwada and Renne 2013: 178).[11] Gumi, who was the director of JNI at the time, did not want to be responsible for running a textile manufacturing operation. He made an arrangement with KTL that the company would take over the operation of NNTM, which was coordinated by Ken Taylor (of David Whitehead and Sons), with Gumi serving as a member of the KTL board of directors (Mohammadu Waziri, interview by Salihu Maiwada, July 16, 2012, Samuru).[12] While printing was not carried out on site, NNTM provided color print facilities for KTL woven cotton cloth.[13] Mohammadu Waziri, who

Figure 7.11. Pakistani businessman Ibrahim Yusuf Gardee (*right*), owner of
NNTM, presenting Abubakar Gumi and members of JNI with copies of the
Qur'ān, Kaduna. He later donated his majority shares in the mill to JNI.
(Photograph by Usman, courtesy of the Kaduna State Ministry of Information).

worked at KTL–NNTM as a designer during his National Youth Service Corps
year, from August 1981 to August 1982, described the equipment and techniques
used in printing at the NNTM, which presaged the subsequent decline in textile
manufacturing in Kaduna: "What I can say about Kaduna Textiles Limited is
that its machinery was out-dated. . . . [T]he weaving looms were using wooden
attachments to throw the shuttles, so that the shuttle could fly off the loom at any
time and harm the weaver. . . . When I was at KTL there was also the problem
of raw materials and also management problems. . . . [T]he production manager, he trained as a colorist and rose to the rank of production manager—he
got his experience on-the-job" (interview by Salihu Maiwada, July 16, 2012, Samaru). Waziri's experience of working at KTL enabled him to see the problems
of the company firsthand. Yet KTL continued to market a line of printed textiles,
known as Super Print, until it closed in February 2002.

The Decline of Textile Manufacturing in Kaduna

Growing political and economic instability undermined the ability of textile mills to operate in Kaduna. The succession of political leaders in the 1980s, from President Shehu Shagari (1979–1983) to General Muhammadu Buhari (1983–1985) to General Ibrahim Babangida (1985–1993)—three heads of state in ten years—contributed to disjunctures in industrial policies. The fall in international oil prices in the early 1980s (Andrae and Beckman 1999: 38) also contributed to a reduction of government support for textile manufacturing in northern Nigeria. Muhammed Buhari worked at Arewa Textiles, the other large textile mill in Kaduna that was founded through Ahmadu Bello's efforts, for fifteen years until it closed in 2005.[14] Buhari's observations of the issues at Arewa Textiles clarify the particular production problems that contributed to the decline of textile manufacturing in Kaduna:

> I began as supervisor, then I became a Team Manager, and then Manager in charge of production control and maintenance. Most of the machines were from Japan, a few were from China, and a few from Germany. Printed textiles [*atamfa*] were the main cloths we produced, both wax prints and roller prints—which were sold under the names Superprint, Africa Print, and Arewa Superwax. We also produced textiles for special requests such as army khakis during the civil war.
>
> There were serious problems, even at the beginning in 1990 when I started. The major problem was obsolete equipment. This equipment had not been replaced in thirty-five years, since the company started. . . . The problem started after SAP [structural adjustment program]—because the devalued naira made getting new machinery very expensive. And the materials for production also became more expensive. So they could not compete with the price of foreign imported textiles but also the quality. They actually tried a private generator for power, but it was so expensive, their costs increased threefold. The black oil/fuel that they used was too expensive. (Muhammed Buhari, interview by the author, July 8, 2010, Samaru)[15]

SAP, sponsored by the International Monetary Fund (IMF), was signed by former president Ibrahim Babangida in 1986–1987 as part of an agreement by the Nigerian state to reduce public spending and to devalue its currency in order to receive future IMF/World Bank loans. Yet as Buhari notes, currency devaluation contributed to the decline of KTL, for as the cost of imported spare parts for power stations and mill equipment skyrocketed, managers made due with obsolete equipment. One oft-cited reason for the mills' decline was that outdated textile equipment was neither repaired nor replaced because the unfavorable foreign exchange rate prevented managers from obtaining needed spare parts and new equipment. Yet even if spinning machines, winders, and looms had been replaced, they became prohibitively expensive to operate due to the irregular supply of electricity and the need to use black oil as a source of power for textile mills in Kaduna. This situation was one of the main reasons for textile mill closings cited in the literature, in newspaper articles, and by textile workers alike.

The lack of working equipment and the expense of black oil led to temporary shut-downs and stoppages (Onyeiwu 1997: 244–245), which affected mill managers' ability to pay workers in a timely fashion and led to periods of compulsory leave. Mills continued operations after 1984, although at KTL the workforce was reduced—not by dismissals but by attrition—and a new manager was put in place who streamlined production by closing mills 3 and 4, by refurbishing equipment using spare parts salvaged from decommissioned machinery, and by putting fewer workers in charge of more machines (Andrae and Beckman 1999: 104). While these actions improved production and even led to a slight profit in 1986, inefficiencies of production and relatively high prices of KTL products contributed to their lack of competitiveness, particularly with respect to increasing Chinese-manufactured textile imports in the 1990s.

This situation also reflected industrial attrition associated with the military regime of Sani Abacha (1993–1998) (Andrae and Beckman 1999: 286). Without government support, public companies such as KTL were "on the verge of collapse," Steve Onyeiwu noted in 1997 (244). KTL closed its doors in February 2002, signaling the end of an era of textile manufacturing in Kaduna. As with the assassination of Bello in 1966, when all his possessions—his books, robes, and turbans—were burned (Alhaji Aliyu Mai Mota Sarkin, interview by the author, July 10, 2012, Kaduna), this closing marked the end of a particular form of leadership and manufacturing in Kaduna.

The Fragmentation of Izala

The religious and political concerns associated with the founding of Jama'atu Nasril Islam in 1962 as an umbrella organization that would provide a united forum for Muslim issues in northern Nigeria was intertwined with the establishment and growth of industrial textile manufacturing in Kaduna during the period from 1957 to 1965. Both initiatives were supported by Ahmadu Bello: the former with the direct support and the latter with the indirect support of Gumi. The subsequent disunity within JNI after the death of Ahmadu Bello was complicated by the leadership of Gumi, who then served as the director of JNI while also supporting the founding of Izala in 1978. In subsequent years, Gumi wrote a column ("Nasiha ga Musulmi—Advice for Muslims") for the northern Nigerian newspaper *Gaskiya Ta Fi Kwabo*. He also presented educational programs in Hausa that aired on Radio Kaduna (Loimeier 1997: 162–163) explaining why he considered *tariqa* practices not only un-Islamic but also parochial. Gumi's close ties with scholars in Saudi Arabia—he received the King Faisal Prize for his achievements as an Islamic scholar in 1987 (156)—also strengthened his Salafist position. Much like the joint ventures with foreign backers (British, Chinese, Japanese, Pakistani, and Sudanese) that enabled the building of large textile manufacturing mills in Kaduna, Izala (and initially JNI) used outside funding—mainly from Saudi Arabia and Kuwait—to establish mosques and schools in Kaduna and elsewhere in northern Nigeria.

However, just as dissent within JNI undermined its effectiveness as a national Islamic organization, divisions within the Izala movement itself also emerged and resulted in the formation of several splinter groups (Mustapha and Bunza 2014: 68). This process began in Kano in the mid-1980s with Aminu d-Din Abubakar (Loimeier 1997: 169, 248), who had formerly joined Gumi in promoting the Izala movement. He later established an organization named Daawa, which took a less confrontational position toward Kano *tariqa* groups. Under Abubakar's leadership, this group carried on the Izala movement's concern with improving Muslim women's education. As part of his efforts to foster Islamiyya education for married women, he also supported the establishment of a *hijab* factory managed by the Federation of Muslim Women of Nigeria (FOMWAN) in Shahuci in Kano in 1987 (249)[16] as well as training programs for women preparing to perform the hajj (see fig. 6.9).

Other members' disenchantment stemmed from Gumi's continuing association with the Nigerian federal government and national political leaders, first with his support for President Shehu Shagari and later for President Ibrahim Babangida, the military dictator who named Gumi as his religious advisor and appointed him as Amir al-Hajj. Consequently the two factions that emerged in the late 1980s reflected dissatisfaction with older Izala leaders' control of positions within the organization. One faction, Izala A, was based in Jos and was associated with the original organization founded there, while a younger generation dominated the Izala B faction in Kaduna. Not surprisingly, members of Izala A continued to wear turbans while young Izala B members often did not (Mustapha and Bunza 2014: 69).

Following the death of Gumi in 1992, Izala *malamai* began their own groups that built on Izala practices but reformed them in line with their own interpretations of Islam. Men and women followers of one such group, Darul Islam, based in Niger State, wore turbans and long *hijab*, respectively. This group was closely monitored by the state government and was eventually forced to move.[17] Two other groups were begun in Kaduna State. Malam Isiyaka Salisu formed Kala Kato,[18] which focuses solely on the Qur'ān, not the hadith, as the source of all Islamic practice (Sa'idu 2009a, 2009c). Initially located in Samaru, near the campus of Ahmadu Bello University–Zaria, Kala Kato followers distinguished themselves from Izala members by condemning ritual baths, funeral prayers, and the use of shrouds to bury the dead.[19] Another Izala *malam*, Sheikh Muhammad Auwal Albani, who began attracting students in Zaria in the early 2000s, established his own movement known as Salafiyya. Albani founded the Darul Hadith School and mosque in the Gaskiya area of Zaria—not far from the Kaduna Polytechnic campus—which grew to attract many students. Like Izala, the basis of the Salafiyya movement was the Qur'ān and hadith. However, Albani saw Gumi and the Izala leadership as too supportive of the federal government, which Albani had criticized on several occasions (Ibrahim et al. 2011). Preferring what they saw as a more exacting interpretation of the Qur'ān, Salafiyya members emphasized the moral importance of reviving "the time of the Prophet" in their actions and words. Salafiyya women attended school wearing long *hijab* and *niqab* (face veils), along with socks to cover their feet, while Salafiyya *malamai* wore caps and *hizami* "little turbans" but without a tail to distinguish its wearers from Izala clerics.

In an interview conducted in 2012 (Sa'idu 2012b), Albani described earlier discussions with Malam Mohammed Yusuf, who had recently left the Shi'a Muslim Brotherhood. Albani said that he had tried to persuade Yusuf to encourage Western education in his teaching, but Yusuf declined this advice.[20] Yusuf then started his own religious group in Maiduguri, Jama'atu Ahlus-Sunnah Lidda'Awati Wal Jihad, or People Committed to the Propagation of the Prophet's Teachings and Jihad. The group is popularly known as Boko Haram (literally, Western education is forbidden) because of the group's rejection of Western education (Anonymous 2012). The trajectory of Yusuf's transformation from a follower of earlier Salafi Islam to a more radical and violent leader of Boko Haram is discussed in chapter 8.

Conclusion

In his 1956 poem, "Song of Freedom" ("*Wakar 'Yanci*"), Sa'adu Zungur expresses his contempt for northern Nigerian Muslims—"people of the gown [*mutane riguna*]"—who supported the emirate system of politics and traditional rulers whom he saw as "mere imitations of the traditional authorities," as pawns for "the Resident, the District Officer and others" during the period of colonial rule:

> They say that authority over everything rests with the ruler
> Because we are told the town is in his hands,
> But the Resident, the District Officer and others
> Are [mere] advisors, without full responsibility of carrying it out.
> A useless lie, an empty lie!
> They have the thread, *they* lay out the warp,
> They have the knife, they do the flaying—
> Rule over the people to their discomfort

The chiefs are mere imitations
Of the traditional authorities in the town.
. . .
Everything in the North is different
From what is found in a hundred [other] communities
Their trading is different, their occupations are different,
Their knowledge is different, for it is not well organized.
Their trading is like their trousers that have no value
Their wide loose trousers that have no value.
Their occupations are like their turbans,
A useless tangled bunch, not carefully planned
Their knowledge is like their gown,
Voluminous but making no useful contribution (Quoted in Hiskett 1975a)

It is not insignificant that Zungur uses weaving and textile metaphors to express this situation. On the one hand, colonial officials "have the thread, *they* lay out the warp"—they have political authority as well as the means of cloth production, with textile mills in the United Kingdom, and of trade, through the importation of British textiles. On the other hand, northern Nigerians have only useless trousers, turbans, and gowns—dress associated with traditional rulers and Qādiriyya Islam. Ahmadu Bello sought to mix these metaphors by both establishing textile manufacturing in Kaduna and supporting the system of traditional rule, reflected in his dress, his prayer beads, and particularly his turbans. While he and Gumi disagreed regarding these visual markers of Islam, they did agree on the importance of modernizing the north industrially, agriculturally, and educationally; on the training of prospective pilgrims traveling to Mecca; and on the improvement of Islamic education—particularly for women—evidenced by their collaborative work in the founding of Jama'atu Nasril Islam. They also both supported industrial development in Kaduna, with Bello actively soliciting foreign backers to establish textile mills in southern Kaduna and Gumi serving on the board of directors of Kaduna Textiles Limited. However, Gumi's condemnation of Qādiriyya and Tijāniyya practices, which he voiced more clearly in his sermons after the establishment of the Izala movement, underscored the fragility of Islamic unity, particularly in the face of growing unemployment and economic uncertainty, reflecting the oil boom and bust as well as the declining textile industry in Kaduna. The growing political instability associated with military coups and civilian governments, as well as growing economic inequality, also contributed to schisms within the Izala movement, as former Izala members founded their own groups to lead their followers to what they saw as a more just, Islamic society (Last 2008: 59). These political and economic factors also contributed to declining infrastructure and the later collapse of the Kaduna textile industry.

Figure 7.12. Veils and *hijab* on display at a stall in Tian Xiu building, Guangzhou, China, December 2014. (Photograph by the author).

However, despite the closure of the textile mills in Kaduna and the fragmentation of Islamic reform groups such as Izala, Muslim women and young girls continue to wear the *hijab* to Islamiyya classes. Yet these *hijab* (and the materials for making them) come from overseas, as in the period before Ahmadu Bello's efforts to bring industrial textile manufacturing to Kaduna—although they come from China and not Great Britain (fig. 7.12). They may be imitations of earlier, beloved *atamfa* printed textile patterns and have trademarks that are be proudly displayed. But they are no longer made from textiles manufactured at Kaduna Textiles Limited and printed on the premises of the Northern Nigerian Textiles Mill. The efforts of Ahmadu Bello, the donations by Yusuf Gardee of copies of the Qur'ān and his factory to Jama'atu Nasril Islam (see fig. 7.11), and Abubakar Gumi's service as the director of Jama'atu Nasril Islam and board member of Kaduna Textiles Limited, all are things of the past.

The character of Kaduna as a regional (and later state) capital, as a manufacturing center, and as an urban and urbane multiethnic and multireligious city has changed over the years. While the establishment of Izala mosques and schools paralleled the city's growth in industrial, educational, and health infrastructure, it also reflected a particular political and economic period of Nigeria's social history. The optimism of independence followed by civil war, the oil boom years, then subsequent drop in oil prices, the implementation of a structural adjustment program, and widespread unemployment associated with the decline of the textile industry affected people's confidence in their government and strengthened the sense that perhaps new Islamic reform groups were in a better position to address the problems of society. Anti-Sufi groups such as Salafiyya and Kala Kato in Zaria, Yusufiyya in Maiduguri, and the Shi'a Islamic movement of Nigeria,[21] which emerged in the 1980s also in Zaria, were established by individual leaders with their own visions of religious practice, requisite texts, and Islamic dress (Anonymous 2012; Mustapha and Bunza 2014). Their distinctive uses (or rejection) of cloth as well as styles of dress worn by men (turbans) and women (veils) distinguish them from earlier and coexisting groups.

The positive uses of textiles and dress—to distinguish Islamic group identities and to strengthen group unity—may, however, have other, less positive consequences, which have been recently witnessed in the increasing violence associated with the reformist Islamic group Boko Haram. One particularly poignant example of the use of cloth for concealment and deception took place in February 2016 when three young girls wearing *hijab* to hide explosive devices were sent to an IDP camp in Dikwa, Borno State. Two of the girls set off their devices, killing fifty-eight people and wounding seventy-eight others (Searcey 2016a). The third girl, on recognizing members of her own family in the camp, surrendered and her bomb was defused. The reasons for and the consequences of the continued use of veils, turbans, and to some extent, uniforms and *hijab* as both markers of Islamic reform identity and as dangerous duplicity are considered in greater detail in chapter 8.

Notes

1. Along with improving Islamic education, Ahmadu Bello was instrumental in the founding of the first university in northern Nigeria, Ahmadu Bello University (ABU), which opened in Zaria in 1962. Various centers at ABU have contributed to Islamic learning; the Institute of Education offers a diploma in Islamic education, while the School of Law includes a program in Shari'a Law (for a listing of the university's departments, see https://abu.edu.ng/programmes.html).

2. The 1927 film *Black Cotton*, later released by British Instructional Films as *Cotton Growing in Nigeria*, was presented to British audiences both to show Nigerian cotton growing and textile production processes as well as to explain the benefits of British cotton-marketing improvements and Nigerian cotton exports for Great Britain (see also Candotti 2015; United Africa Company 1950).

3. See Roberts 1996 for a discussion of French colonial efforts to develop cotton production for the textile industry in France.

4. On January 11, 1980, the head of the Department of Textile Technology, Kaduna Polytechnic, Dr. A. V. Mbaka, sent a letter of thanks to the general manager of United Nigerian Textiles Limited for the donation of dyestuff, chemicals, and reagents to the

department's chemical processing laboratory. The textile departments at Ahmadu Bello University (ABU) received similar support (Cha Chi Ming 2006).

5. For more detailed accounts of the Izala movement and its founding in Nigeria, see Gumi 1992, Kane 2002, Loimeier 1997, and Umar 1993.

6. There are various names for these beads, which include *tesba* (Arabic; Mustapha and Bunza 2014: 66) and the Hausa terms *carbi* and *casbi* (Newman 2007: 19). While Abdul Raufu Mustapha and Mukhtar Bunza note that the digital counters used by Izala members are "Made in China," many of the prayer bead *carbi* are made in China as well (2014: 66).

7. I was told that during a dispute (now settled) between Jos and Kaduna factions of Izala, the *hizami* turban with the tail hanging down on the left shoulder was changed by the opposing faction to the right shoulder. Presently, many Izala *malamai* do not wear a tail at all but rather tuck the tail of the cloth into their caps (Ya'u Tanimu, interview by the author, November 2012, Zaria).

8. Loimeier (1997: 257) notes that Mohammad Sani Umar also argues that economic factors contributed to the popularity of Izala among working-class men and women.

9. In 2011, *hizami* prices ranged from about N750–3,500, depending on the materials and patterns, while *rawani* prices ranged from N2,000 (organdy) to N10,000–20,000 (imported white *harsa sarauta*) in the Zaria City market (see chapter 4, note 4).

10. According to Nich Rutherford, a David Whitehead and Sons official working at KTL at the time of the proposed merger, KTL margins on the two basic cloths—unbleached and bleached baft materials—were being squeezed by Chinese textile imports (interview by the author, June 11, 2011, Minchinhampton, UK).

11. While Loimeier (1997: 144) has written that Gardee decided to leave after the implementation of the first indigenization decree in 1973 (which placed limits on foreign investors), Rutherford noted that Gardee's NNTM had "effectively gone bust" (Nich Rutherford, interview by the author, June 11, 2011, Minchinhampton, UK). Thus, this merger was beneficial for both companies.

12. Ibrahim Dasuƙi was secretary general of JNI (1971–1988) and also chairman of Zamfara Textiles Industries Ltd. until he was named sultan of Sokoto in 1988 (Loimeier 1997: 140).

13. NNTM operated until KTL ended production in 2002.

14. According to Buhari, "In 1960, the Sardauna went to Japan and the Japanese backers came to Nigeria to set up the company. The major shareholders were Japanese—the Overseas Spinning Investment Company—others were the Nigerian federal government. After 1992, they packed up [and returned] to Japan, then the management became Nigerian" (interview by the author, July 8, 2010, Samuru).

15. According to Sola Akinrinade and Olukoya Ogen, "Low Pour Fuel Oil (LPFO) also known as 'Black oil,' [is] an industrial fuel for powering the industrial machines in textile firms. The incessant hike in the price of LPFO has led to an unending escalating cost of operation" (2008: 165).

16. This factory is no longer extant.

17. Following the violence associated with Mohammed Yusuf and Boko Haram, Niger State and federal military officials moved to disband the Darul Islam community at Tegina, Mokwa Local Government Area, in Niger State in August 2009 (Abubakar, Jimoh, and Ebije 2009). Members were later compensated by the Niger State government for their buildings and farmland.

18. Mustapha and Bunza translate the phrase *kala kato* as "a mere man (i.e., the Prophet Muhammad) said it," referring to the hadith, the words of the Prophet, as passed down by Islamic scholars (2014: 79).

19. Kala Kato leaders also established a mosque in Kaduna (Mustapha and Bunza 2014: 79).

20. On February 1, 2014, Albani, his wife, and his son were killed as they drove to their home in the Gaskiya area of Zaria (Sa'idu 2014). While government officials initially could not identify the killers, the Boko Haram leader Abubakar Shekau—"dressed in military fatigue and a turban"—claimed responsibility for the murder, as Albani had frequently criticized the group (Mustapha and Bunza 2014: 82). Nonetheless, Albani himself was a well-known critic of the federal government and had been arrested in June 2011 by the Nigerian police on charges of criminal conspiracy, illegal possession of firearms, and intent to commit culpable homicide (Ibrahim et al. 2011). When four men confessed to the crime and were imprisoned, they were said to have attempted to escape and were subsequently shot and killed. This situation reinforced some Zaria residents' belief that the government was involved in Albani's death.

21. Men followers of the Shi'a Islamic movement of Nigeria may be identified by their black turbans (Kane 2002: 95), while women followers wear black *jellabiya* and *hijab*. Although they initially wore black *niqab*, they later abandoned this form of veil to distinguish themselves from Izala women who wore them.

8 Failures of Modernity and Islamic Reform

Dress and Deception in Northern Nigeria in the Twenty-First Century

> [Shehu dan Fodio] said, "Show by your dress who you are and what you intend. Make up your minds what to do and be prepared."
>
> —Nana Asma'u, quoted in Beverly Mack and Jean Boyd, *One Woman's Jihad*

ON FRIDAY, APRIL 13, 2007, Sheikh Ja'far Mahmoud Adam, who served as imam for the Masallacin al-Muntada in the Dorayi neighborhood of Kano, was gunned down as he led the morning (*fajr*) prayer. Earlier that week, he had received threatening messages and a white burial shroud (*likkafani*) (Brigaglia 2012: 2). As was the case with the Salafist religious leader Sheikh Muhammad Auwal Albani, who was assassinated in Zaria seven years later, those responsible for this killing were never confirmed by the police, although many rumors have circulated over the years.[1] One rumor that predominates is that members of the Islamic group Jama'atu Ahlus-Sunnah Lidda'Awati Wal Jihad (People Committed to the Propagation of the Prophet's Teachings and Jihad), colloquially referred to as Boko Haram ("Western education is forbidden"), were responsible for the killing of both men for their criticism of the group and its founder, Mohammed Yusuf. However, the continuing circulation of other rumors means that it is probably impossible to know the truth of this situation. Many subsequent attacks on government officials, the military and police, and institutions in northern Nigeria have been attributed to Boko Haram, whose leader, Yusuf, and his followers have supported Salafi principles—Islam as practiced in the time of the Prophet, according to the Qur'ān and hadith (Maiangwa et al. 2012; Mustapha 2014). Their rejection of Western moral values, represented by secular education and governance, includes their instruction to followers to wear Islamic or Shari'a dress—specifically, turbans for men and veils for women (Stillman 2000: 158).

Following the extrajudicial killing of Yusuf on July 30, 2009 (fig. 8.1) (Mustapha 2014), violence escalated in 2010, with Boko Haram members attacking government officials (both state politicians and traditional rulers), police officers, soldiers, and customs officials and also the bombing of schools, newspaper offices, and churches (Anonymous 2012; Maiangwa et al. 2012; Thurston 2015). The government attempted to address this violence using military officers and security officials of the federal Joint Task Force (JTF), which ordered massive house-to-house searches, road blocks, arrests, and, at times, retaliatory attacks, particularly when fellow soldiers or police officers had been killed (Amnesty International 2012). These attacks and counterattacks associated with Boko Haram's "seven-year rebellion has left 20,000 people dead and more than two million displaced" since 2009 (*BBC News* 2016). Yet as with the killings of Adam and Albani, many northern Nigerians suspect that actions blamed on Boko Haram cover a range of individuals and groups acting in their own interests—particularly political factions and politicians who use this insecure situation to enhance their political standing in the north.[2] But there are also robbers, kidnappers, and those with personal vendettas who are also believed to be involved.[3] As discussed in this chapter, uncertainty about who is responsible for this violence is compounded by the deceptive use of uniforms and *hijabs*.[4]

The chapter begins with an examination of the evolving situation regarding the activities and constraints on Boko Haram and the splinter group Jama'atu Ansarul Muslimina Fi Biladis Sudan (Ansaru), mainly in northeastern Nigeria, following the death of Yusuf in July 2009 (Chothia 2013; Comolli 2015; Walker 2016). After a short lull, violence erupted in 2010 in several parts of northern Nigeria, with bombing and shootings in six states: Bauchi, Borno, Kano, Katsina, Plateau, and Yobe (Armed Conflict Location and Event Data Project [ACLED] 2016). Despite claims that the federal government was resolved to end Boko Haram–related violence in the northeast—for example, through the passage of Act 2 of the Terrorism (Prevention) (Proscription Order) Notice 2013[5]—not only did violence continue to escalate, but logistical support for the military was waning. It was during the period from 2013 to 2014 that the Boko Haram fighters' use of military uniforms emerged.

By early 2015, the general discontent surrounding Boko Haram violence and its control of fourteen local government areas in northeastern Nigeria contributed to the unprecedented election of the alternative All Progressives Congress (APC) presidential candidate, Muhammadu Buhari, in March 2015; he and Yemi Osinbajo were inaugurated as president and vice president, respectively, on May 29, 2015. Improvements in funding for equipment and the transfer of the base for military operations from Abuja to Maiduguri began almost immediately (Najakku 2016). Buhari also announced his resolve to end Boko Haram attacks by December 2015 (Wakili 2015a). While reports from fleeing captives and captured Boko Haram fighters suggest that the group's strength in late 2015 was much reduced, Boko Haram fighters continue to rely on new strategies such

Figure 8.1. Mohammed Yusuf's image is on the upper right corner of the DVD cover of *Rise and Fall of Boko Haram Fight*. This video, purchased in Zaria in 2010, shows Yusuf in detention and later, his dead body in the back of a pickup truck. (Photograph by the author)

as sporadic attacks, mainly against small villages to obtain food and recruits (Abubakar and Sawab 2015), and at times, IDP camps (Abubakar and Olatunji 2016) and mosques (Sawab et al. 2017), mainly in Bornu and Yobe States. Also, their use of women's Islamic dress, particularly *hijab*, as both pious covering and deadly disguise, while not new, occurred more frequently in their efforts to maintain control of their diminished area of operation. In December 2015, there were several disturbing examples of young women who detonated bombs, having hidden them under their *hijabs*, as described in the conclusion of chapter 7. Although less common, some villagers continue to be deceived by Boko Haram members wearing Nigerian military uniforms. For example, in January 2016, two groups of Boko Haram fighters entered the village of Walori (not far from Maiduguri); the first wore everyday dress and took food and livestock, then set houses on fire. The second group, wearing military uniforms, "arrived at the edge of the village pretending to be soldiers that were there to rescue civilians. That was how they deceived most of the people and killed them," according to one witness (Abubakar, Olatunji, and Sule 2016).

The deceptive use of military uniforms, *hijabs*, and other forms of dress complicates an already confusing situation whereby people are uncertain as to who the actual perpetrators of the violence are—members of Boko Haram, thieves, kidnappers, politicians or their hired thugs, or even the military itself.[6] Nonetheless, Boko Haram's use of military uniforms as duplicitous disguise is paradoxical, considering the long and respectable use of uniforms in the history of northern Nigeria (Barnes 1960). During the colonial era, government officials spent considerable time and funds on uniforms, which both attracted men to government service and also delineated them according to a particular political hierarchy. The Nigerian armed forces have continued to wear uniforms since independence, and uniforms played an integral part in attracting men to fight in the Nigerian Civil War. Ken Saro-Wiwa depicted this dynamic in the words of the protagonist in his novel *Sozaboy*: "When I see all their uniform shining and very very nice to see, I cannot tell you how I am feeling. Immediately, I know that this soza is a wonderful thing. With gun and uniform and singing" (1985: 53).[7] Playing on the function of uniforms in identifying legitimate political authority, Boko Haram leaders and others have complicated this picture for their own ends while taking advantage of other types of uniforms as well: in 2014, for example, a young Boko Haram member wearing a school uniform detonated a bomb in boy's school in Potiskum (Nossiter 2014).

Along with increased military efforts to end Boko Haram violence, the new administration also gave its full support for the Economic and Financial Crimes Commission's (EFCC) investigations of those accused of diversion of funds consisting of billions of naira, which have undermined both the Nigerian military and the economy more generally. One such case, known as Dasuƙigate, refers

Figure 8.2. *Mazaje a Dajin Sambisa* (Men of Sambisa Forest) poster, purchased in Zaria in 2016, showing military victories over Boko Haram leaders and members. President Muhammadu Buhari is pictured top left with Lt. General Tukur Buratai, chief of army staff, to his right. Other images show victims as well as a young girl revealing a belt of bombs strapped to her body. (Photograph by the author)

to charges that the former national security advisor, Colonel Sambo Dasuƙi, diverted $1.2 billion, some of which had been allocated for the military's efforts to fight Boko Haram. Others who have come under investigation are alleged to have stolen from government accounts established to address the problems of inadequate power supply, road maintenance, hospitals, and schools (Opoola 2016). Along with increasing poverty and unemployment in northern Nigeria (*BBC News* 2012), such blatant theft complicates the Nigerian government's claims of moral authority and gives credence to arguments made by antigovernment groups such as Boko Haram and Ansaru as well as the Shi'a Islamic Movement of Nigeria, each claiming that the Nigerian government is not morally fit to rule. Yet since the 2015 elections, Nigerian political leaders at the national and state levels have made both small and larger changes in order to address these problems (*Daily Trust* 2016c). These efforts will not convince intransigent followers of ultra-orthodox Salafist groups such as Boko Haram of the legitimacy of the Nigerian state, yet they may convince others—if not to support it, then to tolerate what is presently possible (Maiangwa et al. 2012). Indeed, as of December 2016, the main Boko Haram stronghold in Sambisa Forest was taken by government soldiers (fig. 8.2). It was reported that as part of this operation, they recovered the Qur'ān belonging to Boko Haram leader Abubakar Shekau (Mutum 2016b) as well as the group's flag, which was presented to Buhari by General Lucky Irabor on December 30, 2016 (*Daily Trust* 2016b). Despite these military successes, however, Boko Haram violence against civilians has continued, with a similar number of attacks in 2017 as in 2016 (Ibrahim 2017; Wilson 2018).

Boko Haram Transformations

Following widespread attacks against the police in Borno State and an earlier confrontation during a funeral procession for four Boko Haram group members (Maiangwa et al. 2012: 47), Mohammed Yusuf was arrested and taken into police custody in Maiduguri in late July 2009 (Mustapha 2014: 150). There he was interrogated by military officials about his group and its practices (Abubakar 2009). When asked whether *boko* [Western knowledge] was sinful, he replied, "Yes, it is *haram* [forbidden]." He was then pressed further about his use of computers and syringes—products of Western knowledge, to which he responded, "They are purely technological things, not Boko . . . and westernization is different." Here he was making a distinction between mere technological things, which may be used and discarded at will, and the more invidious assimilation of a broader secular perspective acquired through Western education to which he and his Islamic followers were opposed.

This assessment was strengthened through his reading of Bakr b. Abdullah Abū Zayd's book *al-Madāris al-ʿālamiyya al-ʿajnabiyya al-ʾistiʿmāriyya: tārikhuha wa makhāṭiruha* (*Global, Foreign and Colonialist Schools: Their*

History and Dangers). In it, Abū Zayd argues—in a way not unlike Michel Fou-cault's notion of governmentality, that "the colonialist conspiracy embedded in modern secular education is more pernicious in perpetuating Western hege-mony than outright military conquest and political domination because both are apparent and can be resisted accordingly whereas the educational conspiracy is not so apparent, hence it is imperative for Muslim religious leaders to wage unrelenting opposition to modern secular education by unmasking the real but hidden colonialist agenda" (Anonymous 2012: 124).

For Yusuf, the hidden political agenda of those promoting secular education was to undermine the moral Muslim way of being in the world, which included separate gender roles and "solid Islamic individual and communal identities built on Salafi notions of piety and righteousness" (Anonymous 2012: 123). For Yusuf and many of his followers, this critical analysis underscored the importance of knowing the Qur'ān and hadith as the only legitimate foundation for human be-ings' life on earth. To follow this vision most precisely, members were encouraged to physically model themselves on the Prophet: "Like other Muslims who strive to emulate the Prophet (PBUH [peace be upon him]) in appearance and action, such as by keeping beards, wearing turbans, trousers slightly below the knees,[8] using *miswak* (chewing stick) to brush the mouth, etc, members of [Mohammed Yusuf's] group also practice these strictly while their women wear *niqab* (a cover-ing for the face), with hijabs (gown) that reach to the ground" (Salkida 2009). As in earlier Islamic reform movements in northern Nigeria, turbans played an im-portant role in reformist identities—during the nineteenth-century Sokoto Ca-liphate, in the twentieth-century groups in Ilorin (Bamidele, Tabligh), and more recently, among followers of Darul Islam and Boko Haram. Thus, even as Boko Haram fighters took up the wearing of camouflage military uniforms in 2012, they continued to wear turbans with them.

Following Yusuf's death, Boko Haram members dispersed and subsequently reorganized themselves, carrying out a series of attacks under the leadership of Shekau beginning in late 2010.[9] In the first half of 2011, over 160 people were killed—soldiers, civilians, and government officials—"mainly in Borno State, but dozens of other attacks, for which the group has claimed responsibility, have oc-curred in Kaduna, Bauchi, Yobe, Gombe, Niger, and Plateau States, and lately the Federal Capital Territory (FCT), Abuja" (Abbah 2011). Particularly difficult for villagers and townspeople were the actions of the Joint Task Force, a select group of military and police, including, at times, their extreme measures to stop Boko Haram terror. These measures included house-to-house sweeps with wide-spread arrests, harassment of Boko Haram sympathizers, and extrajudicial kill-ings, which led to a citizenry that was terrified both by Boko Haram fighters and by government JTF soldiers and police. Thus, in October 2011, when a newspaper vendor in Maiduguri failed to allow some soldiers to read his newspaper for free, he was arrested by JTF police and taken to the notorious Giwa barracks. His colleagues, who went from one police station to another until they finally found him, were told that he would be released the following day (Idris 2011).

There were also several examples of violence and counterviolence. In 2012, Amnesty International published a report that provided examples of this circular carnage: "At least 23 people were killed by police following a bomb blast on Saturday in the north-eastern city of Maiduguri. . . . The bomb, allegedly set off by the Islamist group Boko Haram, went off in the Budum market in central Maiduguri and injured three soldiers. According to reports received by Amnesty International, the Nigerian Joint Military Task Force (JTF) responded by shooting and killing a number of people, apparently at random, before burning down the market."

This confusion over who, precisely, was responsible for civilian deaths contributed to the ominous uncertainty of this situation. This uncertainty was compounded by Boko Haram fighters' use of uniforms worn by the Nigerian military.

Escalating Violence and Transgressive Use of Uniforms

In their attacks, Boko Haram fighters wore turbans wrapped around their heads and faces (fig. 8.3), more as a way to hide their identities than as a form of veiling, perhaps making references to Tuareg rebel fighters in Mali. They also often wore the *keffiyeh*-style turbans associated with Palestinian nationalism (Weir 1989). Some Boko Haram fighters began wearing khaki kaftan or camouflage military uniforms,[10] although the use of Nigerian military uniforms as disguise was not mentioned in news reports until 2013. In a raid on Benisheik, Borno State, on September 17, 2013, Boko Haram fighters surrounded the town, selectively killing those attempting to escape while soldiers were unable to repel the attackers:

> A soldier who spoke to correspondents in confidence said the insurgents had superior power. "The terrorists were using anti-aircraft guns while we were using AK47 rifles and some RPGs. They came in droves, driving about 20 pickup trucks accompanied with two light-armored tankers, all wearing military colors. We had to retreat to our base to reinforce after running out of ammunition," he said. "However, they followed us down and surrounded our base and began to shell our building. We couldn't stand the heat of their superior fire power. We had to retreat into the village after they killed two of our soldiers and three policemen." (Idris 2013a)

The use of "military colors" in this attack marks the shift from Islamic dress to military uniforms, just as their access to sophisticated weaponry indicated a professionalization of their activities. Furthermore, in some cases, these uniforms were precisely those worn by Nigerian soldiers: "Witnesses said the over 200 insurgents were dressed in the latest uniforms being used by the military deployed to Borno, Yobe and Adamawa States shortly after the declaration of state

Figure 8.3. Boko Haram members wearing kaftans with black and brown *keffiyeh*-type *hizami* turbans. "Millions of people in Kano State are supporting us," said the man on the right (Nossiter 2012). (Courtesy of Samuel James, *New York Times*/Redux)

of emergency by President Goodluck Jonathan in May" (Idris and Sawab 2013a). This situation puts a transgressive twist on the use of military uniforms as they were worn by Boko Haram fighters, to bring about the downfall of the Nigerian state rather than to support it.[11]

Authority and the State: Uniforms as Allegiance and Dissent

The significance of military and other government uniforms in reinforcing group unity, discipline, and loyalty to the state has been widely observed (Abler 1999; Barnes 1960; Brady 1954; Craik 2005). In Nigeria, the use of khaki-style uniforms began in 1899 with the establishment of the Nigeria Regiment (Barnes 1960: 276).[12] During the colonial era, the regiment became part of the Royal West African Frontier Force (RWAFF), and specific uniforms were worn according to military or official rank (fig. 8.4). Indeed, numerous files in the Nigerian National Archives document the time and effort colonial officials put into ordering materials, deciding on particular styles and decorations, and outlining precisely who could wear what types of uniforms and when (Premier's Office–Kaduna 1956). While khaki materials were purchased from British textile manufacturing firms such as Ollivant and United Africa Company, the actual construction of most uniforms were restricted to government workshops and not private tailors (Province of Ilorin 1932–1954).[13] Presumably, this rule was followed to maintain control over styles and materials as well as to reduce the likelihood of copies being made for private individuals. This practice continued during the independence era when the former RWAFF uniforms were replaced with khaki uniforms consisting of long-sleeved shirts, trousers, boots, a peaked cap, and a new emblem (Renne 2004a: 135).

These uniforms belonged to the state, so that after service, they were returned to the appropriate offices. Yet not all uniforms were returned, and some circulated in local markets. One of the most common uses of surreptitiously acquired uniforms was as disguise by thieves and extortionists. From 2010 to 2012, the northern Nigerian newspaper, the *Daily Trust*, reported at least six cases of thieves wearing uniforms for robbery, blackmail, and extortion. However, in 2013, this situation changed. Although there was one case of a trio of men in Kaduna wearing uniforms as false army recruiters (Ahmadu-Suka 2013), the majority of stories that year concerned Boko Haram fighters' use of uniforms—as a political statement, as disguise,[14] and as lures. While Boko Haram assailants also wore women's Islamic dress as disguise, they were less successful. In one attempted attack in Baga, Borno State, three men were killed while others were arrested: "Witnesses said over 20 men, clad in Hijab (flowing cloth and veil, popular among Muslim women) and Abaya (a long robe also popular among women in Borno) were arrested around the Police station. A security source said the incident happened around 2pm, adding that all the suspects had AK47 Rifles and Rocket Propelled Grenades (RPGs) concealed in beneath their cloth" (Idris and Sawab 2013b).

They were more successful wearing military uniforms, as in the attack on Benisheik described earlier and on the town market in Gajiran, Borno State, both in September 2013. An estimated fifteen traders were killed in the Gajiran attack, allegedly for collaborating with security forces (Idris 2013b). Boko Haram fighters used uniforms in more invidious ways as well when they duped fourteen young Civilian Joint Task Force (CJTF) volunteers, who helped the military with local security: "Alhaji Baba Shehu Gulumba, chairman of Bama local council, told Reuters in Maiduguri that insurgents disguised as soldiers lured the youths into a trap. 'They were on guard duty when the sect members dressed in military camouflage came and told them that they were needed at a meeting nearby,' he said. 'When they had been lured away from their duty posts they were then attacked and killed'" (Ibrahim 2013).

In 2013, at least seven such attacks were reported in the *Daily Trust*.[15] Although much reduced in subsequent years, these attacks have continued. In January 2016, Boko Haram members dressed in military uniforms attacked three villages surrounding Maiduguri, tricking villagers into thinking that they were

Figure 8.4. Private Joseph Ogundiji, Nigeria Regiment–
RWAFF, served as an instructor in the signal school at the
Zaria Depot, March 9, 1932. By 1937, RWAFF soldiers were
issued sandals as footwear. (Courtesy of the Nigerian
Army Museum, Zaria)

Nigerian soldiers who would assist them: "At Kofa village, suicide bombers in
military uniform were said to have assembled so many fleeing villagers close to a
steak stand before detonating a bomb that killed many people" (Abubakar, Olatunji, and Sule 2016).

These attacks by Boko Haram fighters wearing camouflage military uniforms raise the question of how these uniforms were obtained. There are several
possibilities. With the increasing battles between government and Boko Haram
forces, presumably some uniforms were taken from soldiers' dead bodies. There

were also reports of soldiers who, without sufficient ammunition and supplies, deserted their posts, removing their uniforms as they ran away (Ajobe, Doki, and Mutum 2015); other deserting soldiers were captured by Boko Haram militants who took their uniforms from them (interview by the author, March 6, 2016, Zaria). Additionally, there are published accounts of customs agents intercepting shipments of uniforms from abroad. In 2009, customs agents stopped a truck in Jos, Plateau State, that contained a quantity of Nigerian army uniforms (Abdulsalami 2009). In 2014, another customs agent discovered a container of uniforms and boots at Omne, in Rivers State: "During our routine examination and checks we discovered that a container owned by 24 people has all this stuff inside. What we discovered is 240 numbers of Army camouflage uniforms and we have also discovered during examination 24 pairs of Army boots" (Edozie 2014).

While some of these illegal uniforms may have been imported by those involved in armed robbery, some may have been bought by Boko Haram supporters.[16] Consequently, the chief of army staff, General Kenneth Minimah, announced in July 2014 that new camouflage uniforms were being made exclusively at the Nigerian Army Tailoring Department in Yaba, in Lagos (Agha 2014). In February 2016, Nigerian air force officials announced that they would use the same camouflage uniform as the army and navy, following a 2015 presidential directive. This step was taken "due to the proliferation of different sets of camouflage [as it has been noticed which breached the security in general in the country," one official explained (Mutum 2016a). This change, with the use of identical camouflage uniforms worn by all three branches of the Nigerian armed forces, was paralleled by a report in April 2016 that Boko Haram, too, had changed its uniforms: "The Nigerian army says [troops of 22 Brigade Garrison and 3 Battalion on long range fighting patrol on Monday around Gima village in Ngala Local Government Area in Borno state discovered that Boko Haram fighters now have new uniforms. Army spokesman Colonel Sani Usman . . . said troops were able to apprehend two terrorists in their new styled uniform of green colour with rope as bracelet around their legs and necks" (Mutum 2016c).

Precisely why Boko Haram leaders ordered this change is unclear. Nonetheless, reports of Boko Haram fighters wearing Nigerian military uniforms *are* much reduced. One psychologist, Dr. Abba Sandami, even declared, at the end of the first three months of President Buhari's administration, that "the era of people coming in military uniform to kill some prominent people in a community being guarded by police and soldiers is over" (Mac-Leva, Ibrahim, and Abubakar 2015).

However, Boko Haram members have used other types of uniforms, reflecting both the flexibility of its leaders in planning attacks and their different reasons for selecting particular targets. Thus, shortly after midnight on September

Figure 8.5. The 'Yan Agaji uniform is worn by Izala members who provide first-aid care to people in their communities in Zaria, March 5, 2016. (Photograph by the author)

29, 2013, thirty armed gunmen entered the compound of an agriculture college in Yobe State, opening fire on students as they slept in their dormitory. "'At first we thought they were security personnel on surveillance,' a survivor told *Daily Trust*, adding that the gunmen were in military fatigue" (Matazu, Bashir, and Sule 2013). About one year later, at the Government Senior Science Secondary School in Potiskum, Yobe State, a young man in school uniform was asked by the school prefect at the morning assembly why he was not wearing the school badge;

he then detonated the bomb he was carrying (Nossiter 2014). In both cases, wearing uniforms facilitated Boko Haram members' entry on school grounds.

In November 2015, two young Boko Haram men attempted to attend weekly meetings held in the Zaria area by 'Yan Agaji first-aid volunteers, who were members of Izala (discussed in chapter 7). According to Malam Mustapha Imam Sitti, the national director of Izala, the "vigilance and new security measures that were put in place by the group led to the recent arrest of two suspected Boko Haram members," who wore the group members' uniform in order to infiltrate their meetings (Sa'idu 2015b). Every Saturday members meet in a different Izala mosque around Zaria to discuss group activities, wearing their 'Yan Agaji uniforms (fig. 8.5). While they attempt to monitor the making of their uniforms, one member admitted that it was hard to restrict their production because they hired local tailors. "But we do make sure that the material used to make them is special," the member explained (interview by the author, March 5, 2016, Zaria). This material, plus the placement of special accoutrements such as badges, helped them recognize the imposter Boko Haram members. By identifying the two men, they prevented the possible bombing at the Izala mosques where they met.

Uniforms and Their Social Implications

In his essay on fashion, Georg Simmel notes the social dynamics of imitation seen in various forms of dress: "The charm of imitation in the first place is to be found in the fact that it makes possible an expedient of power, which, however, requires no great personal and creative application, but is displayed easily and smoothly, because its content is a given quantity" (1971b: 295). Uniforms are a type of dress that, as Simmel suggests, are "an expedient of power" because of their standardization—that is, their "content is a given quantity." Nigerians recognize uniforms as articles of dress associated with the power of the state to enforce its laws and to protect its citizens. In this sense, "the wearing of uniforms attests to clothing's ability to register clear meanings for persons wishing to establish an unambiguous role identification for themselves" (Davis 1992: 11; Joseph 1986). Yet as the frequent use of illicit uniforms by robbers and extortionists reported in Nigeria suggests, it is precisely this easy assumption of legitimacy that makes uniforms an excellent means for deception.

Uniforms as Deceptive Disguise

Boko Haram fighters' deadly use of Nigerian military and school uniforms is particularly ironic in that they would disguise themselves as representatives of the Nigerian state or as students attending schools that promulgate Western education, both institutions that they sought to destroy. Yet Boko Haram is not the only reformist group to wear military-style and school uniforms. Reformed Qādiriyya Nasiriyya members observe Maulidin Abdulkadir (The birthday of the Prophet) wearing paramilitary-style white uniforms (see fig. 7.2), as do members of the Shi'a Islamic Movement of Nigeria. Indeed, under the leadership of Sheikh Ibrahim El-Zakzaky, the IMN has developed an elaborate hierarchy of military-style uniforms associated with different units within this order. Although they do not use uniforms for deception, their members wear uniforms as a way of counterposing the authority of the Nigerian state with their own Islamic authority.[17] In their use of military uniforms more generally, all these reformist Islamic groups distinguish their members from everyday affairs and make a point of displaying their group's unity.

Yet the deceptive use of military uniforms by Boko Haram fighters as well as armed robbers and extortionists confirms the continuing need to change uniforms in order to address the problem of uniforms as disguise. The Nigerian military has developed new camouflage uniforms to be worn only by members of the armed forces, while school officials have adapted uniforms with distinctive badges, and 'Yan Agaji members closely observe the material used in their uniforms. Perhaps this heightened alertness as well as increasing military pressure discouraged Boko Haram fighters from continuing the frequent use of military uniforms in their attacks after 2014.

Hijab as Pious Protection and Concealment

The shift of Boko Haram fighters' strategy to swift and targeted terror has led to their increasing use of women and even young girls as bombers, encouraging them to hide their explosives under their *hijabs* (see image in fig. 8.2 of young woman with belt of bombs strapped to her body) and detonate them in public places, such as IDP camps (Abubakar and Olatunji 2016) and soft targets such as mosques and markets in towns and cities in northern Nigeria (Mudashir and Muktar 2014; Searcey 2016a): "A female suicide bomber yesterday at the Maiduguri Monday Market blew herself up and killed many unsuspecting traders and buyers, vigilantes and security sources said. . . . It was gathered that the suicide bomber hid three explosives under her hijab (veil) and approached a busy entrance at the market which is popularly known as Shonekan Gate" (Idris and Sawab 2015a).

The use of *hijab* in this way might seem particularly sacrilegious considering Shehu 'Uthmān dan Fodio's prescription to "show by your dress who you are and what you intend" (cited by his daughter Nana Asma'u in the chapter epigraph). However, along with the belief by some that these young women's sacrifice will be rewarded in paradise, the ending of the Nigerian state justifies the means for this violent deception in the eyes of Boko Haram members.

Yet it is not always clear that young women and girl bombers know what they are doing (Matfess 2017). For example, in December 2014, three young women ('*yan mata*) were instructed to go to Kantin Kwari market to detonate the bombs hidden under their *hijabs* (*BBC News* 2014; Mudashir and Muktar 2014). According to one young man who witnessed this event, the girls seemed quite ordinary but also not quite right:

> What happened that time, we were sitting, talking with our friends. We saw three girls come toward the shops [where we were sitting]. Because when I saw them, I even went up to them and asked one of them, "Hajiya, what do you want to buy?" They were touching the curtain rods—which at that time sold for N3,000. I was even telling my friend that these type of women, they cannot afford to buy such things. My friend asked jokingly, "Can you tell the type of women who can afford these things?" Because when you saw them, you would say they looked like *talakawa* [poor/working class]. I left them and came and sat down.
>
> One thing that I can remember. All of the girls were wearing *hijab*—the type of *hijab* made of *lylon* [nylon or another synthetic material], the *lylon hijab* young girls used to wear—only it was the ordinary short one [in a brownish color]. They didn't look *kwaliya* [decorated or fashionable] and even if they did not dress fashionably, you will see people looking decent and clean—but they didn't look like that. When you saw them, you will realize that they are poor and also that they are not in their right minds (*ba su cikin kwanciyan hankali*). (Interview by the author, January 23, 2017, Kano)

After two of the young women detonated their bombs, this young man—who was wounded by the second woman's bomb—later learned that the third young woman, while wounded herself, had taken a *daidaita sahu* (a form of tuk tuk, or public transport) to a village near Kano where she had formerly lived: "When the driver of the *daidaita sahu* took her to the place, an old man said that he recognized her. Because she was wounded and the old man recognized her, the driver took her to the hospital and when they got there, she left her belongings in the vehicle. She had removed her bomb and left it there. That was how they realized that there was a bomb, that was how people knew she was the third bomber" (interview by the author, January 23, 2017, Kano).

Another trader present at the market that day was struck by the ordinariness of the girls: "Many people saw them because one of the girls . . . even came to one of the shops and begged for money [*sadaka*]. I gave her N50. They took a long time walking around the market so nobody paid attention to them. . . . People never expected that [they had bombs], they didn't care about them" (interview by the author, January 23, 2017, Kano).

The association of *hijabs* with Muslim women's modest piety and the ordinariness of *hijabs* as Muslim women's dress combined to make people oblivious to their wearers. While this incident led people to suspect women wearing *hijab*, particularly women who seemed nervous or disoriented, it has been difficult to stop women bombers wearing *hijab*. In December 2017, two young women detonated bombs strapped to their bodies at a market in Biu, Borno State, killing twenty-five people and injuring many others (Sawab and Olatunji 2017). Nonetheless, two young women suicide bombers in another incident were intercepted by a hunters' vigilante group and blew themselves up before reaching their target in Tsamiya village in the Madagali area of Adamawa State in June 2017 (Anwar 2017). While the government floated a proposal to ban the wearing of the *hijab* in late 2015, many Muslim women, including the leadership of the Federation of Muslim Women of Nigeria (FOMWAN), protested (Jimoh 2015b), and the idea was dropped.[18] However, in 2015, several government and women's groups became involved in rehabilitating women associated with these bombings (Wakili 2015b), and the number of these suicide bombings was somewhat reduced in 2016. Military and school uniforms used as disguise by Boko Haram fighters and *hijab* worn by women to cover bombs have been effective because both countered expectations: the former assumed official authority and the latter Islamic piety.[19]

Failures of Modernity

A frequent refrain during the height of Boko Haram violence in 2013 and 2014 was that government officials were corrupt and were it not for government mismanagement of the crisis, the problem would have long been settled.[20] Indeed, this view was voiced by the protesting soldiers' wives in Maiduguri in August 2014:

> The women burnt tyres along the streets, accusing army commanders of exploiting the war on terror for pecuniary gains. . . . The protesters alleged that top military commanders in both the North East and Abuja were "endangering" the lives of their husbands by forcing them to the frontlines without the appropriate weapons to fight. During the earlier protest on Saturday, the women, accompanied by their grown up daughters and little children, alleged that most of the arms being used by their husbands were old with limited ammunitions. They added that the armoured tanks being deployed to the frontlines were obsolete and unserviceable. (Idris and Ibrahim 2014)

With inadequate ammunition and equipment, some soldiers refused to fight and some faced secret court-martials. Thus, in early January 2015, 203 soldiers were dismissed for dereliction of duties:

> One of the sacked soldiers said on condition of anonymity that they were dismissed for asking for support equipment following the army's plan to convey them in a tipper [truck] for an operation in Bama and Gwoza, two strongholds of the Boko Haram insurgents. . . . The soldier said his unit reconvened in Maiduguri last August after they were dislodged by the insurgents in Damboa in an operation where their commanding officer and several other soldiers were killed. He said they were given two weeks' pass and that at the expiration of their pass, they were issued new uniforms, boots and 30 rounds of bullets each

as opposed to the statutory 60 rounds. He said having engaged the insurgents in several past battles, [a] majority of the soldiers argued that the operation would be fierce, and therefore requested support equipment.

"So we asked for support weapons. No support weapon was provided. Our Commanding Officer [CO] said he would discuss with the GOC [General Officer Commanding] of the 7 Division at the headquarters. When he came back, he said we should stand down. We thought all was well," our source said. The next day, their new CO . . . ordered them to submit their weapons and uniforms or be charged with mutiny. (*Daily Trust* 2015a)

The problem of lack of support equipment was widely reported in early 2015 by the Nigerian press, despite the fact that government funds had been allocated for their procurement. During his talk at Chatham House (a London-based think tank) in January 2015, the former national security advisor Colonel Sambo Dasuki responded to the question, "Do you actively seek direct feedback from the troops fighting Boko Haram?" The chair, Richard Gozney, summarized Dasuki's answer in the question-and-answer session: "The government does receive direct feedback from soldiers. Dasuki said that claims that the Nigerian army is ill-equipped are disingenuous. He said that news reports have showcased the high level of sophistication of the weapons that Boko Haram has taken from the army in recent battles. . . . The government believes that many of these claims were made by people who simply wanted an excuse not to fight" (2015: 5).

While people speculated at the time about corrupt practices by government officials, it was not until Buhari's support for Economic and Financial Crimes Commission investigations that the truth of allegations against Dasuki and others associated with military contracts was documented (Wakili 2016c). Indeed, Leah Wawro, of Transparency International, was outraged as she described the hypocrisy of Dasuki's claims: "Dasuki allegedly created phantom arms contracts for helicopters, fighter jets and ammunition," stressing that his arrest for allegedly diverting $2.1 billion meant for arms purchases "shows just how appalling these statements [at Chatham House] were" (Chonoko 2016).[21] Meanwhile, a special presidential committee set up specifically to investigate the Office of the National Security Advisor under Dasuki was able to recover over N7 billion from the indicted companies and individuals, who had received payment without "any contractual agreement or evidence of jobs executed" (Wakili 2016c). Indeed, the "[EFCC] recovered N473 billion and $98.2 million in 2017" (Krishi 2018).

Islamic Belief and Practice and the Failures of Modernity

Islamic reform groups have a long history in northern Nigeria, and their moral evaluation of the political and social practices of their contemporaries has often been the basis for their reformist stance (Last 2014). For Shehu dan Fodio, the decadent practices of the Habe states influenced his decision to pursue jihād. In

Bayān Wujūb al-Hijra 'ala 'l-'Ibad, he defined jihād as fighting "to make God's law supreme" (1978: 80), in other words, to live according to the precepts of the Qur'ān and Islamic law. His assessment of the Habe states in Chapter 53, "On Practices Wherewith a State Cannot Survive," is paralleled by subsequent assessments of the twenty-first-century Nigerian state: "It is stated in *Diya al-khulafa*: When God desires to destroy a state, He hands its affairs over to extravagant sons of the rulers whose ambition is to magnify the status of kingship, to obtain their desires and indulge in sins. . . . Other practices [destructive of sovereignty] are arrogance and conceit which take away virtues. There are six qualities which cannot be tolerated in a ruler: lying, envy, breach of promise, sharpness of temper, miserliness and cowardice" (1978: 142).

Shehu dan Fodio's writings have influenced Islamic reformers who have followed him, even while they may not have followed his precepts entirely. Thus, although many northern Nigerians may have agreed with Yusuf's assessment of the failures of the Nigerian government to provide a modicum of well-being for its citizens, many were opposed to antistate violence and the subsequent brutality of Yusuf's successor, Shekau. For him, dan Fodio's admonition concerning those who should not be killed during jihād, which included "women, unless they are engaged in fighting, boys, the insane, as well as decrepit old men, the chronically ill, the blind and monks secluded in a monastery," was ignored (1978: 86).

Nonetheless, a prevailing sense of insecurity associated with what Yusuf saw as the westernization of social and political life in northern Nigeria persists (Last 2008). Precisely how the *dar al-Islam*, the Islamic community (known as the *umma*), can be strengthened and cultural practices associated with Western education contained—particularly those associated with gender and dress—are questions that remain unanswered. Several northern Nigerian religious scholars have sought to address these concerns, including Dahiru Bauchi (Tijāniyya), 'Abd Allāh Bala Lau (Qādiriyya), Ja'far Mahmoud Adam (Ahlus-Sunnah), Muhammad Albani (Salafiyya), and Ahmad Gumi (Izala), among others. For these are difficult questions, as Max Weber observed, citing Tolstoy: "What shall we do, and how shall we arrange our lives?" (1946: 152–153). With the blockade of the Sambisa Forest and surrender of many Boko Haram fighters (Abubakar 2015), as well as the arrest of Khalid al-Barnawi, the leader of Ansaru in Lokoja, in April 2016 (*Daily Trust* 2016a),[22] these are the matters that northern Nigerian religious and political leaders are attempting to address as the Boko Haram era comes to an end.

Conclusion

Islamic reformers in northern Nigeria have followed various paths toward addressing what they view as un-Islamic, unjust, and corrupt political rule. Some, such as dan Fodio (1978), performed jihād against the kingdoms of Gobir and Zazzau in order to establish a more just and Islamic form of governance. Others such as Sheikh Adam al-Iluri established Islamic schools in Abeokuta, Lagos, and Ilo-rin, and "in his literary interests as well as his Islamic activities," the sheikh "was closely linked to Islamic reformism within Egypt and the Arab World" (Reich-muth 1997: 244), indirectly countering British colonial rule (Last 2008: 48). Alter-nately, Bashir Suleiman of Darul Islam founded a separate community in a remote rural area in Niger State to distance the group from the Nigerian government (Abubakar, Jimoh, and Ebije 2009). Malam Mohammed Yusuf, largely self-taught as an Islamic scholar, began the Yusufiyya movement to counter the corruption and harmful governance of Borno State, establishing his headquarters, *Markaz Ibn Taymiyya*, with its mosque, Islamic school, and clinic, in Maiduguri. As Ab-dul Raufu Mustapha has noted, "Yusuf also criticized the conspicuous consump-tion and opulence of the wider Western-educated elect in the midst of the abject poverty of the bulk of the population" (2014: 149). He countered this situation by providing his followers with employment, Islamic education, and funds for their marriages (Salkida 2009). It was this combination of his convictions, his astute-ness in attending to the spiritual and economic needs of his followers, and govern-mental and military corruption, as well as the government's mishandling of this movement, that contributed to the transformation of Boko Haram into a powerful and violent religious group by 2014. Reclaiming the funds that have been misal-located and stolen, rearming the military and reinforcing its unified force through the provision of adequate weapons and new camouflage uniforms, managing IDP camps, and rehabilitating former Boko Haram fighters have all contributed to the group's decline after the 2015 election. Furthermore, efforts by Buhari and Osin-bajo to reclaim stolen assets continue, despite legal impediments and comments such as those made by former British prime minister David Cameron about Ni-geria as "a fantastically corrupt country." "[When] asked if he wanted an apology from Cameron, Buhari said, 'No. I am not going to demand any apology from any-body. What I am demanding is the return of assets. What would I do with an apol-ogy? I need something tangible'" (Jega 2016). As President Buhari aptly pointed out, he wanted the stolen assets that were invested or hidden in British properties, companies, and banks. Similarly, he requested assistance from the World Bank in reclaiming assets ($320 million) held in Swiss bank accounts opened by the Sani Abacha family (Soniyi 2016). One need not point out that this corruption repre-sents a relationship between those who steal money and those who benefit from its investment. Funds from the Abacha account and the return of an estimated N1.34 trillion stolen between 2006 and 2013 would go a long way in providing for new roads, hospitals, and schools as well as provide funds for planned cash transfers to women and children, job training, and educational programs.

Yet even with these efforts and World Bank loans to rebuilt northeastern Nigeria (*Daily Trust* 2015b), the fear and insecurity associated with the violence perpetrated by Boko Haram fighters and, in some cases, the Nigerian military, will not be soon forgotten. The uncertainty perpetuated by Boko Haram's use of uniforms as dissemblance and disguise contributes to continued suspicion and apprehension. Thus, in February 2015, young members of the Civilian Joint Task Force mistook the soldiers accompanying two trucks carrying ammunition for the Seventh Division in Maimalari Barracks, Maiduguri, for mercenaries and stopped the trucks: "On interrogation, the soldiers accompanying the truck told the youths that they were conveying rice but the youths insisted on checking. The result was the discovery of weapons and bombs. The soldiers who were in uniform admitted [the weapons shipment] and showed their identity cards to the youth" (Idris and Sawab 2015b). When the young men attempted to burn tires on the truck roofs, they were shot by the soldiers, who feared an explosion; three were killed, and twenty were injured. This suspicion also carries over to those who were kidnapped and imprisoned by Boko Haram fighters. Young women, some of whom were impregnated by Boko Haram members, with infants have been ostracized in IDP camps (Searcey 2016b). People fear that they, like the Boko Haram fighters in military uniforms, are not what they appear to be and cannot be trusted.

Women members of Boko Haram have worn *niqab* and later *hijab*. While their men counterparts have worn turbans and, initially, shortened pants (see chapter 3), they subsequently wore military camouflage uniforms with *keffiyeh* turbans, which they also used to cover their faces to hide their identities. These distinctive configurations of dress reflect the historical context in which particular prescriptions for Islamic dress and forms of Islamic practice have taken place in northern Nigeria. One of the most recent Islamic groups to emerge in Kaduna State in 2016 (Sa'idu 2016a), the Gawsiyya sect, follows Tijāniyya prescripts with the exception of the timing of the requisite five daily prayers. The group's leader, Sheikh Isma'il Yusha'u, has established the group's main mosque at Madinatu Zaria, a small rural settlement about fifteen miles from Zaria City's Kofar Gayan gate. Wearing a large white turban, Sheikh Yusha'u explained that he had received his early Islamic education in Zaria City and then studied under Sheikh Atiku in Sanka, Kano, before being selected as Gawsiy, an individual whom "Allah chooses [from among] one of his servants to lead Muslims globally" (Sa'idu 2016a). As Murray Last has observed, "Today's dissidents, such as the notorious Boko Haram, are part of a tradition of dissidence; and neither are they a new phenomenon nor will they be the last of their kind" (2014: 19).

Notes

1. Andrea Brigaglia (2012: 18–21) cites at least four possibilities—namely, the involvement of (1) Kano State government politicians, (2) local *tariqa* clerics, (3) the CIA, or (4) members of Boko Haram.

2. For example, some attribute the killing of Mahmoud Adam to Kano State gubernatorial election politics (Brigaglia 2012: 19).

3. Even confidence men have taken advantage of the situation: in 2012, one man was arrested for taking payments from worried families in Maiduguri, anxious to get their relatives released from police custody.

4. Uniforms were deceptively used during an earlier period of uncertainty: "After the conquest of Kano in 1903, there was a very brief period of confusion when 'bush soldiers' (*sojojin gona*) pretended to be British soldiers and roamed the countryside extorting food and goods from the frightened villagers. Shortly, however, peace and security on the roads were restored" (Shea 1975: 86).

5. On June 4, 2013, the Terrorism (Prevention) (Proscription Order) Notice 2013 was approved by President Goodluck Jonathan, as was set out in Section 2 of the Terrorism Prevention Act 2011. This act states that "anyone found to have collaborated with a terrorist group or supported the commission of an act of terrorism will be sentenced to a minimum of 20 years imprisonment" (Wakili 2013).

6. For example, in February 2012, JTF officials announced that they had killed eight Boko Haram fighters at the Baga fish market in Maiduguri. However, witnesses said that several bystanders were killed during the shoot-out. A nurse at the University of Maiduguri Teaching Hospital described what he saw: "'I am not sure of the exact number but I saw more than 20 bodies,' he said, adding that most were wearing traditional Islamic Kaftans worn by men in the area. None were in military uniforms" (Idris and Ibrahim 2012).

7. During the colonial era, British officials received letters from textile manufacturers in the United Kingdom extolling the virtues of their khaki products (Province of Ilorin 1932–1954), and during the civil war, several textile manufacturing firms in Kaduna, Kano, and Lagos provided khaki materials for their construction (see chapter 7; see also Renne 2004a).

8. During his interrogation, the police also suggested that Yusuf's trousers, made of industrially manufactured cloth, represented a Western innovation: "Yusuf: (cuts in) . . . it is pure cotton and cotton belongs to Allah" (Abubakar 2009).

9. In September 2009, the sultan of Sokoto, Muhammad Sa'ad Abubakar, noted that "although the leader of the sect, Mohammed Yusuf, was killed, his followers are very much in operation, a situation which poses security threat in the country" (Yahaya 2009).

10. The Nigerian *Daily Trust* article by Omirin Olatunji (2016) includes a photograph of Boko Haram fighters wearing camouflage uniforms with *keffiyeh* turbans extended to cover their faces.

11. While Jennifer Craik discusses the transgressive uses of uniforms in her book *Uniforms Exposed* (2005), she does so in the context of unconventional Western styles and practices.

12. Uniforms were worn by the Gold Coast Constabulary beginning in 1844, which was later renamed the Lagos Hausas in 1865 (Barnes 1960: 176).

13. However, after independence, local tailors were engaged to make uniforms for officers of the legislature (Premier's Office–Kaduna 1964–1967).

14. Paul Richards (2009: 504) describes soldier-rebels' use of thick vests made of handspun, handwoven cotton material that were worn for protection during the 1991–2002 civil war in Sierra Leone. He does not report military uniforms used as disguise, however: "Stories circulated that new army pattern fatigues had been ordered by the regime, only to

disappear. Yet most sightings of actual rebel groups (whether RUF [Revolutionary United Front] or army splinters) tended to reveal not fine new uniforms but a wild miscellany of old clothing" (499), suggesting a different dynamic at play in being "dressed to kill" in Sierra Leone.

15. This figure involves incidents concerning uniforms in 2013. I downloaded 156 *Daily Trust* stories pertaining to Boko Haram specifically for that year. However, not all incidents received newspaper coverage: ACLED reported 269 Boko Haram–related incidents in 2013 (ACLED 2016).

16. Perhaps more information about sources and the logistics of these shipments will become available in the future. In 2016, at least four Chinese companies offered camouflage uniforms for sale on the Alibaba website. In 2017, a shipment of pump-action rifles from China was intercepted by customs agents in Lagos (Jega 2017).

17. Nigerian authorities and IMN have clashed in two major altercations over the use of public spaces for their processions, mainly in Zaria, Kaduna State. In a major confrontation during the procession to recognize Id el Maulud on December 12, 2015, in Zaria, over sixty people were killed, and the group's leader, El-Zakzaky, was arrested (Sa'idu 2015a). Amnesty International (2016) issued a statement condemning the military's handling of this situation in March 2016, and months later, the violence associated with this incident was still under investigation and a trial was ongoing (*Daily Trust* 2016d).

18. In support of his position against the president's proposed *hijab* ban, Ishaq Akintola, director of Muslim Rights Concern (MURIC), noted: "If army and police uniforms are not banned although they are often used by bandits, why should we ban hijab? Security agents know how they often fish out hoodlums who use police and soldiers' uniforms to commit atrocities. The same method should be used to prevent the use of hijab for bombing" (Jimoh 2015a).

19. *Hijabs* have been associated with deception in other ways as well. For example, women wearing *hijab* have been suspected of shoplifting and, in Kano, as disguised prostitutes (Sa'idu 2009d).

20. Buhari himself made such an assessment when meeting with Grand Imam of Al-Azhar, Dr. Ahmed El-Tayeb on May 18, 2016: "Corruption was largely responsible for the inability of the Nigerian military to quickly defeat Boko Haram" (Wakili 2016a).

21. More recent estimates say that the amount diverted may have been as much as $15 billion (Agbese 2016).

22. One escapee describes the blockade of the Sambisa Forest: "I am an Islamic scholar. [Boko Haram fighters] have been consulting me for spiritual assistance. . . . Those ones left behind [in the Sambisa Forest] know that their days are numbered. They may not surrender because of stubbornness or because of the belief they have that they are fighting a religious war. There are several old people and children that cannot trek from the bush that need to be evacuated. No, the insurgents are not holding them" (Abubakar 2015).

Epilogue

Moral Imagination, Material Things, and Islamic Reform

On the day of passing away
It is only five yards of white cloth,
That you will be wrapped in,
One grave will be made,
Ten graves will not be dug,
Simply because you are rich,
You will be buried in there,
It is the same with the poor
When passed away
It is only five yards of white cloth,
That he will be wrapped in,
One grave will be made
Not up to ten
Because he is poor
If you study this (case) well
You are equally treated.

> —Dan Maraya, "Rich and Poor" (*"Mai Akwai da Mai Babu"*),
> translated by Habibu Daba

CLOTHING AND TEXTILES often serve as metaphors for social relations. In the story "The Monk of Changqing," Pu Songling describes the death of an elderly monk in seventeenth-century China, whose wandering soul entered the body of a young nobleman who had suddenly died in Henan Province. When the nobleman came back to life, but with the soul of an austere monk, he subsequently rejected worldly things and went back to live in his former monastery in Changqing: "His wife sent a household steward with rich gifts of gold and silk, all of which he refused, except for the plain cotton robe, which he kept for his own use. From time to time, his friends from Henan Province would call on him if they were in the neighbourhood. They found a man of quiet dignity and sincerity, barely thirty years old but with the wisdom of a man fifty years his senior"

(Songling 1958: 58). His retention of the cotton robe, while rejecting gold and silk, captures in a material way his spiritual asceticism, similar to the ways that some Islamic reformers and their followers in northern Nigeria have often preferred to dress simply and live in remote rural areas away from the world. Indeed, regarding the sensuous pleasure of pure silk garments, Shehu 'Uthmān dan Fodio (1978: 91–92) wrote that Muslim men were forbidden to wear them, even during jihād, while women were allowed to do so, marking a particular form of gender distinction.[1] Similarly, members of the Darul Islam group residing in rural Niger State (until they were expelled in 2009) wore simple garments—men wore kaftans with short pants and turbans and women wore long black *hijab* (*Daily Trust* 2009). The Islamic reform group Maitatsine, the group that perhaps is most similar to Boko Haram in its rejection of Western ways and its urban base (however in Kano, not Maiduguri), went still further by condemning "automobiles, radios, watches, televisions and even buttons" (Lubeck 1985: 370). This way of thinking is expressed in a poem composed in northern Nigeria in the 1930s:

> Whatever article of their clothing, if you wear it, I tell you that you may understand,
> If you pray a thousand times you will not be vindicated—
> And the same applies to the maker of hurricane lamp globes—
> Your short trousers together with your tight-fitting trousers,
> Whoever puts them on, his unbelief is wide.
>
> . . .
>
> Whoever wears suits with buttons, he has apostatized,
> He has no religion at all, only pride,
> His state is the state of the makers of silver dollars,
> They are beyond our power to imitate,
> One should not wear shirts with collars,
> Whoever wears them, his unbelief is wide.
>
> . . .
>
> Khaki and pyjamas, whoever it is
> Who wears them and prays in them, he has committed a crime (Hiskett 1973: 164)

Thus, the camouflage uniforms worn by Boko Haram fighters, however subversive of the prevailing government, would neither have been approved by this poet nor have been permitted during the Maitatsine revolt.

Although the meaning of successive Islamic reform movements in northern Nigeria may not be understood without considering their historical, political, and economic contexts, more general social dynamics at play may help to explain these recurring efforts of religious reform. In many places and times, people have attempted to find an optimal way of being in the world, to find the right path and the virtuous way. Textiles and dress have often been an integral part of this process as members of reform movements express their religious beliefs, in part, through material means. These material things—*abin duniya* (things of the world)—may nonetheless be used to represent spiritual ideals and distinguish the identities of successive reform groups. Textiles and clothing are particularly salient because of their close association with the human body and its techniques (Mauss 1973), as when a woman dons a *hijab* before kneeling in prayer or when a man carefully winds twenty yards of cloth around his head to secure his turban. The profound significance of various forms of Islamic dress may also be seen in the responses of others to its different manifestations, as when Izala women who wore *hijab* were harassed by Qādiriyya and Tijāniyya men in Zaria City in the 1980s—or later, when *hijab*-wearing women and girls are feared as sources of deadly Boko Haram violence.

Religion and Material Things

The importance of material things—particularly textiles and dress—in expressing the moral position of their users and conveying religious ideas and sentiments has often been observed. In the relationship between people and ordinary things, *abin duniya* may be imbued with ideas, yet the material qualities of these things may, in turn, shape individuals' perceptions of them. In India, for example, the historically close connection between a moral social identity and cloth was conveyed through patterning, colors, and material qualities of the thread from which it was made. With the influx of British-manufactured textiles in the early twentieth century, which undermined the extensive Indian handweaving industry, the commodification of textiles—as factory-made, impersonal things—was countered by nationalists such as Mahatma Gandhi, who promoted *swadeshi* (home industries), which included hand spinning and the handweaving of cloth, which "could evoke powerful symbols of community and right conduct" (Bayly 1986: 285). Moral qualities such as association, cooperation, and diligence are necessarily related to the myriad processes involved in making handwoven cloth. Furthermore, cloth—because of its flexibility and absorbency as well as the relative ease with which it travels—can be used to transmit associated moral qualities, as when turbans and veils obtained in Mecca convey special spiritual blessings on their original and subsequent wearers (van Santen 2013; Renne 2015). How individuals as members of Islamic reform groups imagine Islamic dress—for example, as dress in the time of the Prophet—reinforces their identity as a group and visually asserts a particular moral positioning with respect to others, who may or may not accept these claims. T. O. Beidelman notes two aspects of this imaginative dynamic: for while "imagination involves contemplation and speculation about the ideas or symbols that stand for [the coherence of] one's world . . . at other times, imagination provides vent for profound disquiet and hostility by centering on these very contradictions [in prevailing visions of the world]" (1985: 6).[2] Thus, just as medieval Islamic scholars in North Africa depended on both imaginative contemplation as well as a chain of authority to legitimate their reading of the Qur'ān (Touati 2010), so Islamic reformers in northern Nigeria have used imaginative thinking to redress contradictions in religious beliefs and moral practice. Particular material things have often been used as part of this process. During the Sokoto Caliphate, Shehu dan Fodio insisted that Muslim men wear turbans; he also favored the wearing of particularly colored clothing—for example, green, in reference to the dress of the Prophet (dan Fodio 1978: 92). A later reformer, Malam Isiyaka Salisu, of the 'Yan Kala Kato group, which in 2009 was based in Zaria (Sa'idu 2009a, 2009c), distinguished his group's doctrine by focusing on the Qur'ān as the only source of Islamic knowledge and jurisprudence, thus rejecting study of the hadith. Salisu also represented this distinction in a material way by ending the use of white cloth shrouds (*likkafani*) as part of Muslim burial practices because they are not specifically mentioned in the Qur'ān: "We also differ from the way other Muslims make graves for their dead. Our way of making graves is only to dig a hole and put the deceased in and return back the dug-sand. This is how Allah commanded. We don't waste time in decorating graves" (Sa'idu 2009c). Thus, reformist efforts to address a world seemingly amiss and return it to moral rightness continue to be distinguished by distinctive interpretations of Islamic texts and uses of material things.

However, like the moral reimagining of reformist Islamic concepts with which particular textiles and clothing are associated, their specific meanings are continually being reproduced, modified, and challenged. The *keffiyeh* "little turbans" worn by Boko Haram members follow dan Fodio's precept that Muslim men wear turbans. Yet they differ visually from the solid white or shiny blue-black dan Kura turbans worn in the nineteenth century and also suggest a modified meaning—namely, religious and political support for Palestinians, who are associated with these checked cloths. Also, by wearing kaftans rather than the more local Hausa *babban riga*, they assert a global Muslim identity rather than one associated with traditional Hausa-Fulani emirs, whom they view as collaborators with the Nigerian state (see fig. 8.3). Nonetheless, many men in northern Nigeria have taken to wearing lighter-weight and less costly kaftans for convenience and fashion, not necessarily to distance themselves from emirate rulers. The voluminous *babban riga*, covered with elaborate hand (or machine) embroidery, continue to be worn, but mainly by those associated with traditional rule—emirs, royal families (*sarauta*), and traditional district heads—although northern Nigerian state and national political leaders such as Buhari also wear them on occasion. This sartorial shift reflects a dramatic change in the ways that one particular form of Islamic dress—embroidered robes—are being used, commissioned, and distributed as gifts, which has contributed to a sense of social disintegration and of moral disorder for some.

Robes, Cars, and Distributions of Gifts

Babban riga are particularly useful material things with which to consider changing obligations between political rulers and their subjects in northern Nigeria, changes that have contributed to a general sense of a world gone awry. As described in earlier chapters, the distribution of robes as gifts was an important expression of emirate political hierarchy among court officials, district leaders, and community members. The dynamic of obligations and rights associated with these distributions served to maintain the political authority of the emir and good social relations with his subjects. Yet this material means of marking and sustaining social and political order also included a system of production of these robes that entailed a parallel set of social relations among designers, embroiderers, tailors, washers, beaters, and traders. Thus, as in the Mughal empire, which controlled much of northern India from the early sixteenth to mid-eighteenth centuries, it was "the duty of the king . . . to consume the wares of his subjects and to make his court the great engine of redistribution" (Bayly 1986: 298). Indeed, moral and material values may be reinforced through the exchange of such textiles (Appadurai 1986).

However, this consumption and distribution of robes has significantly changed in northern Nigeria in recent years. While emirs may continue to commission and distribute robes—although at a reduced rate as compared with the past—government officials have largely opted out of the system of robe distribution. In 2012, Jimi Magajiya (fig. E.1), a robe designer in Zaria city, explained the basis for this change:

> The years 2000–2007, I can say that there were more sales for *babban riga* but in 2009–2012, there is so much reduction . . . after these years, things have changed. Especially since three years ago [2009], we have so many problems, there is no money and there is no market. And I think the reason why is because the people now, in their minds, they only care about government and the government takes away everything from the people.
>
> You see the [local government] chairman, before he could do things for people. But now he cannot because they are not given so much money [from the state]. All they get now is enough to take care of themselves. And there are so many people who need things from the government. Some people get into politics just to get money to buy cars, they don't care about people. Before, politicians used to buy *babban riga* and distribute them to people, so that those who are doing the robes can have a market. . . . Now instead of buying robes, they prefer to buy expensive cars to give to the person [political boss] who can

Figure E.1. Jimi Magajiya drawing patterns on cotton damask (*shadda*) in preparation for hand-embroidery work in his home in Anguwar Magajiya, Zaria City, July 2, 2012. (Photograph by the author)

help them to win the election. Because of that, he knows he has no problems with the masses because he doesn't need their vote. That is why things have become worse now. (Jimi Magajiya, interview by the author, July 4, 2012, Zaria)

While the demand for *babban riga* has also declined due to changing fashion tastes and men's preference for lighter-weight kaftans with simpler designs, Jimi Magajiya's assessment of the impact of government officials' spending on cars rather than on robes or "other things [they] can do for people," is a trenchant observation. Reports emerging from recent EFCC investigations have shown the enormous amounts spent on cars by governors and the Nigerian legislature. For example, in 2014 at the end of his term as governor of Katsina State, Ibrahim Shema sold to himself state vehicles worth N400 million for a fraction of their price. "Can you imagine a car of N78 million bought in 2014 was sold [to the former governor] for just N3 million, another N10 million vehicle for N990,000?" asked the present governor, Aminu Masari (Aminu 2016). More recently, in May 2016 Nuruddeen Abdallah (2016b) of the *Daily Trust* reported that many state governments distributed expensive official vehicles for legislators' use ("mostly 2016 SUV models of Toyota Land Cruiser Prado, Escape Ford, as well as . . . Toyota Camry, Hyundai and Peugeot brands"), while at the same time, "a majority of Nigeria's 36 states owe workers between one to nine months in unpaid salaries."

This situation hardly corresponds to an ideal of austerity and caring for the poor promulgated by Islamic reformers such as dan Fodio, who observed that there was a "difference between the governments of the Muslims and the governments of the unbelievers. . . . One of the ways of their government is to shut the door in the face of the needy" (Hiskett 1960: 569).

* * *

The economy of the Sokoto Caliphate was based on agriculture, craft production, and trade, which reflected a particular intersection of work, worship, and seasonal changes. Unemployment was not an issue, and in any event such figures were not recorded. However, the continuing practice of slavery suggests that it was people, not work opportunities, who were in shorter supply (Guyer 1995). This particular configuration of labor enabled the caliphate to become a major producer and exporter of textiles throughout West Africa, as Philip Shea (1975, 2006) has observed. With some modifications, this form of textile production and trade persisted, even during the colonial period when quantities of manufactured textiles and machine-spun thread were imported and alternative employment opportunities—in Western forms of teaching, medicine, and local government—began to emerge. New Islamic groups such as Ansar ud-Deen and the Bamidele group in Ilorin and Ibadan, in southwestern Nigeria, reflected the different responses to these changes.[3] With independence in 1960 and the opening of textile mills in northern Nigeria, industrial textile manufacturing grew, although men's narrow-strip handweaving continued in rural areas, particularly in Kano State (United Nations 1968).

These relationships between religious practice, textile-related work, and governance continued through the mid-1960s, when, after the assassinations of Abubakar Tafawa Balewa and Ahmadu Bello, civil war broke out in 1967. It was not until 1970, when relative peace returned, that the economy began to grow, especially in response to a favorable exchange rate supported by high oil prices. Yet rather than provide for the majority of citizens, the so-called oil boom years led to growing inequality, reflected in the Maitatsine rebellion of 1980, as the shift from rural craft, agriculture, and trade to capitalist manufacturing and oil wealth favored a relative urban few (Lubeck 1985, 1986). This was also a period of considerable religious change and political instability, when the Salafist Islamic group Izala emerged, challenging older Qādiriyya and Tijāniyya beliefs and practices, and when a series of military coups led to four changes in national leadership in ten years, from 1983 to 1993. Furthermore, in the years following the implementation of a structural adjustment program in 1986, the continuing drop in the value of the naira contributed to infrastructural decay and the decline of the northern Nigerian textile industry, with a concurrent loss of jobs. The fragmentation of Izala after the death of Sheikh Abubakar Gumi in 1992 resulted in

Figure E.2. Unemployment in northern Nigeria increased with the closing of the many textile mills there, leading one writer to observe that the "collapse of industries [is] worse than Boko Haram" (Isuwa 2012). Seven years after the closing of the Kaduna Textiles Limited mill, the condition of one of the main weaving rooms suggests the devastation of the industry, Kaduna, June 17, 2011. (Photograph by the author)

the emergence of new Islamic reform groups: Salafiyya in Zaria, Ahlus-Sunnah in Kano, and Boko Haram in Maiduguri.

None of the founders of these new groups were alive in 2016, and all had violent deaths. Furthermore, the carnage perpetuated in the aftermath of the extrajudicial killing of Mohammed Yusuf, the founder of Boko Haram, continues to mark parts of northeastern Nigeria. Yet some have argued that other factors—such as unemployment, poverty, and corruption (Salkida 2009)—have not only contributed to the growth of Boko Haram but have been even more destructive. For example, Sanusi Abubakar (2016) cites the present high rate of unemployment (12.1 percent) as "a threat worse than Boko Haram" (fig. E.2). Similarly, Sheikh Ahmad Gumi, the son of Abubakar Gumi, has conflated economic and religious offense when noting the huge sums stolen by government officials, bankers, and wealthy businessmen: "The people that live on corruption, that is their religion" (Sa'idu 2016b).

It would be comforting to think that a return to agriculture, textile production, and trade as practiced during the Sokoto Caliphate would bring about widespread employment. The nineteenth century was also a time of violence, in part because of the continuing practice of slavery but also because of continuing conflict over territorial sovereignty and political power. Yet increased participation of young people in agriculture, a revived textile industry, and small and medium-sized enterprises (SMEs) are mentioned as possible solutions to the contemporary problem of unemployment (Meagher 2010; World Bank 2016a, 2016b). There are also "palliatives" being offered by the federal government, which include technical and digital education that may improve young northern Nigerians' work opportunities (*Daily Trust* 2016c). A recent tree-planting program outlined for Kaduna State is projected to involve a minimum of 27,000 women who will be paid to plant and care for economic trees—cashew, neem, shea butter, and moringa—in a shelter belt from Ikara to Birnin Gwari (Alabi 2016). Additionally, a pilot solar power project, funded by the United Kingdom Agency for International Development (UKAID), provided 49,000 homes with basic solar power systems in early 2016 (Sunday 2016). These programs are all important contributions toward improving the well-being of northern Nigerians.

However, it is the regular provision of electricity through solar power or other means that is the critical element for improving business, industry, and trade in the north: "the biggest constraint to productivity in Nigeria is power" (World Bank 2016a: 15). Indeed, for northern Nigerian cities such as Kano to provide employment for their growing populations due to rural–urban migration, the provision of basic infrastructural services such as electricity and water are essential (World Bank 2016a).

Work, Worship, and Everyday Moral Virtues

The shift from wealth based on oil extraction to wealth based on various forms of urban-based commerce—material and digital as well as manufacturing and trade—and improved agriculture has much to offer those living in northern Nigeria. In some ways, it recalls the nineteenth- and early twentieth-century family trading networks, such as the successful family businesses based in Kano described by Abdulkarim DanAsabe (2000), Paul Lovejoy (1980), and Abdullahi Mohammed (1978). Through a combination of business acumen, hard work, cooperation, social and political connections, and prayer, cloth and kola were profitably traded throughout Nigeria and West Africa. Similarly, the caravan trader Madugu Mohamman Mai Gashin Baki, described by Eduard Flegel ([1885] 1985), exhibited the socially valued skills of cooperation, modesty, and diligence in his organization and leadership of caravans to Adamawa and beyond. In other words, in thinking about the future, "it would be useful to look at cultural norms and social structures that seem to work well and from which lessons could be extrapolated" (Fischer 2014: 215).

In the mid-nineteenth century, caravan leaders (*madugu*) from Kano who traveled west toward Salaga in what is now eastern Ghana brought goods loaded on donkeys from the Kano region—cloth, jewelry, and leather goods—and returned to Kano with kola nuts from the Ashanti region (Goody and Mustapha 1967). Successful *madugu* shared several characteristics: they were wealthy traders in their own right, they came from certain ethnic groups whose members provided social support, and "they had to be well-respected, confident, but not overly ambitious" (Lovejoy 1980: 103). One aspect of caravan trade was its improvisational quality—*malamai* needed to be consulted in order to determine an auspicious date for departure; dates were not openly announced but rather were spread by word of mouth and by rumor so that the flexibility to organize last-minute preparations was an important skill. Another characteristic of a successful *madugu* was the psychological preparedness about possible dangers facing a caravan and sufficient knowledge and materials to prevent them. Things that brought luck or protection included *layoyi* (amulets that consisted of small folded pieces of paper covered with writing from the Qur'ān, enclosed in leather packets; Hassan 1992; Heathcote 1974; Rubin 1984); certain items of clothing or hats; and special swords or knives. Lovejoy (1980: 105) also mentions the increasing importance of Islamic knowledge, and several of the successful Kano businessmen discussed by DanAsabe (2000) had memorized the Qur'ān as children. Some of these men also kept written records of caravan trade, which suggests that literacy was another valuable trading asset. Finally, the personal ability to attract a sufficient number of loyal followers was also critically important in establishing a reputation as a famous *madugu*.[4]

While not all leaders of Islamic reform groups in northern Nigeria have exhibited all of these qualities,[5] the reputation for prayer, sermons, and scholarship, generosity, flexibility, and modesty—personally and in appearance—attracted the loyalty of followers to Shehu dan Fodio and his son Muhammad Bello. Simplicity in dress and the distribution of clothing, epitomized by 'Attāb b. Usayd's giving out the two gowns he had received (noted by dan Fodio in *Bayān Wujūb al-Hijra* [1978; see chapter 1 epigraph]), exemplifies this ideal of generous modesty. Through their assessment of the excellence, the good character, of Islamic reformers, their followers hope to follow the path that is straight and to become better people and live better lives (Hiskett 1960: 570).

Islamic Reform and Imagined Moral Communities

Despite the appeal that good character has contributed to the successful leadership of several Islamic reformers and has figured in improvements in education, pilgrimage, and trade, the importance of Islam in considering the right way forward, "the path that is straight," has sometimes resulted in conflict (Mustapha 2014: 6). Shehu 'Uthmān dan Fodio led the Sokoto jihād against the leaders—political and religious—for what he saw as their lax observance of

Islam (Last 1967), while Qādiriyya leaders challenged the practices introduced by the Tijāniyya leader Sheikh Ibrahim Niass. Subsequently, Abubakar Gumi condemned a range of religious practices performed by followers of Tijāniyya and Qādiriyya movements, while Sheikh Ja'far Mahmoud Adam established the Ahlus-Sunnah movement in response to what he saw as the harshness of Gumi's pronouncements. Yet these conflicting views of the straight path may also be seen as forms of social interaction, with opposing views and practices defining the boundaries of one group with respect to others and thus providing the grounds by which future resolution of differences may be achieved. For example, the terrible violence of Boko Haram has strengthened unity among different Islamic groups in northern Nigeria, even as differences in religious practices and dress persist.

One aspect of this unity is "oriented around recognized moral virtues" (Fischer 2014: 217), which in the case of members of different Islamic reform groups include knowledge of the Qur'ān and hadith as well as observance of the five daily prayers and of Ramadan. Most northern Nigerian Muslims, even those with only basic knowledge of the Qur'ān, know Al-Fātihah (The Prologue; Sura 1) by heart:

ALL PRAISE BE to Allah,
Lord of all the worlds,
2. Most beneficent, ever-merciful,
3. King of the Day of Judgement.
4. You alone we worship, and to You
alone turn for help.
5. Guide us (O Lord) to the path that is straight,
6. The path of those You have blessed,
7. Not of those who have earned Your anger,
nor those who have gone astray (*Al-Qur'ān* 1993)

Yet it is naïve to think that all Muslims in northern Nigeria interpret "the path that is straight" in the same way. Some, such as the Muslim government officials responsible for the theft of billions of naira, which would have gone far in building basic infrastructure in the country,[6] have interpreted "the path of those You have blessed" in a particular way. Others, such as Mohammed Yusuf and followers of Boko Haram, have interpreted "the path that is straight" differently; for them, a separate Islamic state, distinct from the secular Nigerian state, is the only proper path.[7]

These two distinctive views of the "path that is straight" also reflect the continuing tension between the wealth and power of politicians and the austerity and knowledge of Islamic scholars that contributed to conflict associated with the nineteenth-century Sokoto jihād and that continued even during the relative unity of the Sokoto Caliphate. In the twenty-first century, economic inequality, unemployment, lack of basic infrastructure, and insecurity ("shut[ting] the door in the face of the needy," as Shehu dan Fodio put it [Hiskett 1960: 569]) have been attributed not to emirate leaders and their courts but largely to officials of the Nigerian state—ministers, governors, and other "public servants" (Opoola 2016). The 2015 election of the opposition party APC candidates reflects an attempt by Nigerians to elect leaders who will address these problems. Since May 2015, numerous investigations of the misuse of government funds have been initiated and some funds have been recovered.[8] Efforts to address unemployment and malnourishment through job-creation initiatives, training courses, and school food programs have been initiated, yet the questions raised by Islamic reformers in northern Nigeria about the moral basis of work remain. How can economic inequality be addressed and how can employment opportunities be increased? How can one follow "the path that is straight" that will ensure one's presence in paradise in the afterlife while also living a better material life in this world?

Perhaps some earlier practices may help in imagining this future. During the 1960s, the textile industry in Kano and Kaduna prospered alongside small hand-weaving and hand- and machine-embroidery businesses. Even with secondhand equipment and the employment of expensive expatriate staff, the demand for textiles and clothing by the growing population of Nigeria ensured the success of these endeavors. However, by the end of the twentieth century, textile mills were foundering and fewer young men were engaged in handweaving work. While less costly textile imports, mostly from China, are often blamed for the industry's subsequent decline, it was mainly infrastructural problems—electricity and water—along with a devalued currency that made replacement equipment prohibitively expensive that were ultimately to blame.

Yet the revitalization of the textile industry has been a recurring aspiration of several politicians and government agencies. In July 2010, Namadi Sambo, who was then Nigeria's vice president, set up a committee to reorganize revival efforts by the federal government (Shehu 2010). By the end of March 2011, Salisu Umar, chairman of the textile sector of the Manufacturers Association of Nigeria, reported that "at least 60 per cent of textile companies in the country have accessed loan[s] from the N100 billion textile revival fund" (Shosanya 2011). However, without infrastructural improvements, this initiative was doomed to fail. In May 2015, calls for reviving Kaduna's textile industry by the governor of Kaduna State, Nasir el-Rufai, reflected an Action Democratic Party (ADP) election promise. He noted that "reviving the textiles is a significant campaign promise of General Buhari and he is committed to it. Besides, Buhari lives in Kaduna and knows the impact of the textile industry on the economy. Kaduna used to be Manchester of the textile industry. We have met at forum of northern governors-elect and we have decided to ensure the revival of the textile companies" (Adama 2015).

Later, in April 2016, Vice President Yemi Osinbajo met with members of the Implementation Committee on the National Cotton, Textile and Garment Policy concerning their proposal for "a 'Wear Naija Day' when public officials and employees of corporate organisations would all wear locally made fabrics" (Wakili 2016b). A year later, however, the government's order to patronize "Made in Nigeria" textiles had largely been ignored (*Daily Trust* 2018a). Similarly, despite the optimistic announcement by the New Nigeria Development Company in August 2017 about plans to reopen the KTL mill negotiated with Turkish textile manufacturer SUR (*Daily Trust* 2017), it is unlikely that production will begin without a large government order for uniform materials (interview by the author, November 13, 2017, Kaduna).

If the needs of the industry for electricity and water can be met, it is possible that some of the funds recovered by the federal government may be used to refurbish the main textile mills in Kaduna and Kano and to provide updated equipment and training. If current tariffs on textile imports can be enforced, the production of Nigerian-manufactured textiles would have a price advantage, even if efficiencies of production cannot compared with those of Chinese mills. One Nigerian textile trader who buys textiles from China and works out of Kano would prefer local products if they were available:

> If they put the textile industry in order, we prefer to deal with our own people in Nigeria. Because our country will improve and people will get more work to do. And sometimes we don't like to go outside to buy things, but if we can't get it in our country, we have to.
>
> What I will say is that our government should look at the textile problem. If the government can make the production of textiles like China—because China, they can be using their land for cotton farming—and here in Nigeria we have that too. We have people who can produce the cotton. So we can produce just like China. Because the factory can get cotton and at a cheaper price. But it is power that is the main problem. Because if there is no light, the production will be costly because they have to buy diesel and other things. When the government solves all these problems, we will come back to "Made in Nigeria" instead of "Made in China." The economy of our country will improve and can even go to other countries to sell. (Alhaji Yakubu Nuhu, interview by the author, August 28, 2012, Zaria)

Alhaji Yakubu Nuhu mentioned cotton production, and this agricultural component is another aspect of textile manufacturing revitalization that has been discussed.[9] However, other smaller-scale textile-related possibilities would be particularly appropriate given the cultural "combination . . . of norms, dispositions, practices, and histories, [that have] frame[d] the good life" (Appadurai 2013: 292) in the northern Nigerian past. The valued qualities of piety, flexibility, generosity, literacy, and modesty, which facilitated an elaborate system of textile

Figure E.3. Thread sales expert at one specialty shop in
Kantin Kwari market, Kano. This shop consists of floor-to-
ceiling shelves filled with different types of thread, mainly
for hand and machine embroidery, Kano, March 7, 2016.
(Photograph by the author)

production and trade, could be a resource for the future. For example, in 2014,
several Chinese textile manufacturing firms began advertising narrow-strip textiles on the Chinese website Alibaba. These strips are woven on narrow band
looms (also sold on Alibaba). With sufficient electricity and local sources of raw
cotton and cotton thread, weavers could establish small businesses to fill this
continuing demand for narrow-strip textiles that could be used for, among other
things, *saki* cloth for turbans. Other smaller-scale textile manufacturing businesses could produce thread for weaving and embroidery as well as made-to-
order blankets and ready-to-wear clothing and underwear and thrive in places

such as Kano, where the famous Kantin Kwari market already has many small, well-organized businesses involved in the textile trade (fig. E.3).

＊ ＊ ＊

As Marcel Mauss has observed, "These pages of social history, theoretical sociology, political economy and morality do no more than lead us to old problems which are constantly turning up under new guises" (1967: 2). If these suggestions seem unrealistic, particularly during the hard times that Nigeria is facing with the decline in oil prices beginning in 2015 and the weakened value of the naira in 2016, as well as with expensive recovery efforts estimated at $5.9 billion needed in northeastern Nigeria in 2016 (Sule 2016), it is important to recall that textiles have not only played an important historical role in the material well-being of many living in northern Nigeria but also an important part in the perpetuation of Islamic beliefs and practices there. Indeed, Islamic learning and worship have long intersected with textile trade and production: from the young boys who memorize passages from the Qur'ān written on *allo* boards and learn how to weave; to itinerant textile traders who studied with Islamic scholars as they traveled; to *hijab*-clad married women as they attend *Islamiyya Matan Aure* classes; and to daily prayers performed by mill workers at the small mosques built on the grounds of textile mills in Kaduna. Textiles have also played in integral role in Islamic reform movements, visually delineating Muslim followers of particular Islamic leaders, including dan Fodio, Salami Bamidele, Abubakar Gumi, and Yusuf. It remains to be seen whether these long-standing connections can be reimagined and revived in new ways that "can structure the economy and . . . lives to best promote the common good" (Fischer 2014: 216). If Mauss is correct about "old problems which are constantly turning up under new guises," then it is likely that the problems that faced Shehu dan Fodio in the nineteenth century, particularly the ostentatious wealth of the political elite and a disregard for the common good, will turn up "under new guises" in the future, just as new Islamic reform movements—including distinctive forms of dress and, at times, disguise—will emerge to address them.

Notes

1. While he noted that some scholars had written that wearing silk in battle was permissible because "it makes a man feel proud and overawes the enemy in battle," dan Fodio rejected this argument (1978: 91). Nonetheless, as Colleen Kriger (2010) has observed and museum collections confirm, some Muslim men in the nineteenth-century Sokoto Caliphate certainly wore a range of styles of large silk robes (Worden 2010).

2. There is another aspect of imagination that differs from these two polarities—namely what might be called immoral imagination—that is neither a positive envisaging of the group

nor a questioning of its contradictions but rather is purely negative and immoral. Holocaust survivor Primo Levi's observation about Nazi misuses of one particular thing—a Jewish prayer shawl—exemplifies this sort of imagination: "I remember here, in passing, that the vilification of the prayer shawl is as old as anti-Semitism—from those shawls, taken from deportees, the SS would make underwear which was then distributed to the Jews imprisoned in the Lager" (1984: 5).

3. The Islamic reform group Ansar ud-Deen, founded in Lagos in 1923, has schools in Ibadan and Ilorin, with branches in Abuja and Kaduna. It supports women's education and freedom of movement (Gbadamosi 1978a), while the Bamidele movement emphasizes seclusion and women's wearing of *burqa* (Doi 1969).

4. Many of these qualities, evidence of the moral character of Hausa caravan leaders, are also characteristics that are valued in Hausa men and women, referred to more generally as having *kirki*, excellence of character (Salamone and Salamone 1993).

5. For example, one of the leaders of Boko Haram, Abubakar Shekau, has vociferously bragged on YouTube about the prowess of this group, which may explain why, along with the terrible violence he perpetuated, many Hausa-Fulani found his leadership so untenable and revealing of his lack of *kirki*.

6. Out of the N1.34 trillion allegedly stolen by fifty-five individuals over a six-year period, from 2006 to 2013, it is estimated that "one third of the stolen funds could have provided 635.18 kilometres of road; built 36 ultra modern hospitals, that is one ultra modern hospital per state; built 183 schools; educated 3,974 children from primary to tertiary level at 25.24 million per child; and built 20,062 units of 2-bedroom houses" (Opoola 2016).

7. Many northern Nigerian Muslims would agree that the moral basis of this particular example of jihād is belied by a 2016 World Bank "Post Insurgency Recovery and Peace Building Assessment Report," which reports that "Borno State lost 20,000 citizens and suffered property damage worth $5.9bn . . . in the hands of Boko Haram insurgents in the last seven years" (Sule 2016).

8. On June 4, 2016, the minister of information, Lai Mohammed, noted that the government had recovered over N115 billion—"in local and hard currencies," during the previous year, from June 2015 to May 2016 (Wakili, Mudashir, and Opoola 2016).

9. In July 2016, the director general of the Raw Materials Research and Development Council (RMRDC) announced that over ten tons of improved cotton seeds had been distributed to farmers over the past two years (Agbo 2016).

Glossary

abawa: type of loosely spun silk or rayon thread

abaya: woman's gown

abin duniya: things of this world

adiko: type of women's head tie

ajami: Hausa words written in Arabic script

akoko: unpatterned white cotton cloth; baft

alfuta: handkerchief

alhaji (male), *hajiya* (female): person who has performed the hajj

alharini: imported magenta waste silk

alkyabba: embroidered capes with hoods, worn by royalty

allo: board used by students to memorize portions of the Qur'ān (*wala* in Yoruba)

almajiri: itinerant Islamic student

amawali: men's face veil

aska biyu: embroidered pattern on men's robes; literally, two knives

aska tara: embroidered pattern on men's robes; literally, ten knives

atamfa: printed textile (from English, stamped)

atamfa hajji: printed cloth specially made for Nigerian hajj pilgrims

babban riga: large men's robe

ƙaƙin rawani: black turban made with indigo-dyed ɗan Kura cloth

barka: blessings

bid'a: religious innovation; some viewed as heretical by different groups

black oil: oil used to power textile mills when electricity is unavailable

burqa: a robe-like garment worn by women, which covers both the body and face

carbi: prayer beads, also called *tesba*; refers to modern digital counters as well

chop marks: trademarks used on manufactured textiles

ɗan Kura: type of blue-black indigo-dyed cloth; literally, son of Kura (town)

ɗankwali: headscarf (Zaria)

dar al-Islam: the Islamic community (*umma* in Arabic)

da'wah: Islamic proselytization; literally, invitation in Arabic

ɗinkin hannu: hand embroidered

ɗinkin keke: machine embroidered

dogarai: palace guards

duniya: this world

eleeha: Yoruba Muslim women who wear *burqa*-like cloth coverings; literally, owner of seclusion in Yoruba

falke (or *farke*): traveling trader

fari: white cotton cloth

fiqh: Islamic jurisprudence

gele: see *gyale*

gyale: stolelike veil; *gele* (Yoruba)

gyale-hijab: style of *hijab* made with two *gyale* veil-like flaps of cloth

hadith: traditions of the Prophet Muhammad

harami: *ihrām* dress worn by men during the hajj

harsa sarauta: stiff white cloth used in royal turbans

hijab: type of head and body covering, a form of veil

hisab: divination

hizami: a strip of cloth used as head covering, also referred to as a "little turban"

hula: cap

iboju: face veil (Yoruba)

iborun: stole; cloth worn over shoulder or around waist (Yoruba)

ihrām: the period during the performance of the hajj when pilgrims are said to be in the state of *ihrām* and are subject to numerous restrictions

'imāma: Arabic word for turban; *rawani/rawuna* (Hausa); *lawani* (Yoruba)

Islamiyya Matan Aure: Islamic classes for married women

jaji: women teachers organized by Nana Asma'u, the daughter of Shehu dan Fodio in mid-nineteenth century Sokoto

jellabiya: all-encompassing *burqa*-like garment worn by Yoruba Muslim women; also referred to as *jilbab*

jilbab: see *jellabiya*

kaftani mai rumi: kaftan with *mai rumi* (*passementerie*) embroidery

kallabi: headscarf (Kano)

katsi: dyebath residue removed from the bottom of dye pots, used to make *laso* cement

kayan gabas: things from the Middle East

kayan Mecca: things from Mecca; items obtained on hajj for gifts and mementos

keffiyeh: checked black and white (or red and white) cloth, used as *hizami* (men's "little turbans") and face coverings, associated with Palestinians

khadi: handwoven cloth made under Mahatma Gandhi's leadership during the nationalist movement in India

kirki: excellence of character

kiswa: black silk cloth with Qur'ānic verses hand embroidered in gold and silver thread, used to cover the Ka'aba in Mecca (robe in Arabic) *kore:* type of dark, indigo-dyed robe

kunne: literally, ears; tying of turbans to produce earlike projections

kunya: modesty

kwatanniya: large clay pots used for indigo dyeing

Lahira da Aljannat: afterlife in paradise

laso: cement made from *katsi* dyebath residue, used to make large dye pits

lawani: Yoruba word for turban; *rawani/rawuna* (Hausa); *'imāma* (Arabic)

layoyi: protective amulets consisting of small folded pieces of paper covered with writing from the Qur'ān enclosed in leather packets

likkafani: white cloth burial shroud

madugu: caravan leader

mai roba: fashion *hijab* made with light nylon fabrics

mai rumi: type of embroidery using *abawa* thread and couched stitching, related to *passementerie* embroidery

maiyafi: sueded cotton material used for *hijabs*; literally, sand

makawiya: Saudi headdress, *'aqal*; also known as *kambu* in Hausa

malafa, malfa: type of straw hat worn by men over a turban or cap, or by women teachers in Sokoto

malam (s), malamai (pl): Islamic teacher(s)

malum malum: type of large embroidered robe with large checkered design

mayafi: large cloth worn by women that covers the head and body

mujadded: Islamic reformer (Yoruba)

mutane riguna: Muslims; literally, people of the gown

mutawwif: hajj guide in Saudi Arabia

muwardi: turban with woven pattern

naɗi: winding of turban; also spinning of cotton to make yarn

neman girma: the practice of appearing big, looking important; literally, looking for greatness

niqab: type of face veil

oniwala: supplementary weft pattern on narrow handwoven cloth strips depicting wooden board (*wala* in Yoruba, *allo* in Hausa) on which students write Qu'rānic verses

rawani (s), rawuna (pl): turban(s); *lawani* (Yoruba); *'imāma* (Arabic)

rawani ɗan Sardauna: bright multicolored turban associated with Ahmadu Bello

rawani Sunnah: turban of Muslims

ribats: garrison towns

rigar giwa: large embroidered robe; literally, the robe of an elephant

rigar sarki: refers to horse riders who accompany the emir during processions; literally, the robe of the king

saki: guinea fowl cloth woven with black and white warp and weft threads, giving it a speckled appearance; known as *etu* in Yoruba

Salafi: Islamic group that advocates a return to the time of the Prophet and places emphasis on the Qur'ān and hadith; associated with Saudi Arabia

Sallah: Muslim holiday of Eid-el-Fitr marking the end of the Ramadan fast

sarauta: royalty

sarki: emir, king

shadda: cotton damask, also known as guinea brocade; *aso Ateginni* (Yoruba)

Shari'a: Islamic law

sha rubutu: practice of writing portions of the Qur'ān on a wooden *allo* board, then washing off the ink and drinking the resulting ink-water mixture

shuni: concentrated indigo paste used to produce shiny black cloth

soro: raised dome in the roof of a compound's entry room (*zaure*)

Sufi: Islamic group associated with Sunni Islam

tafsir: commentary on a Qur'ānic text

talakawa: commoners, poor people

tariqa: Sunni Islam groups in northern Nigeria: Qādiriyya and Tijāniyya

tikaris: undocumented Nigerian pilgrims in Saudi Arabia

tokare: costly robes made from doubled cloth strips

tsamiya: local wild silk

tu'ɓe: removing an emir from office; literally, taking off of a garment

turkudi: very narrow handwoven cloth strips (approximately half an inch wide) that are sewn together to make the required size cloth

wazifa: white cloth used in Tijaniyya *zhikr* ritual associated with physical presence of the spirit of the group's founder, Sheikh Ahmad al-Tijani

'yar Dikwa: embroidery pattern on *babban riga*; literally, daughter of Dikwa (town)

'yar Madaka: embroidery pattern on *babban riga*; literally, daughter of Madaka (town)

zabuni: jacket embroidered with *mai rumi* work

zane: cloth wrapper worn by women as skirt or body/head covering

zawiya: enclosed place for Tijaniyya seclusion, also a prayer group

zhikr: remembrance; Tijaniyya ritual performed to remember founder Ahmad al-Tijani using white *wazifa* cloth

References

Unpublished Work

Armed Conflict Location and Event Data Project (ACLED). 2016. "Nigeria, 1997–2015" (version 6). Accessed May 17. http://www.acleddata.com.

Balewa, Abubakar Tafawa. 1958. Letter to Ahmadu Bello. May 23. File 18/S.7, Premier's Office, 2nd Collection, Nigerian National Archives, Kaduna.

Bello, Omar. 1983. "The Political Thought of Muhammad Bello (c. 1781–1837) as Revealed in His Arabic Writings, More Especially *Al-Ghayth al-Wabi fi Strat Al-Imam Al-'Adl*." PhD thesis, University of London.

Candotti, Marisa. 2015. "Cotton Growing and Textile Production in Northern Nigeria: From Caliphate to Protectorate, c. 1804–1914." PhD thesis, University of London.

Cha Chi Ming. 2006. Miscellaneous unpublished files, Department of Industrial Design, Ahmadu Bello University, Zaria.

Danmole, Hakeem Olumide Akanni. 1980. "The Frontier Emirate: The History of Islam in Ilorin." PhD diss., University of Birmingham, UK.

E. H. D. L. 1925. "Tijani Missionaries in Nigeria." ZAR PROF 7/1, c. 4013. Nigerian National Archives, Kaduna.

Hartley, Gordon. 2012. Unpublished report on Kaduna Textiles Limited. February 18. In the author's possession.

Heathcote, David. 1979. "The Embroidery of Hausa Dress." 2 vols. PhD diss., Ahmadu Bello University, Zaria, Nigeria.

Ministry of Internal Affairs. 1960. Document prepared for the Office of the Premier regarding his upcoming trip to Niger. December 7. Arewa House, Kaduna, Nigeria.

Mohammed, Abdullahi. 1978. "A Hausa Scholar-Trader and His Library Collection: The Case Study of Umar Falke of Kano, Nigeria." PhD diss., Northwestern University, Evanston, IL.

Ndatsu, P. N. 2002. "Nurses Uniform." Unpublished memorandum, Nursing and Midwifery Council of Nigeria, Lagos.

North Central State Government of Nigeria. 1975. "Program for the Installation of Alhaji Shehu Idris, Emir of Zaria, 11th April 1975." Emir's palace, Zaria.

Northern Region of Nigeria. 1954. *Report on the Exchange of Customary Presents*. Lagos: Government Printer. Library of African Studies, Northwestern University, Evanston, IL.

O'Hear, Ann. 1983. "The Economic History of Ilorin in the Nineteenth and Twentieth Centuries: The Rise and Decline of a Middleman Society." PhD diss., University of Birmingham, UK.

Oladimeji, Lateef Folorunsho. 2005. "Da'wah Trend in Islam: A Case Study of the Jamā'atut-Tablīgh in Nigeria." PhD thesis, University of Ilorin, Nigeria.

Premier's Office–Kaduna. 1956. "Ceremonial Robes." File 335/s.1, PRE 1/1 (fourth collection), Nigerian National Archives, Kaduna.

Premier's Office–Kaduna. 1964–1967. "Officers of the Legislature—House Uniforms." Vol. 1. File 396/s.1, PRE 1 (third collection), Nigerian National Archives, Kaduna.

Province of Ilorin. 1932–1954. "Uniforms for Prison Wardens and Native Administrative Police." File 1485, Nigerian National Archives, Kaduna.

Shea, Philip J. 1975. "The Development of an Export-Oriented Dyed Cloth Industry in Kano Emirate in the Nineteenth Century." 2 vols. PhD diss., University of Wisconsin-Madison.

Published Work

Abba, Isa Alkali. 1981. "Sir Ahmadu Bello: The Sardauna of Sokoto's Conversion Campaign 1964–1965 in Adamawa Division and Northern Sardauna Province." *Kano Studies* 2 (2): 53–60.

Abbah, Theophilus. 2011. "Six Months of Terror: 160 Killed in Boko Haram Attacks." *Sunday Trust*, June 19, p. 1.

Abdallah, Nuruddeen. 2016a. "EFCC Recovers N593m Jewellery from Diezani, Omokore's Wife." *Daily Trust*, April 27. https://www.dailytrust.com.ng/news/general/efcc -recovers-n593m-jewellery-from-diezani-omokore-s-wife/144281.html.

———. 2016b. "States Spend Billions on Legislators' Cars." *Daily Trust*, May 24. https://www .dailytrust.com.ng/news/general/states-spend-billions-on-legislators-cars/148121.html.

Abdullah, Abdul, ed. 2005. *Islamic Dress Code for Women*. London: Darussalam Research Division.

Abdulsalami, Isa. 2009. "Customs Intercept Vehicle with Army Uniform in Jos." *The Guardian*, July 19, p. 17.

Abler, Thomas. 1999. *Hinterland Warriors and Military Dress: European Empires and Exotic Uniforms*. Oxford: Berg.

Abubakar, Nasiru. 2009. "Interrogation of Mohammed Yusuf." *Daily Trust*, July 30. https:// maxsiollun.wordpress.com/2009/08/03/videos-of-boko-haram-suspects-being- interrogated-and-executed.

Abubakar, Nasiru, Abbas Jimoh, and Ayegba Ebije. 2009. "Darul-Islam: Concerns over Rights Violation." *Daily Trust*, August 17.

Abubakar, Sanusi. 2016. "A Threat Worse than Boko Haram." *Daily Trust*, May 24. https:// dailytrust.com.ng/news/tuesday-column/a-threat-worse-than-boko-haram/148043.html.

Abubakar, Shehu. 2015. "Escapees Tell of Distress within B/Haram." *Daily Trust*, November 5. https://www.dailytrust.com.ng/news/general/escapees-tell-of-distress-within-b-haram /118152.html.

Abubakar, Shehu, and Omirin Olatunji. 2016. "58 Killed, 78 Injured in Borno IDP Camp Suicide Blast." *Daily Trust*, February 11. https://www.dailytrust.com.ng/news/ general/58-killed-78-injured-in-borno-idp-camp-suicide-blast/133136.html.

Abubakar, Shehu, Omirin Olatunji, and Ibrahim Sule. 2016. "Attack on Maiduguri Villages . . . 85 Corpses Recovered." *Daily Trust*, February 1. https://www.dailytrust.com.ng/news /general/attack-on-maiduguri-villages-85-corpses-recovered/131671.html.

Abubakar, Shehu, and Ibrahim Sawab. 2015. "'Boko Haram Desperate, Recruiting Randomly.'" *Daily Trust*, September 12. https://www.dailytrust.com.ng/news/news /-boko-haram-desperate-recruiting-randomly/110477.html.

Adama, Dickson. 2015. "Why We Must Revive Textile Industry—El-Rufai." *Daily Trust*, May 22. https://www.dailytrust.com.ng/daily/index.php/business/55330-why-we-must -revive-textile-industry-el-rufai.

Agbese, Andrew. 2016. "Dasukigate: $15b May Have Been Stolen—Lai Mohammed." *Daily Trust*, May 11. https://www.dailytrust.com.ng/news/general/dasukigate-15b-may-have-been-stolen-lai-mohammed/146260.html.

Agbo, Ahmed. 2016. "RMRDC Moves to Revive Cotton Farming, Distributes Seeds to Farmers." *Daily Trust*, July 7. https://www.dailytrust.com.ng/news/agriculture/rmrdc-moves-to-revive-cotton-farming-distributes-seeds-to-farmers/154221.html.

Agha, Eugene. 2014. "Army to Get New Uniform." *Daily Trust*, July 30. https://www.dailytrust.com.ng/daily/news/30424-army-to-get-new-uniform.

Ahmadu-Suka, Maryam. 2013. "Military Officer, 2 Others Arrested over Fake Recruitment." *Daily Trust*, August 31. https://www.dailytrust.com.ng/weekly/index.php/newnews/13830-military-officer-2-others-arrested-over-fake-recruitment.

Ahmadu-Suka, Maryam, and Nathaniel Bivan. 2017. "Why I'm Always Given Villainous Roles—Kasimu Yero." *Daily Trust*, September 4. https://www.dailytrust.com.ng/news/general/why-i-m-always-given-villainous-roles-kasimu-yero/212857.html.

Ajobe, Ahmed, Terna Doki, and Ronald Mutum. 2015. "Nigerian Army's Season of Courts-Martial." *Daily Trust*, January 10. https://www.dailytrust.com.ng/weekly/index.php/top-stories/18702-nigerian-army-s-season-of-courts-martial.

Akinrinade, Sola, and Olukoya Ogen. 2008. "Globalization and De-industrialization: South-South Neo-liberalism and the Collapse of the Nigerian Textile Industry." *Global South* 2 (2): 159–170.

Akou, Heather. 2011. *The Politics of Dress in Somali Culture*. Bloomington: Indiana University Press.

Alabi, Christiana. 2011. "Sellers of Caps Make Brisk Business as Sallah Approaches." *Daily Trust*, August 25.

———. 2016. "27,000 Women to be Engaged for Tree Planting." *Daily Trust*, May 24. https://www.dailytrust.com.ng/news/general/27-000-women-to-be-engaged-for-tree-planting/148144.html.

Al-Naqar, Umar. 1972. *The Pilgrimage Tradition in West Africa*. Khartoum: Khartoum University Press.

Al-Oadah, Salman bin Fadh. 2006. *Alleviating the Difficulties of the Hajj*. Riyadh: Islam Today.

Al-Qur'ān. 1993. Translated by Ali Ahmed. Princeton, NJ: Princeton University Press.

Aminu, Habibu. 2016. "How Former Gov Shema Took Away N400m State Vehicles—Masari." *Daily Trust*, April 22. https://www.dailytrust.com.ng/news/katsina/how-former-gov-shema-took-away-n400m-state-vehicles-masari/143658.html.

Amnesty International. 2012. *Nigeria: Trapped in a Cycle of Violence*. London: Amnesty International. https://www.amnesty.org/en/documents/AFR44/043/2012/en.

———. 2016. "Nigeria—'Unearthing the Truth': Unlawful Killings and Mass Cover-Up in Zaria." https://www.amnesty.org/en/documents/afr01/3883/2016/en.

Andrae, Gunilla, and Björn Beckman. 1999. *Union Power in the Nigerian Textile Industry*. New Brunswick, NJ: Transaction.

An-Nawawī. 1991. *40 Hadith*. Translated by Ezzeddin Ibrahim and Denys Johnson-Davies. Kaduna: Kauran Wali Islamic Bookshop.

Anonymous. 2012. "The Popular Discourses of Salafi Radicalism and Salafi Counter-radicalism in Nigeria: A Case Study of Boko Haram." *Journal of Religion in Africa* 42 (2): 118–144.

Anwar, Kabiru. 2017. "Female Bombers Dead in Failed Attack." *Daily Trust*, June 20. https://www.dailytrust.com.ng/news/general/female-bombers-dead-in-failed-attack/202581.html.

Appadurai, Arjun, ed. 1986. *The Social Life of Things*. Cambridge: Cambridge University Press.

———. 2013. *The Future as Cultural Fact*. London: Verso.

Badmos, Abdul Ganiyu. n.d. *Al-Mujaddid Bamidele*. Ibadan: Muraina Adigun.

Baker, Patricia. 1995. *Islamic Textiles*. London: British Museum Press.

Banire, Buniyamin A. 2006. *"Hijaabah Sister": Alalu Barika Obinrin*. Lagos: Al-Bayaan Islamic Publications.

Bargery, G. P. (1934) 1993. *A Hausa-English and English-Hausa Dictionary*. 2nd ed. Zaria: Ahmadu Bello University Press.

Barnes, Robert M. 1960. *Military Uniforms of Britain and the Empire, 1742 to the Present Time*. London: Seeley Service.

Barth, Heinrich. 1857. *Travels and Discoveries in North and Central Africa*. 3 vols. New York: Harper.

Bayly, C. A. 1986. "The Origins of Swadeshi (Home Industry): Cloth and Indian Society, 1700–1930." In *The Social Life of Things: Commodities in Cultural Perspective*, edited by Arjun Appadurai, 285–321. Cambridge: Cambridge University Press.

BBC News. 2012. "Nigerians Living in Poverty Rise to Nearly 61%." February 13. http://www.bbc.com/news/world-africa-17015873.

———. 2014. "Nigeria Violence: Two Suicide Attacks near Busy Kano Market." December 10. http://www.bbc.com/news/world-africa-30416870.

———. 2016. "Nigeria Boko Haram: Children Starving, Warns Unicef." July 19. http://www.bbc.com/news/world-africa-36831225.

Beidelman, T. O. 1985. *Moral Imagination in Kaguru Modes of Thought*. Bloomington: Indiana University Press.

———. 2012. *The Culture of Colonialism: The Culture of Subjection of Ukaguru*. Bloomington: Indiana University Press.

Bello, Ahmadu. 1962. *My Life*. Cambridge: Cambridge University Press.

———. 1986. *Work and Worship: Selected Speeches of Sir Ahmadu Bello*. Edited by S. Amune. Zaria: Gaskiya Corporation.

Bivins, Mary W. 2007. *Telling Stories, Making Histories: Women, Words, and Islam in Nineteenth-Century Hausaland and the Sokoto Caliphate*. Portsmouth, NH: Heinemann.

Black Cotton (Cotton Growing in Nigeria). 1927. London: British Instructional Films. http://www.colonialfilm.org.uk/node/1322.

Bobboyi, Hamid, ed. 2011. *Principles of Leadership: According to the Founders of the Sokoto Caliphate*. Abuja: Centre for Research and International Development.

Boyd, Jean. 1989. *The Caliph's Sister*. London: Cass.

Boyd, Jean, and Murray Last. 1985. "The Role of Women as 'Agents Religieux' in Sokoto." *Canadian Journal of African Studies* 19 (2): 283–300.

Brady, Michael. 1954. "The Changing Uniforms of RWAFF." *West African Review*, March, pp. 216–217.

Bray, Francesca. 1997. *Technology and Gender: Fabrics of Power in Late Imperial China*. Berkeley: University of California Press.

Brigaglia, Andrea. 2012. "A Contribution to the History of the Wahhabi Da'wa in West Africa: The Career and Murder of Shaykh Ja'far Mahmoud Adam (Daura, c. 1961/1962 –Kano 2007)." *Islamic Africa* 3 (1): 1–23.

Campbell, Robert. 1861. *A Pilgrimage to My Motherland. An Account of a Journey among the Egbas and Yorubas of Central Africa, in 1859–60.* New York: T. Hamilton.

Candotti, Marisa. 2010. "The Hausa Textile Industry: Origins and Development in the Precolonial Period." In *Being and Becoming Hausa: Interdisciplinary Perspectives,* edited by A. Haour and B. Rossi, 187–211. Leiden, Netherlands: Brill.

Chonoko, Ibrahim. 2016. "Dasuki Slammed over Statement on Nigerian Soldiers." *Daily Trust,* May 15. https://www.dailytrust.com.ng/news/general/dasuki-slammed-over -statement-on-nigerian-soldiers/146760.html.

Chothia, Farouk. 2013. "Profile: Who Are Nigeria's Ansaru Islamists?" *BBC News,* March 11. http://www.bbc.com/news/world-africa-21510767.

Christelow, Allen. 1987. "Three Islamic Voices in Contemporary Nigeria." In *Islam and the Political Economy of Meaning,* edited by W. Rott, 226–253. London: Croom Helm.

Clapperton, Hugh. 1829. *Journal of the Second Expedition into the Interior of Africa, from the Bight of Benin to Soccatoo: To Which Is added, the Journal of Richard Lander from Kano to the Sea-Coast.* London: John Murray.

Clarke, Peter. 1982. *West Africa and Islam.* London: Edward Arnold.

Clarke, W. H. 1972. *Travels and Explorations in Yorubaland (1854–1858).* Edited by J. A. Atanda. Ibadan: University of Ibadan Press.

Cohen, Abner. 1969. *Custom and Politics in Urban Africa: A Study of Hausa Migrants in Yoruba Towns.* Berkeley: University of California Press.

Cohn, Bernard. 1989. "Cloth, Clothes, and Colonialism: India in the Nineteenth Century." In *Cloth and Human Experience,* edited by A. Weiner and J. Schneider, 303–353. Washington, DC: Smithsonian Institution Press.

Comolli, Virginia. 2015. *Boko Haram: Nigeria's Islamist Insurgency.* London: Hurst.

Cooper, Barbara. 1997. *Marriage in Maradi.* Portsmouth, NH: Heinemann.

Craik, Jennifer. 2005. *Uniforms Exposed: From Conformity to Transgression.* Oxford: Berg.

Daily Trust. 2009. "We're Treated Like Animals, Darul-Islam Members Cry Out." August 22. https://www.dailytrust.com.ng/news/others/we-re-treated-like-animals-darul-islam -members-cry-out/1868.html.

———. 2015a. "Army Dismisses 203 Soldiers after Secret Trial." January 2. https://www .dailytrust.com.ng/daily/top-stories/43492-army-dismisses-203-soldiers-after-secret-trial.

———. 2015b. "World Bank's $2.1bn Fund to Rebuild the North East." July 27. https://www .dailytrust.com.ng/news/editorial/world-bank-s-2-1bn-fund-to-rebuild-the-north -east/82678.html.

———. 2016a. "Nigerian Army Arrests Leader of Islamist Militant Group Ansaru." April 4. https://www.dailytrust.com.ng/news/general/nigerian-army-arrests-leader-of -islamist-militant-group-ansaru/140860.html.

———. 2016b. "Nigerian Army Presents Captured Boko Haram Flag to President Buhari." December 31. https://www.dailytrust.com.ng/news/general/nigerian-army-presents -captured-boko-haram-flag-to-president-buhari/178493.html.

———. 2016c. "Presidency Rolls Out Palliatives." May 18. https://www.dailytrust.com.ng/news /general/presidency-rolls-out-palliatives/147237.html.

———. 2016d. "Shi'ite/Army Clash: Kaduna Govt Grants 4 Weeks Extension to Commission of Inquiry." April 5. https://www.dailytrust.com.ng/news/general/shi-ite-army-clash-kaduna-govt-grants-4-weeks-extension-to-commission-of-inquiry/141056.html.

———. 2017. "Cheerful News about Kaduna Textile." August 22. https://www.dailytrust.com.ng/news/editorial/cheerful-news-about-kaduna-textile/211060.html.

———. 2018a. "Textile Manufacturers Decry Non-implementation of Local Content Order." January 20. https://www.dailytrust.com.ng/textile-manufacturers-decry-non-implementation-of-local-content-order.html.

———. 2018b. "Troops Destroy Major Bomb Factory in Sambisa Forest." February 7. https://www.dailytrust.com.ng/troops-destroy-major-bomb-factory-in-sambisa-forest.html.

Dan-Ali, Mannir. 2016. "Face-to-Face with a Boko Haram Wife." *Daily Trust*, June 11. https://www.dailytrust.com.ng/news/general/face-to-face-with-a-boko-haram-wife/150681.html.

DanAsabe, Abdulkarim. 2000. "Biography of Select Kano Merchants, 1853–1955." *FAIS: Journal of Humanities* 1 (2): 45–60.

dan Fodio, 'Uthmān. 1978. *Bayān Wujūb al-Hijra 'ala 'l-'Ibad*. Edited and translated by F. H. El Masri. Khartoum: Khartoum University Press.

Danmole, H. O. A. 1984. "Colonial Reforms in the Ilorin Emirate, 1900–1919." *Odù*, no. 26: 84–107.

Davis, Fred. 1992. *Fashion, Culture, and Identity*. Chicago: University of Chicago Press.

Denham, Dixon, Hugh Clapperton, and Walter Oudney. 1831. *Travels and Discoveries in Northern and Central Africa, in 1822, 1823, and 1824*. 2 vols. London: John Murray.

Dixon, P. J. 1991. "'Uneasy Lies the Head': Politics, Economics, and the Continuity of Belief among Yoruba of Nigeria." *Comparative Studies in Society and History* 33 (1): 56–85.

Doi, A. R. 1969. "The Bamidele Movement in Yorubaland." *Orita: Ibadan Journal of Religious Studies* 3:101–111.

Douny, Laurence. 2011. "Silk-Embroidered Garments as Transformative Processes: Layering, Inscribing and Displaying Hausa Material Identities." *Material Culture* 16 (4): 401–415.

Durkheim, Émile. 1915. *The Elementary Forms of the Religious Life*. London: Allen and Unwin.

Edozie, Victor. 2014. "Customs Intercepts Imported Military Uniforms, Boots." *Daily Trust*, June 12. https://www.dailytrust.com.ng/daily/business/26439-customs-intercepts-imported-military-uniforms-boots.

El Guindi, Fadwa. 1999. *Veil: Modesty, Privacy, and Resistance*. Oxford: Berg.

El Masri, F. H. 1978. Introduction to *Bayān Wujūb al-Hijra 'ala 'l-'Ibad*, by 'Uthmān dan Fodio, 1–39. Khartoum: Khartoum University Press.

Fischer, Edward. 2014. *The Good Life: Aspiration, Dignity, and the Anthropology of Wellbeing*. Stanford, CA: Stanford University Press.

Flegel, E. R. 1885. *Lose Blätter aus dem Tagebuche meiner Haussa-Freunde und Reisegefährten*. Hamburg: L. Friederichsen.

———. (1885) 1985. *The Biography of Madugu Mohamman Mai Gashin Baki*. Translated and annotated by Mark B. Duffill. Los Angeles: Crossroads.

Gaudio, Rudolf. 2009. *Allah Made Us: Sexual Outlaws in an Islamic African City*. Malden, MA: Wiley-Blackwell.

Gbadamosi, Tajudeen G. O. 1978a. *The Ansar Ud Deen of Nigeria: Case Study in Islamic Modern Reformist Movement in West Africa*. London: Muslim Institute for Research and Planning.

———. 1978b. *The Growth of Islam among the Yoruba, 1841–1908*. Atlantic Highlands, NJ: Humanities Press.

Giginyu, Ibrahim Musa. 2012. "Pomp as Sanusi Is Turbaned Danmajen Kano." *Daily Trust,*
June 9. https://www.dailytrust.com.ng/news/others/pomp-as-sanusi-is-turbaned
-danmajen-kano/10025.html.

Goody, Jack, and T. M. Mustapha. 1967. "The Caravan Trade from Kano to Salaga." *Journal of
the Historical Society of Nigeria* 3 (4): 611–616.

Gozney, Richard. 2015. "Nigeria's Security: Insurgency, Elections and Coordinating
Responses to Multiple Threats." https://www.chathamhouse.org/sites/files
/chathamhouse/field/field_document/20150122NigeriaSecurityQA_0.pdf.

Gray, Christopher. 1998. "The Rise of Niassene Tijaniyya, 1875 to the Present." In *Islam
et Islamismes au Sud du Sahara*, edited by O. Kane and J-L, Triaud, 59–82. Paris:
Karthala.

Gumi, Abubakar, with Ismaila Tsiga. 1992. *Where I Stand*. Ibadan: Spectrum.

Guyer, Jane. 1995. "Wealth in People, Wealth in Things." *Journal of African History* 36 (1):
83–90.

Hammoudi, Abdullah. 2006. *A Season in Mecca*. New York: Hill and Wang.

Hassan, Salah. 1992. *Art and Islamic Literacy among the Hausa of Northern Nigeria*. Lewiston,
NY: Edwin Mellen.

Heath, Deborah. 1992. "Fashion, Anti-Fashion, and Heteroglossia in Urban Senegal."
American Ethnologist 19 (1): 19–33.

Heathcote, David. 1972. "Hausa Embroidered Dress." *African Arts* 5 (2): 12–19, 82, 84.

———. 1974. "A Hausa Charm Gown." *Man* 9 (4): 620–624.

Hermon-Hodge, H. 1929. *Gazetteer of Ilorin Province*. London: Allen and Unwin.

Hiskett, Mervyn. 1960. "*Kitāb al-farq:* 'A Work on the Habe Kingdoms Attributed to ʿUt̲h̲mān
dan Fodio.'" *Bulletin of the School of Oriental and African Studies* 23 (3): 558–579.

———. 1973. *The Sword of Truth: The Life and Times of Shehu Usuman Dan Fodio*. New York:
Oxford University Press.

———. 1975a. "The Development of Sa'adu Zungur's Political Thought from *Maraaba
DaSooja*, through *Arewa, Jumhuurriyaa Koo Muluukiyaa* to *Waakar 'Yanci*." *African
Language Studies* 16:1–24.

———. 1975b. *A History of Hausa Islamic Verse*. London: School of Oriental and African
Studies, University of London.

———. 1980. "The 'Community of Grace' and Its Opponents, the 'Rejectors': A Debate about
Theology and Mysticism in Muslim West Africa with Special Reference to Hausa
Expression." *African Language Studies* 17:99–140.

———. 1984. *The Development of Islam in West Africa*. London: Longman.

Hocart, A. M. (1936) 1970. *Kings and Councillors: An Essay in the Comparative Anatomy of
Human Society*. Chicago: University of Chicago Press.

Hogben, S. J., and Anthony Kirk-Greene. 1966. *The Emirates of Northern Nigeria*. London:
Oxford University Press.

Houtman, Dick, and Birgit Meyer. 2012. *Things: Religion and the Question of Materiality*. New
York: Fordham University Press.

Hunwick, John, and R. S. O'Fahey, eds. 2016. "'Umar b. Abī Bakr Ramaḍān b. Abī Bakr b.
Muḥammad al-Mujāhid al-Ṭawāriqī al-Kanawī al-Tijānī." In *Arabic Literature of Africa
Online*. Leiden, Netherlands: Brill. http://dx.doi.org/10.1163/2405-4453_alao_COM
_ALA_20007_3_19.

Ibrahim, Abubakar Adam. 2017. "Boko Haram Kills 1,100 since Being 'Technically
Defeated.'" *Daily Trust*, December 3. https://www.dailytrust.com.ng/boko-haram
-kills-1-100-since-being-technically-defeated.html.

Ibrahim, Abubakar Saddiq. n.d. *Hijab: The Shield of the Umma*. Translated by Zakariya Garba Umar. Lagos, Nigeria.

Ibrahim, Hussain, Solomon Chung, Misbahu Bashir, and Isa Liman. 2011. "Sheikh Albani Released on Bail." *Daily Trust*, July 16. https://www.dailytrust.com.ng/news/general /sheikh-albani-released-on-bail/7185.html.

Ibrahim, Yahaya. 2013. "Gunmen Kill 20 Vigilantes in Borno." *Daily Trust*, August 28. https:// www.dailytrust.com.ng/news/general/gunmen-kill-20-vigilantes-in-borno/26323.html.

Idris, Hamza. 2011. "JTF Whisks Away Newspaper Vendor in Maiduguri." *Daily Trust*, October 20.

———. 2013a. "Benisheik Attack Death Toll Now 161." *Daily Trust*, September 20. https:// www.dailytrust.com.ng/news/others/benisheik-attack-death-toll-now-161/28143.html.

———. 2013b. "50 Insurgents, 24 Civilians Killed in Borno." *Daily Trust*, September 7. https:// www.dailytrust.com.ng/news/others/50-insurgents-24-civilians-killed-in-borno/14770 .html.

Idris, Hamza, and Yahaya Ibrahim. 2012. "20 Killed as JTF Pursues Boko Haram." *Daily Trust*, February 21.

———. 2014. "Soldiers' Wives Protest Husbands' Deployment to Fight B/Haram." *Daily Trust*, August 12. https://www.dailytrust.com.ng/news/others/soldiers-wives-protest -husbands-deployment-to-fight-b-haram/53551.html.

Idris, Hamza, and Ibrahim Sawab. 2013a. "Insurgents Sack Benisheik, Kill 50." *Daily Trust*, September 19. https://www.dailytrust.com.ng/news/others/insurgents-sack-benisheik -kill-50/28038.html.

———. 2013b. "'Women' as Boko Haram's New Face." *Daily Trust*, July 6. https://www. dailytrust.com.ng/weekly/index.php/top-stories/13199-women-as-boko-haram-s-new -face.

———. 2015a. "Female Bomber Kills Many at Maiduguri Market." *Daily Trust*, March 11. https://www.dailytrust.com.ng/daily/index.php/top-stories/49123-female-bomber -kills-many-at-maiduguri-market.

———. 2015b. "Three Vigilantes Die in Confrontation with Soldiers." *Daily Trust*, February 17. https://www.dailytrust.com.ng/daily/index.php/news-menu/news/47191-three -vigilantes-die-in-confrontation-with-soldiers.

Ingham, Bruce. 1997. "Men's Dress in the Arabian Peninsula: Historical and Present Perspectives." In *Languages of Dress in the Middle East*, edited by N. Lindisfarne-Tapper and B. Ingham, 40–54. Surrey, UK: Curzon.

Isichei, Elizabeth. 1987. "The Maitatsine Risings in Nigeria, 1980–85: A Revolt of the Disinherited." *Journal of Religion in Africa* 17 (3): 194–208.

Isuwa, Sunday. 2012. "'Collapse of Industries Worse than Boko Haram.'" *Daily Trust*, February 20.

Janson, Marloes. 2005. "Roaming about for God's Sake: The Upsurge of the Tablīgh Jamāʻat in the Gambia." *Journal of Religion in Africa* 35 (4): 450–481.

Jega, Mahmud. 2016. "Fantastically Sharp U-Turn." *Daily Trust*, May 16. https://www .dailytrust.com.ng/news/monday-column/fantastically-sharp-u-turn/146810.html.

———. 2017. "Six Singular Security Sweeps." *Daily Trust*, February 13. https://www.dailytrust .com.ng/news/columns/six-singular-security-sweeps/184987.html.

Jimoh, Abbas. 2015a. "Boko Haram: Outrage Greet Buhari's Hijab 'Ban' Comment." *Daily Trust*, December 31. https://www.dailytrust.com.ng/news/news/boko-haram-outrage -greet-buhari-s-hijab-ban-comment/126888.html.

———. 2015b. "FOMWAN, MURIC to FG: Ignore Call for Hijab Ban." *Daily Trust*, July 27. https://www.dailytrust.com.ng/daily/index.php/news-menu/news/60925-fomwan -muric-to-fg-ignore-call-for-hijab-ban.

———. 2015c. "Hajj Stampede: 87 More Nigerians Confirmed Dead." *Daily Trust*, November 14. https://www.dailytrust.com.ng/news/general/hajj-stampede-87-more-nigerians -confirmed-dead/119351.html.

Johnson, Marion. 1973. "Cloth on the Banks of the Niger." *Journal of the Historical Society of Nigeria* 6:353–363.

———. 1974. "Cotton Imperialism in West Africa." *African Affairs* 73 (291): 178–187.

———. 1976. "Calico Caravans: The Tripoli-Kano Trade after 1880." *Journal of African History* 17:95–117.

———. 1978. "By Ship or by Camel: The Struggle for the Cameroons Ivory Trade in the Nineteenth Century." *Journal of African History* 19 (4): 539–549.

Johnson, Samuel. 1921. *The History of the Yorubas*. London: Routledge.

Joseph, Nathan. 1986. *Uniforms and Nonuniforms: Communication through Clothing*. New York: Greenwood.

Kaba, Lansine. 1974. *The Wahhabiyya: Islamic Reform and Politics in French West Africa*. Evanston, IL: Northwestern University Press.

Kane, Ousmane. 2002. *Muslim Modernity in Post-colonial Nigeria*. Leiden, Netherlands: Brill.

Kenny, Erin. 2007. "Gifting Mecca: Importing Spiritual Capital to West Africa." *Mobilities* 2 (3): 363–381.

Kisch, Martin. 1910. *Letters and Sketches from Northern Nigeria*. London: Chatto and Windus.

Kriger, Colleen. 1988. "Robes of the Sokoto Caliphate." *African Arts* 21 (3): 52–57, 78–79, 85.

———. 1993. "Production and Gender in the Sokoto Caliphate." *Journal of African History* 34 (3): 361–401.

———. 2006. *Cloth in West African History*. Lanham, MD: AltaMira.

———. 2010. "Silk and Sartorial Politics in the Sokoto Caliphate, 1804–1903." In *The Force of Fashion in Politics and Society: Global Perspectives from Early Modern to Modern Times*, edited by B. Lemire, 143–163. Surrey, UK: Ashgate.

Krishi, Musa. 2018. "EFCC Recovered N473bn, $98m in 2017—Magu." *Daily Trust*, February 6. https://www.dailytrust.com.ng/efcc-recovered-n473bn-98m-in-2017-magu.html.

Kumm, Herman K. W. 1910. *From Hausaland to Egypt through the Sudan*. London: Constable.

Lamb, Venice, and Judy Holmes. 1980. *Nigerian Textiles*. Hertingfordbury, UK: Roxford.

Lander, Richard, and John Lander. 1854. *Journal of an Expedition to Explore the Course and Termination of the Niger: With a Narrative of a Voyage Down That River to Its Termination*. 2 vols. New York: Harper.

Last, Murray. 1966. "An Aspect of the Caliph Muhammad Bello's Social Policy." *Kano Studies* 1:56–59.

———. 1967. *The Sokoto Caliphate*. London: Longman.

———. 1970. "Aspects of Administration and Dissent in Hausaland, 1800–1968." *Africa* 40 (4): 345–357.

———. 1974. "Reform in West Africa: The Jihād Movements of the Nineteenth Century." In *History of West Africa*, vol. 2, edited by J. F. A. Ajayi and M. Crowther, 1–29. Essex, UK: Longman.

———. 1979. "Some Economic Aspects of Conversion in Hausaland (Nigeria)." In *Conversion to Islam*, edited by N. Levtzion, 236–246. New York: Holmes and Meier.

———. 2008. "The Search for Security in Northern Nigeria." *Africa* 78 (1): 41–63.

———. 2014. "From Dissent to Dissidence: The Genesis and Development of Reformist Islamic Groups in Northern Nigeria." In *Sects and Social Disorder*, edited by Abdul Raufu Mustapha, 18–53. Woodbridge, Suffolk: Boydell and Brewer.

LeBlanc, Marie. 2000. "Fashion and the Politics of Identity: Versioning Womanhood and Muslimhood in the Face of Tradition and Modernity." *Africa* 70 (3): 443–481.

Lemu, B. Aisha, and Fatima Heeren. 1976. *Women in Islam*. Leicester, UK: The Islamic Foundation.

Levi, Primo. 1984. *The Periodic Table*. New York: Schocken.

Levinson, Jerrold, ed. 1998. *Aesthetics and Ethics: Essays at the Intersection*. Cambridge: Cambridge University Press.

Levtzion, Nehemia. 1987. "The Eighteenth Century: The Background to the Islamic Revolution in West Africa." In *Eighteenth-Century Renewal and Reform in Islam*, edited by N. Levtzion and J. Voll, 21–38. Syracuse, NY: University of Syracuse Press.

Lewis, Reina. 2003. Preface to *Veiling, Representation and Contemporary Art*, edited by D. Bailey and G. Tawadros, 10–15. Cambridge, MA: MIT Press.

Lhote, Henri. 1955. *Les Touaregs du Hoggar*. Paris: Payot.

Liman, Usman Shehu. 1996. *Hajj 91: Travel Notes of a Nigerian Pilgrim*. Zaria: Ashel Enterprises.

Loimeier, Roman. 1997. *Islamic Reform and Political Change in Northern Nigeria*. Evanston, IL: Northwestern University Press.

Lombard, Maurice. 1978. *Les textiles dans le Monde Musulman du VIIe au XIIe siècle*. Paris: Mouton.

Lovejoy, Paul. 1978. "Plantations in the Economy of the Sokoto Caliphate." *Journal of African History* 19 (3): 341–368.

———. 1980. *Caravans of Kola: The Hausa Kola Trade, 1700–1900*. Zaria: Ahmadu Bello University Press.

———. 1981. "Slavery in the Sokoto Caliphate." In *The Ideology of Slavery in Africa*, edited by P. Lovejoy, 201–243. Beverly Hills, CA: Sage.

Lubeck, Paul. 1985. "Protest under Semi-Industrial Capitalism: 'Yan Tatsine Explained." *Africa* 55 (4): 369–389.

———. 1986. *Islam and Urban Labor in Northern Nigeria: The Making of a Muslim Working Class*. Cambridge: Cambridge University Press.

———. 2011. "Nigeria: Mapping a Shari'a Restorationist Movement." In *Shari'a Politics: Islamic Law and Society in a Modern World*, edited by R. Hefner, 244–279. Bloomington: Indiana University Press.

Lydon, Ghislaine. 2009. *On Trans-Saharan Trails: Islamic Law, Trade Networks, and Cross-Cultural Exchange in Nineteenth-Century West Africa*. Cambridge: Cambridge University Press.

Mack, Beverly, and Jean Boyd. 2000. *One Woman's Jihad: Nana Asma'u, Scholar and Scribe*. Bloomington: Indiana University Press.

Mac-Leva, Fidelis, Haruna Ibrahim, and Shehu Abubakar. 2015. "Boko Haram: 881 Killed, 376 Injured in 100 Days." *Daily Trust*, September 6. https://www.dailytrust.com.ng /news/general/boko-haram-881-killed-376-injured-in-100-days/109563.html.

Mahdi, Hauwa. 2013. "Invoking *Hijab*: The Power Politics of Spaces and Employment in Nigeria." In *Veiling in Africa*, edited by E. Renne, 165–185. Bloomington: Indiana University Press.

Maiangwa, Benjamin, Ufo Okeke Uzodike, Ayo Whetho, and Hakeem Onapajo. 2012. "'Baptism by Fire': Boko Haram and the Reign of Terror in Nigeria." *Africa Today* 59 (2): 41–57.

Maiwada, Salihu, and Elisha Renne. 2007. "New Technologies of Machine-Embroidered Robe Production and Changing Work and Gender Roles in Zaria, Nigeria." *Textile History* 38 (1): 25–58.

———. 2013. "The Kaduna Textile Industry and the Decline of Textile Manufacturing in Northern Nigeria, 1955–2010." *Textile History* 44 (2): 171–196.

Maraya, Dan. "Rich and Poor (*Mai Akwai da Mai Babu*)." 1996. In *Poetry, Prose and Popular Culture in Hausa*, by Graham Furniss, 158. Washington, DC: Smithsonian Institution Press.

Masquelier, Adeline. 2013. "Modest Bodies, Stylish Selves: Fashioning Virtue in Niger." In *Veiling in Africa*, edited by E. Renne, 110–136. Bloomington: Indiana University Press.

Matazu, Hamisu, Misbahu Bashir, and Ibrahim Sule. 2013. "50 Yobe College Students Shot Dead." *Daily Trust*, September 30. https://www.dailytrust.com.ng/news/others/50 -yobe-college-students-shot-dead/28754.html.

Matfess, Hilary. 2017. *Women and the War on Boko Haram: Wives, Weapons, Witnesses*. London: Zed.

Mauss, Marcel. 1967. *The Gift*. Translated by I. Cunnison. New York: Norton.

———. 1973. "Techniques of the Body." *Economy and Society* 2 (1): 70–88.

Meagher, Kate. 2010. *Identity Economics: Social Networks and the Informal Economy in Nigeria*. Woodbridge,UK: James Currey.

Meek, C. K. 1925. *The Northern Tribes of Nigeria: An Ethnographic Account of the Northern Provinces of Nigeria*. 2 vols. London: Oxford University Press.

Meyer, Birgit, and Houtman, Dick. 2012. "Introduction: Material Religion—How Things Matter." In *Things: Religion and the Question of Materiality*, edited by D. Houtman and B. Meyer, 1–23. New York: Fordham University Press.

Mockler-Ferryman, A. F. 1892. *Up the Niger*. London: G. Philip.

Mohammed, Ahmed Rufai. 1993. "The Influence of the Niass Tijaniyya in the Niger-Benue Confluence Area of Nigeria." In *Muslim Identity and Social Change in Sub-Saharan Africa*, edited by L. Brenner, 116–134. Bloomington: Indiana University Press.

Mohammed, Kyari. 2014. "The Message and the Methods of Boko Haram." In *Boko Haram: Islamism, Politics, Security and the State in Nigeria*, edited by M-A de Montclos, 9–32. Leiden, Netherlands: African Studies Centre.

Morgan, David. 2010. *Religion and Material Culture: The Matter of Belief*. New York: Routledge.

Mudashir, Ismail, and Abdulkadir Muktar. 2014. "Female Suicide Bombers Kill 5 in Kano Market." *Daily Trust*, December 11. https://www.dailytrust.com.ng/news/general /female-suicide-bombers-kill-5-in-kano-market/63752.html.

Mudashir, Ismail, Abdulkadir Muktar, and Haruna Yaya. 2014. "Jonathan Bows to Pressure over Sanusi." *Daily Trust*, June 13. https://www.dailytrust.com.ng/news/others /jonathan-bows-to-pressure-over-sanusi/48716.html.

Muhammad, Garba. 2015. "Mecca Crane Collapse: Nigerian Survivors Recount Tragedy." *Daily Trust*, September 19. https://www.dailytrust.com.ng/news/general/mecca-crane -collapse-nigerian-survivors-recount-tragedy/111460.html.

Murphy, Robert. 1964. "Social Distance and the Veil." *American Anthropologist* 66 (6): 1257–1274.

Mustapha, Abdul Raufu. 2014. Introduction to *Sects and Social Disorder*, edited by A. Mustapha, 1–15. Woodbridge,UK: Boydell and Brewer.

Mustapha, Abdul Raufu, and Mukhtar Bunza. 2014. "Contemporary Islamic Sects and Groups in Northern Nigeria." In *Sects and Social Disorder*, edited by A. Mustapha, 54–97. Woodbridge,UK: Boydell and Brewer.

Mutum, Ronald. 2014. "SS Detains Sanusi at Lagos Airport, Confiscates Travel Documents." *Daily Trust*, February 20.

———. 2016a. "Air Force Unveils New Camouflage Uniforms." *Daily Trust*, February 29. https://www.dailytrust.com.ng/news/general/air-force-unveils-new-camouflage -uniforms/135898.html.

———. 2016b. "Boko Haram Fighters Have New Uniform—Army." *Daily Trust*, April 26. https://www.dailytrust.com.ng/news/general/boko-haram-fighters-have-new -uniform-army/144161.html.

———. 2016c. "DHQ Establishes Camp for Repentant Boko Haram Members." *Daily Trust*, April 6. https://www.dailytrust.com.ng/news/general/dhq-establishes-camp-for -repentant-boko-haram-members/141195.html.

Na'abba, Ghali. 2011. "Emirs and Politics." *Daily Trust*, March 9.

Najakku, Abu. 2016. "Change Has Come to Boko Haram." *Daily Trust*, April 5. https://www .dailytrust.com.ng/news/opinion/change-has-come-to-boko-haram/140997.html.

Nast, Heidi. 2006. *Concubines and Power*. Minneapolis: University of Minnesota Press.

Newman, Paul. 2007. *A Hausa-English Dictionary*. New Haven, CT: Yale University Press.

Nigeria Magazine. 1944. "Kano." No. 22, p. 35.

Nigerian Citizen. 1964. "Sardauna Wins New Converts—Makarfi." April 8, p. 1.

———. 1965a. "11,000 Become Muslims in Massive Campaign." May 1, p. 1

———. 1965b. "Sardauna Preaches: 800 Converted to Islam, Kotarkoshi, Sokoto Province." February 26, p. 8.

———. 1965c. "Sardauna's 20th Century Islamic Crusade in Northern Nigeria." April 28, pp. 1, 9.

Niven, Rex. 1982. *Nigerian Kaleidoscope: Memoirs of a Colonial Servant*. London: C. Hurst.

Nossiter, Adam. 2012. "In Nigeria, a Deadly Group's Rage Has Local Roots." *New York Times*, February 25. https://mobile.nytimes.com/2012/02/26/world/africa/in-northern-nigeria -boko-haram-stirs-fear-and-sympathy.html.

———. 2014. "Bomb at School in Nigeria Kills Nearly 50 Boys." *New York Times*, November 10. https://www.nytimes.com/2014/11/11/world/africa/nigeria-suicide-bomber-boko -haram.html.

O'Hear, Ann. 1987. "Craft Industries in Ilorin." *African Affairs* 86 (345): 505–522.

———. 1988. "Alhaji Yahaya Kalu Olabintan of Ilorin: Master Weaver." *Nigerian Field* 53 (1–2): 3–10.

———. 1997. *Power Relations in Nigeria: Ilorin Slaves and Their Successors*. Rochester, NY: University of Rochester Press.

Ogunbiyi, I. A. 1969. "The Position of Muslim Women as Stated by 'Uthman b. Fudi." *Odu* 2:43–60.

Okenwa, Saleh. 2016a. "Practical Steps in Performing the Hajj Rites." National Hajj Commission of Nigeria. http://nigeriahajjcom.gov.ng/content/hajj-rites.

———. 2016b. "Tips on the Performance of Umrah (Lesser Hajj)." National Hajj Commission of Nigeria. http://nigeriahajjcom.gov.ng/content/umrah.

Oladimeji, Lateef Folorunsho. 2012. "Jamā'atut-Tablīgh in Nigeria: A Historical Perspective." *Ad-Dirāyah: International Journal of Islamic Studies* 1 (1): 67–88.

Olatunji, Omirin. 2016. "30 Killed in Borno Weekend Attacks." *Daily Trust*, February 14. https://www.dailytrust.com.ng/news/general/30-killed-in-borno-weekend-attacks/133681.html.

Onyeiwu, Steve. 1997. "The Modern Textile Industry in Nigeria: History, Structural Change, and Recent Developments." *Textile History* 28 (2): 234–249.

Opoola, Latifat. 2016. "55 People Stole N1.3tr in 7 Years—Fed Govt." *Daily Trust*, January 19. https://www.dailytrust.com.ng/news/general/55-people-stole-n1-3tr-in-7-years-fed-govt/129701.html.

Orwell, George. (1946) 1984. *Why I Write*. London: Penguin Books.

Paden, John. 1986. *Ahmadu Bello, Sardauna of Sokoto: Values and Leadership in Nigeria*. Zaria: Hudahuda.

Palmer, H. S. 1908. "Kano Chronicles." *Journal of the Royal Anthropological Institute of Great Britain and Ireland* 38:58–98.

Panter-Brick, Keith, ed. 1978. *Oil and Soldiers: The Political Transformation of Nigeria*. London: Cass.

Pedler, Frederick. 1974. *The Lion and the Unicorn in Africa: A History of the Origins of the United Africa Company, 1787–1931*. London: Heinemann Educational.

Perani, J., and N. Wolff. 1992. "Embroidered Gown and Equestrian Ensembles of the Kano Aristocracy." *African Arts* 25 (3): 70–81, 102–104.

Peters, E. E. 1994. *The Hajj: The Muslim Pilgrimage to Mecca and the Holy Places*. Princeton, NJ: Princeton University Press.

Picton, John, and John Mack. 1979. *African Textiles*. London: British Museum.

Porter, Venetia, ed. 2012. *Hajj: Journey to the Heart of Islam*. Cambridge, MA: Harvard University Press.

Rasmussen, Susan. 1991. "Veiled Self, Transparent Meanings: Tuareg Headdress as Social Expression." *Ethnology* 30 (2): 101–117.

Reichmuth, Stefan. 1993. "Islamic Learning and Its Interaction with 'Western' Education in Ilorin, Nigeria." In *Muslim Identity and Social Change in Sub-Saharan Africa*, edited by L. Brenner, 179–197. London: Hurst.

———. 1995. "A Sacred Community: Scholars, Saints, and Emirs in a Prayer Text from Ilorin." *Sudanic Africa* 6:35–54.

———. 1996. "Education and the Growth of Religious Associations among Yoruba Muslims: The Ansar-ud-Deen Society of Nigeria." *Journal of Religion in Africa* 26 (4): 365–405.

———. 1997. "A Regional Centre of Islamic Learning in Nigeria: Ilọrin and Its Influence on Yoruba Islam." In *Madrasa: La Transmission du Savoir dans le Monde Musulman*, edited by N. Grandin and M. Gaborieau, 229–245. Paris: Éditions Arguments.

Renne, Elisha. 2004a. "From Khaki to *Agbada*: Dress and Political Transition in Nigeria." In *Fashioning Nations: Clothing, Politics, and African Identities in the 20th Century*, edited by J. Allman, 125–143. Bloomington: Indiana University Press.

———. 2004b. "The Production and Marketing of *Babban Riga* in Zaria, Nigeria." *African Economic History* 32:103–122.

———. 2012. "Educating Muslim Women and the Izala Movement in Zaria City, Nigeria." *Islamic Africa* 3 (1): 55–86.

———. 2013a. "The Hijab as Moral Space in Northern Nigeria." In *Fashion and Power in Africa*, edited by Karen T. Hansen and D. Soyini Madison, 92–107. Oxford, UK: Bloomsbury Academic.

———. 2013b. "Intertwined Veiling Histories in Nigeria." In *Veiling in Africa*, edited by E. Renne, 58–81. Bloomington: Indiana University Press.

———. 2013c. "The Motorcycle Sallah Durbars of Zaria, 2012." *Anthropology Today* 29 (4): 12–16.

———, ed. 2013d. *Veiling in Africa*. Bloomington: Indiana University Press.

———. 2015. "Photography, Hajj Things, and Spatial Connections between Mecca and Northern Nigeria." *Photography and Culture* 8 (3): 1–27.

Richards, Paul. 2009. "Dressed to Kill: Clothing as Technology of the Body in the Civil War in Sierra Leone." *Journal of Material Culture* 14:495–512.

Roberts, Richard. 1996. *Two Worlds of Cotton: Colonialism and the Regional Economy in the French Soudan, 1800–1946*. Stanford: Stanford University Press.

Robinson, Charles Henry. 1897. *Hausaland; or, Fifteen Hundred Miles through the Central Soudan*. London: Sampson Low, Marston.

———. 1913–1914. *Dictionary of the Hausa Language*. 2 vols. 3rd ed. Cambridge: Cambridge University Press.

Rubin, Arnold. 1984. "Layoyi: Some Hausa Calligraphic Charms." *African Arts* 17 (2): 67–70, 91–92.

Ryan, Patrick J. 1978. *Imale: Yoruba Participation in the Muslim Tradition; A Study of Clerical Piety*. Missoula, MT: Scholars' Press.

Sa'idu, Isa. 2009a. "Heretic Sect Emerges in Zaria." *Daily Trust*, August 28.

———. 2009b. "I Didn't Contravene Dress Code—Sacked ABUTH Nurse." *Daily Trust*, April 14.

———. 2009c. "Kala-Kato: Meet Group with Yet Another Perception of Islam." *Daily Trust*, August 15. https://www.dailytrust.com.ng/news/general/kala-kato-meet-group-with -yet-another-perception-of-islam/1795.html.

———. 2009d. "Red-Light Districts Resurface in Kano—Sex Workers Now Disguise Themselves in Hijabs." *Weekly Trust*, February 14.

———. 2012a. "In Kachia, Chiefs Ordered to Dump Turbans for Leopard Skin." *Daily Trust*, June 9. https://www.dailytrust.com.ng/news/general/in-kachia-chiefs-ordered-to -dump-turbans-for-leopard-skin/9978.html.

———. 2012b. "My Encounter with Moh'd Yusuf over Boko Haram—Sheikh Albani." *Daily Trust*, January 1. https://www.dailytrust.com.ng/sunday/index.php/news/9564-my -encounter-with-mohd-yusuf-over-boko-haram-sheikh-albani.

———. 2014. "The Man Sheikh Albani." *Daily Trust*, February 3. https://www.dailytrust.com .ng/daily/index.php/news-menu/news/15901-the-man-sheikh-albani.

———. 2015a. "Army/Shiites Clash: The Untold Story." *Daily Trust*, December 19. https://www.dailytrust.com.ng/news/general/army-shiites-clash-the-untold-story/125096.html.

———. 2015b. "'How We Arrested Boko Haram Suspects in Izala Uniform.'" *Daily Trust*, November 20. https://www.dailytrust.com.ng/news/general/-how-we-arrested-boko-haram-suspects-in-izala-uniform/120486.html.

———. 2016a. "Inside Kaduna's Unusual Religious Sect." *Daily Trust*, April 16. https://www.dailytrust.com.ng/news/general/inside-kaduna-s-unusual-religious-sect/142691.html.

———. 2016b. "Nigeria's Elite Have Made Corruption Their Religion—Sheikh Gumi." *Daily Trust*, June 11. https://www.dailytrust.com.ng/news/general/nigeria-s-elite-have-made-corruption-their-religion-sheikh-gumi/150680.html.

Sa'idu, Isa, and Aliyu Yusuf. 2009. "Hijab: ABUTH to Reinstate Nurse." *Daily Trust*, April 22.

Salamone, Frank, and Virginia Salamone. 1993. "*Kirki*: A Core Value of Hausa Culture." *Africa: Rivista trimestrale di studi e documentazione dell'Istituto italiano per l'Africa e l'Oriente* 48 (3): 359–381.

Salkida, Ahmad. 2009. "Muhammad Yusuf: Teaching and Preaching Controversies." *Daily Trust*, February 29. http://salkida.com/muhammad-yusuf-teaching-and-preaching-controversies.

Saro-Wiwa, Ken. 1985. *Sozaboy: A Novel in Rotten English*. Port Harcourt, Nigeria: Saros.

Sawab, Ibrahim, and Omirin Olatunji. 2017. "Suicide Bombers Kill 25 at Biu Market." *Daily Trust*, December 3. https://www.dailytrust.com.ng/suicide-bombers-kill-25-at-biu-market.html.

Sawab, Ibrahim, Omirin Olatunji, Isiaku Bara'u Zakka, and Isiaka Wakili. 2017. "Suicide Bomber Kills Prof, 4 Others in Maiduguri." *Daily Trust*, January 17, pp. 1, 5.

Schneider, Jane, and Annette Weiner. 1986. "Cloth and the Organization of Human Experience." *Current Anthropology* 27 (2): 178–184.

Schulz, Dorothea. 2007. "Competing Sartorial Assertions of Femininity and Muslim Identity in Mali." *Fashion Theory. Journal of Dress, Body, and Culture* 11 (2–3): 253–280.

Searcey, Dionne. 2016a. "Boko Haram Using More Children as Suicide Bombers, Unicef Says." *New York Times*, April 12. https://www.nytimes.com/2016/04/13/world/africa/boko-haram-children-suicide-bombers-unicef-report.html.

———. 2016b. "Victims of Boko Haram, and Now Shunned by Their Communities." *New York Times*, May 19. https://www.nytimes.com/2016/05/19/world/africa/boko-haram-victims-nigeria.html.

Shameem, Asma bint. 2011. "Common Mistakes Women Make during Hajj or Umrah." *Muslim Matters*, October 20. https://muslimmatters.org/2011/10/20/common-mistakes-women-make-during-hajj-or-umrah.

Shea, Philip J. 1980. "Kano and the Silk Trade." *Kano Studies* 2 (1): 96–112.

———. 2006. "Big Is Sometimes Best: The Sokoto Caliphate and Economic Advantages of Size in the Textile Industry." *African Economic History* 34:5–21.

Shehu, Mohammed. 2010. "FG Sets Up Committee on Textile Revival." *Daily Trust*, July 28.

Shosanya, Mohammed. 2011. "60% of Textile Coys [Companies] Have Accessed Loan." *Daily Trust*, March 24.

Simmel, Georg. 1950. *The Sociology of Georg Simmel*. Edited by K. Wolff. New York: Free Press.

————. 1971a. "Conflict." In *On Individuality and Social Forms*, edited by D. Levine, 70–95. Chicago: University of Chicago Press.

————. 1971b. "Fashion." In *On Individuality and Social Forms*, edited by D. Levine, 294–323. Chicago: University of Chicago Press.

————. 1971c. "The Poor." In *On Individuality and Social Forms*, edited by D. Levine, 150–178. Chicago: University of Chicago Press.

Smith, Mary F. (1954) 1981. *Baba of Karo: A Woman of the Muslim Hausa*. New Haven, CT: Yale University Press.

Smith, M. G. (1954) 1981. Introduction to *Baba of Karo: A Woman of the Muslim Hausa*, by M. F. Smith, 11–34. New Haven, CT: Yale University Press.

————. 1960. *Government in Zazzau, 1800–1950*. London: Oxford University Press for the International African Institute.

————. 1964. "Historical and Cultural Conditions of Political Corruption among the Hausa." *Comparative Studies in Society and History* 6 (2): 164–194.

Songling, Pu. 1958. *Strange Tales from a Chinese Studio*. London: Penguin.

Soniyi, Toni. 2016. "Buhari Seeks World Bank's Support to Recover Stolen Funds." *This Day*, April 28. https://www.thisdaylive.com/index.php/2016/04/28/buhari-seeks-world -banks-support-to-recover-stolen-funds/.

Staudinger, Paul. (1889) 1990. *In the Heart of the Hausa States*. 2 vols. Translated by J. Moody. Athens: Ohio University Press.

Steiner, Christopher. 1985. "Another Image of Africa: Toward an Ethnohistory of European Cloth Marketed in West Africa, 1873–1960." *Ethnohistory* 32 (2): 91–110.

Stillman, Yedida. 2000. *Arab Dress: A Short History from the Dawn of Islam to Modern Times*. Edited by N. Stillman. Leiden, Netherlands: Brill.

Strassler, Karen. 2010. *Refracted Visions: Popular Photography and National Modernity in Java*. Durham, NC: Duke University Press.

Strümpell, Kurt. 1912. *Die Geschichte Adamauas nach mündlichen Überlieferungen*. Hamburg: L. Friedrichsen.

Sule, Ibrahim. 2016. "World Bank Report: Borno Lost N1.9trn to Boko Haram." *Daily Trust*, March 21. https://www.dailytrust.com.ng/news/general/world-bank-report-borno-lost -n1-9trn-to-boko-haram/138786.html.

Sunday, Simon. 2016. "UKAID Connects 49,000 Homes to Solar Power in 3 Months." *Daily Trust*, June. https://www.dailytrust.com.ng/news/general/ukaid-connects-49-000 -homes-to-solar-power-in-3-months/150876.html.

Tangban, O. E. 1991. "The Hajj and the Nigerian Economy, 1960–1981." *Journal of Religion in Africa* 21 (3): 241–255.

Tarlo, Emma. 2010. *Visibly Muslim: Fashion, Politics, Faith*. Oxford: Berg.

Thurston, Alex. 2015. "Nigeria's Mainstream Salafis between Boko Haram and the State." *Islamic Africa* 6:109–124.

Touati, Houari. 2010. *Islam and Travel in the Middle Ages*. Translated by Lydia Cochrane. Chicago: University of Chicago Press.

Umar, Auwalu. 2011. "KNSG Forces Emir to do Hawan Nasarawa." *Daily Trust*, September 2.

Umar, Muhammad S. 1993. "Changing Islamic Identity in Nigeria from 1960s to the 1980s: From Sufism to Anti-Sufism." In *Muslim Identity and Social Change in Sub-Saharan Africa*, edited by L. Brenner, 154–178. Bloomington: Indiana University Press.

———. 2000. "The Tijaniyya and British Colonial Authorities in Northern Nigeria." In *La Tijaniyya: Un confrérie musulmane á la conquête de l'Afrique*, edited by J.-L. Triaud and David Robinson, 327–355. Paris: Karthala.

———. 2006. *Islam and Colonialism: Intellectual Responses of Muslims of Northern Nigeria to British Colonial Rule*. Leiden, Netherlands: Brill.

United Africa Company. 1950. "Produce Goes to Market. Nigeria: Cotton." *Statistical and Economic Review* 6 (September): 1–45.

United Nations. 1968. "The Textile Industry in the West African Sub-Region." *Economic Bulletin for Africa* 7:103–125.

van Santen, José. 2012. "The *Tasbirwol* (Prayer Beads) Under Attack: How the Common Practice of Counting One's Beads Reveals Its Secrets in the Muslim Community of North Cameroon." In *Things: Religion and the Question of Materiality*, edited by D. Houtman and B. Meyer, 180–197. New York: Fordham University Press.

———. 2013. "Pilgrimage, Veiling, and Fundamentalisms in Cameroon." In *Veiling in Africa*, edited by E. Renne, 137–161. Bloomington: Indiana University Press.

Vaughan, James, and Anthony Kirk-Greene, eds. 1995. *The Diary of Hamman Yaji: A Chronicle of a West African Muslim Ruler*. Bloomington: Indiana University Press.

Vogelsang-Eastwood, Gillian. 2010. *Embroidery from the Arab World*. Leiden, Netherlands: Primavera.

Vogelsang-Eastwood, Gillian, and Willem Vogelsang. 2008. *Covering the Moon: An Introduction to Middle Eastern Face Veils*. Leuven, Belgium: Peeters.

Wakili, Isiaka. 2013. "Jonathan Bans Boko Haram, Ansaru." *Daily Trust*, June 5. http://allafrica.com/stories/201306050975.html.

———. 2015a. "Boko Haram Won't Last Beyond Dec–FG." *Daily Trust*, October 15. https://www.dailytrust.com.ng/news/general/boko-haram-won-t-last-beyond-dec-fg/115132.html.

———. 2015b. "FG Rehabilitates 22 Female Would-be Bombers." *Daily Trust*, July 1. https://www.dailytrust.com.ng/daily/index.php/news-menu/news/58760-fg-rehabilitates-22-female-would-be-bombers.

———. 2016a. "Buhari: Corruption Prevented Military from Defeating B/Haram." *Daily Trust*, May 19. https://www.dailytrust.com.ng/news/general/buhari-corruption-prevented-military-from-defeating-b-haram/147417.html.

———. 2016b. "Osinbajo Wants Stronger Patronage of Nigerian Goods." *Daily Trust*, April 6. https://www.dailytrust.com.ng/news/general/osinbajo-wants-stronger-patronage-of-nigerian-goods/141193.html.

———. 2016c. "Presidential C'ttee Indicts Dasuki, 300 NSA Contractors." *Daily Trust*, March 25. https://www.dailytrust.com.ng/news/general/presidential-c-ttee-indicts-dasuki-300-nsa-contractors/139476.html.

Wakili, Isiaka, Ishmael Mudashir, and Latifat Opoola. 2016. "FG Recovers N115bn from Looters." *Daily Trust*, June 5. https://www.dailytrust.com.ng/news/general/fg-recovers-n115bn-from-looters/149762.html.

Walker, Andrew. 2016. *"Eat the Heart of the Infidel": The Harrowing of Nigeria and the Rise of Boko Haram*. London: Hurst.

Ware, Rudolph, III. 2014. *The Walking Qur'an: Islamic Education, Embodied Knowledge, and History in West Africa*. Chapel Hill: University of North Carolina Press.

Weber, Max. 1946. *From Max Weber: Essays in Sociology*. Edited by H. H. Gerth and C. W. Mills. New York: Oxford University Press.

Weir, Sheilagh. 1989. *Palestinian Costume*. Austin: University of Texas Press.

Wilson, Mark. 2018. "Nigeria's Boko Haram Attacks in Numbers—as Lethal as Ever." *BBC World News*, January 25. http://www.bbc.com/news/world-africa-42735414.

Worden, Sarah. 2010. "Cloth and Identity: How Can Museum Collections of Hausa Textiles Contribute to Understanding the Notion of Hausa Identity." In *Being and Becoming Hausa: Interdisciplinary Perspectives*, edited by A. Haour and B. Rossi, 213–234. Leiden, Netherlands: Brill.

World Bank. 2016a. *From Oil to Cities: Nigeria's Next Transformation*. Washington, DC: World Bank. http://documents.worldbank.org/curated/en/711661468010811972 /pdf/106150-PUB-ADD-DOI-ISBN-SERIES-OUO-9.pdf.

———. 2016b. *More, and More Productive, Jobs for Nigeria: A Profile of Work and Workers*. Washington, DC: World Bank. http://documents.worldbank.org/curated /en/650371467987906739/pdf/103937-WP-P146872-PUBLIC-Nigeria-Jobs-Report.pdf.

Yahaya, Nasidi. 2009. "Boko Haram Crisis Not Over—Sultan." *Daily Trust*, September 23. http://allafrica.com/stories/200909230341.html.

Yamba, C. Bawa. 1995. Permanent Pilgrims: The Role of Pilgrimage in the Lives of West African Muslims in Sudan. Edinburgh, UK: Edinburgh University Press.

Index

Abdullahi, Ahmadu: and *mai rumi* embroidery, 134–135; pilgrim from Zaria, 128–129, *129*, 133–134; reformed Tijānniya, 136

Adam, Ja'far Mahmoud: assassination of, 180; criticism of Mohammed Yusuf, 180; establishment of Ahlus Sunnah, 213; and Islamic community, 198

Agbaji, Yusuf: Islamic scholar in Ilorin, 56–57, 71n16; as teacher of Salami Bamidele, 50, 56–57

Ahlus-Sunnah, 174, 180, 210, 213

Albani, Muhammad Auwal, 5, 93; assassination of, 179n20, 180; as founder of Salafiyya, 174; and Izala, 174

Alibaba website, 202n16, 216

almajiri, 82

alms, 11

amulets (*layoyi*), 71n9, 158; and caravan traders, 44n14, 132, 212

Ansaru (Jama'atu Ansarul Muslimina Fi Biladis Sudan), 9, 185; as Boko Haram splinter group, 181; and Khalid al-Barnawi, 198

Ansar ud-Deen Society, 63, 209, 218n3

Arab influences: Bamidele on *jilbab*, 58, 66, 70; dress, 27, 37; traders, 27, 37, *38*, 108; turban (*imāma*), 44n5, 73, *74*

Arabic language: fluency of Abubakar Gumi, 157; literacy, 50, 69, 110, 140, 162, 163; schools, 69

Asma'u, Nana: as daughter of 'Uthmān dan Fodio, 5; *jaji* teachers, 109; *A Warning, II*, 5–6

austerity, 40; and hajj, 150; ideal of, 8, 209; opposition to wealth, 8, 9; and scholarship, 8, 213

Baba of Karo, 120

babban riga (big robes), *14*, 20, 29, *34*, 42, 46, 47, 53, 86, 88, 91, 93, 160, 207;

hand-embroidered, 57, 58, 66, 80; machine-embroidered, *75*; neck embroidery (*kwado da linzami* or "frog and harness"), 132. *See also* exchange, forms of; Muslim holidays: Eid-el-Fitr

babban riga embroidery patterns: *aska biyu* (two knives), 81, 85, 86; *aska tara*, 85; *kwado da linzami* (frog and harness), 132; *malum malum*, 81; 'yar Dikwa, 85

Balewa, Abubakar Tafawa, 15, 95n4, 131, 141–142, 143, 168, 209

Bamidele, Abdul Salami: and Bamidele movement, 50, 73, 209; as "conservative reformer," 49; and *eleeha*, 58, 59, 60, 61, 62–63, 64, 66; emphasis on Islamic dress, 6, 50, 57, *58*, 59, 63, 64, 217; Islamic school in Ibadan, 57, 59; masquerade incident, 61–62; opposition to Western education, 60

Bamidele, Khalifa Ahmadu (son of Abdul Salami Bamidele), 57, *58*, 60

Beidelman, T. O., 205–206

Bello, Ahmadu (Sardauna of Sokoto), 67, *68*, *161*; assassination of, 95n11, 155, 157, 179, 209; attractive dress, 73, *75*, *76*, 80, *81*, 82, 160, *161*; and Muhammad Bello, 91, 95n10; development of Northern Nigeria, 92, 153; and Kaduna textile manufacturing, 75, 80, 153, 165, 167, *167*, 168, 171, 176; and *kiswa*, 146; on modernity and tradition, 87, 93–94; Muslim unity, 87; support for emirs, 92; support for power of Nigerian state and undermining emirs, 92; turbans as markers of Islamic identity, 74, 78, 86–87, 92. *See also* Gumi, Abubakar

Bello, Muhammad (son of 'Uthmān dan Fodio), 19, 30, 31, 42; establishment of garrison towns (*ribats*), 20, 30, 31; indigo and cotton plantations, 31; Islamic scholarship, 51; security and communal prayer, 33; security and textile production,

al-Adab, 56, 71n16, 71n19; Adam al-Iluri, 56, 69, 199; Abu Ikororo, 46, 56, 71n16; Sheikh Kamalu 'd-deen, 56, 69; Sheikh Korede, 56–57, 62–63, 64, 65, 67, 69, 71n18

Yusuf, Mohammed, 5, 201n9, 213; extrajudicial killing of, *182*, 185; founder of Boko Haram, 15, 180, 199, 210; rejection of western education, 174, 186. *See also* Boko Haram (Jama'atu Ahlus-Sunnah Lidda'Awati Wal Jihad); Maiduguri; violence

Zaria, 2, 10, 15, 16, 17n6, 21, 29, 30, 36, 39, 53, 73, 80, 83, 86, *89*, 93, 98, 105, 109, 110, 111, 115–116, 118, 122, 126n11, 128, 130, 134, 136, 139, 140, 147, 150, 155, 157, 163–164, 173, 174, 177, 177n1, *190*, *192*, 193, 202n17, 206, 210; Emirate, 18n11, 110; Province, 83, *168*; Zaria City (*birnin* Zazzau), 7, 9, *12*, 24, 45n18, *76*, *84*, 85, 86, 90–91, 110, *112*, 113–115, *117*, *119*, *121*, 124, *129*, 133, *135*, 150, *159*, 163, 178, 200, 205, 207–208, *208*

Zaria emirs (*sarkin*): Muhammadu Aminu, *168*; Shehu Idris, 88; Ja'afaru Dan Isyaku, *100*; Muhammad Sambo, 10, 29, 94n9, 122; Aliyu Sidi, 94n9, *101*, 139

Zumuratu Muminu (Zumratul Mumeenun), 58

Zungur, Sa'adu, 174; "Song of Freedom" ("*Wakar 'Yanci*"), 174–175

ELISHA P. RENNE is Professor Emerita in the Department of Afroamerican and African Studies (DAAS) and in the Department of Anthropology at the University of Michigan–Ann Arbor. She is author of *Cloth That Does Not Die*, *Population and Progress in a Yoruba Town*, and *The Politics of Polio in Northern Nigeria* and editor of *Veiling in Africa*.

Lightning Source UK Ltd.
Milton Keynes UK
UKHW01f0627191018
330815UK00020B/555/P